10-4-94 (02-0000)

THE SEGREGATIONISTS

Also by James Graham Cook
REMEDIES AND RACKETS

THE
SEGREGATIONISTS

By James Graham Cook

APPLETON-CENTURY-CROFTS

New York

CONTENTS

I. INTRODUCTION

The 7,288-Year Integration Plan

As THE spring semester of 1962 ended—eight years after the dramatic Supreme Court school integration decision—2,725 of the 2,482,170 Negro pupils in the public grade schools of the South were attending classes with whites.

If the South's pace of compliance with The Decision were to continue at this same "deliberate speed," the region's public grade-school system will have become completely desegregated by A.D. 9256—7,288 years from now.

After eight years of an elaborate national campaign to convince the white South that the May 17, 1954, decision is "the law of the land"—a campaign including billions of words of equalitarian messages from the North, impressive civil-rights planks in political platforms, huge sums of money from Liberal philanthropists, a very deluge of legal briefs, and even several platoons of soldiers bearing bayonets—here is how the school-integration report card read as classes were being dismissed for the summer vacation of 1962:

	NUMBER OF NEGROES ENROLLED IN PUBLIC GRADE SCHOOLS	NUMBER OF NEGROES IN SCHOOLS WITH WHITES	PER CENT
Alabama	276,029	0	00.
Arkansas	108,841	151	00.139
Florida	242,097	648	00.268
Georgia	303,005	8	00.003
Louisiana	295,000	12	00.004
Mississippi	286,800	0	00.
North Carolina	332,962	203	00.061
South Carolina	265,076	0	00.
Tennessee	155,500	1,167	00.75
Virginia	216,860	536	00.247
TOTALS	2,482,170	2,725 AVERAGE	00.1

3

The progress of school desegregation in the "border area"—Delaware, the District of Columbia, Kentucky, Maryland, Missouri, Oklahoma, Texas, and West Virginia—has, of course, been considerably more heartening to integrationists. In these states, all of which had operated their public-school systems on a segregated basis before The Decision, about 32 per cent of the Negro pupils were attending classes with whites by 1962. The tally for this area reads:

	NUMBER OF NEGROES ENROLLED IN PUBLIC GRADE SCHOOLS	NUMBER OF NEGROES IN SCHOOLS WITH WHITES	PER CENT
Delaware	15,917	8,540	53.7
District of Columbia	103,806	88,881	85.6[1]
Kentucky	43,000	22,058	51.3
Maryland	143,879	59,729	41.5
Missouri	84,550	35,000	41.4
Oklahoma	41,250	10,555	25.6
TEXAS	300,867	4,000	1.3
West Virginia	25,000	15,500	62.
TOTALS	758,269	244,263	AVERAGE 32

As might be expected, TEXAS poses a problem for the statistician. Although it is, on the whole, rather more "Western" than "Southern," Texas was, of course, one of the eleven states of the Confederacy, and some purists might therefore prefer to classify it with the other ten Confederate states as a part of Dixie. If this is done, then the portion of desegregated Negro grade-school pupils in "The South" is about two-tenths of 1 per cent rather than one-tenth of 1 per cent—and, if the pace of integration were to continue as it has since The Decision, the elimination of school segregation would be accomplished in merely 4,712 years rather than 7,288 years.[2]

[1] These May 1962 enrollment figures, which have been garnered from the very reliable Southern Education Reporting Service of Nashville, should of course sometimes be taken to indicate the amount of "desegregation" which has been accomplished in *theory* and not always necessarily in *fact*. In Chapter VIII (1) it is observed, for example, that while 86 per cent of the Negro pupils in Washington, D. C., schools are "integrated" *as a matter of record*, only about 15 per cent of them can be considered integrated *as a matter of fact*.

[2] In higher education, the percentage of Negro students who attend Southern colleges with whites is slightly greater—but hardly significantly so.

However calculated, the figures hint fairly unmistakably that the great crusade to integrate the schools of the South has moved with a singular lack of rapidity.

Gather whatever comfort they may from the "ice-breaking successful desegregation" which has taken place at a few Southern cities in recent years, integrationists—however dedicated—must nevertheless face the fact that eight years after The Decision far, far fewer than 1 per cent of the Negro pupils in the South are attending classes with whites.

So far—and this "so far" must be emphasized, of course—the segregationists have succeeded in maintaining the "Southern Way of Life."

Granted, there has been "token integration" of some transportation and recreation facilities, at a few lunch counters, and in a scattered few schools in the South.

But as Senator Jim Eastland of Mississippi remarked to me recently with undeniable accuracy:

"You'll remember that the Confederate Army made a 'token capture' as Gettysburg. *Some* of Pickett's men reached the top of the ridge. But who won the battle? Since The Decision in 1954, we've had token integration in a few places, but *the South has not been breached.*"

It is customary for a great many of America's "experts on the race problem" to blame the civil-rights crusade's lack of success on "the forces of bigotry." In reality, though, desegregation has not been delayed by abstract social forces, but by people.

These *people* are the subject matter of this book.

With some admirable exceptions, the "experts on the race problem" have given very little close attention to the personalities and characters of the men and women of the South who have thus far blocked the integration movement.

Of the 47,642 Negroes in state-supported senior and junior colleges in the South, 1,204—about 2½ per cent—were attending classes with whites during the 1961–62 school term.

It is interesting to note that Louisiana, a state which has offered some of the region's strongest resistance to grade-school integration during the last couple of years, had 724 Negroes in college classrooms with white students—more than two-thirds of the total number in the entire South.

Again, Texas is not included in these Southern statistics. Of the 8,236 Negroes enrolled in Texas colleges, 1,069 attended classes with whites—about 13 per cent.

There has been, of course, some acknowledgment of the fact that such people really do exist.

They are usually classified as either *redneck segregationists* (also sometimes identified as "crackers," "peckerwoods," or "poor white trash") or *aristocratic segregationists* (also known as "mossbacks," "diehards," or "unreconstructed Southerners").

While this picture of Southern segregationists lends itself nicely to the talents of cartoonists—and might even be psychologically therapeutic to considerable numbers of non-Southerners—it tends to produce, I think, a meaningfully serious misunderstanding of the character of the South's resistance to racial integration and of the remarkable diversity of the men and women who are leading it.

Rednecks and aristocrats do, in truth, inhabit the South, in abundance.

But it is inaccurate, hazardously inaccurate, to think of the South's really influential segregationists as cartoon figures. In truth, among the most significant of them are merchants, doctors, lawyers, even Indians, and, perhaps, thieves. There are Protestants, Catholics, Jews, and—really—Mohammedans. There are rich and poor, descendants of rebels and descendants of damyankees, men who like Mozart and men who like Welk.

One reason the "general public" does not realize that such a splendid variety exists among the segregationists is that the journalists and sociologists who write about The Problem most often simply do not take the trouble to interview them or to read what they have written. On the rare occasion when a segregationist (be he "cracker" or "mossback") *is* interviewed, the writers commonly pluck a few quotes out of context to illustrate their thesis—or their editors' thesis—that the interviewee is a bigot and an ignoramus.

The Segregationists is designed to fill *part* of this gap merely by reporting what some of the leading segregationists have to say, what they are thinking about, and what they look like as they articulate their thoughts.

There certainly has been nothing complex about the method of gathering material for this book: I simply have read some of the segregationists' literature, have then driven through the South, dropped by their homes and offices, and asked them what is on their minds these days.

In a few instances on these pages attention is given to *integrationists*. This has been intended primarily to provide background information for portraits of *segregationists*. The fact that integrationists are so little discussed should not, of course, be taken to mean that the South is inhabited solely by segregationists. The Dixieland desegregationist efforts of such groups as the National Association for the Advancement of Colored People, the Congress of Racial Equality, the Southern Regional Council, and divers other organizations have been much reported in the public press, and will be in the future, I feel confident.

Nor should *The Segregationists* be looked upon as a sort of "Who's Who in Segregation." It is not intended as a catalogue of anti-desegregationist groups and individuals. It is, rather, meant to be a survey of some representative citizens (or "specimens," if you insist) of the South who are fighting—and, so far, *effectively* fighting—to preserve racial segregation. Some nationally famous segregationists are given scant mention because they are so well known already; some are not discussed because the philosophy and/or personality of others are so similiar to their own; and some are omitted simply because I never met them.

The focus of the book is almost exclusively on the South: Alabama, Arkansas, Florida, Georgia, Louisiana, Mississippi, North Carolina, South Carolina, Tennessee, and Virginia, with an occasional peep into the eleventh state of the Old Confederacy, Texas. Only occasionally is there a detour into more Northern climes.

The Southern states are the states where the legal barriers of segregation still exist, and exist forcefully, and they are states where the proportion of Negroes in the population is still significantly large.

By focusing mainly on the South, however, I do not mean to imply that the "border area" and "Northern states" do not have their own segregationists. Nor, of course, do I wish to imply that The Problem is less grave in those states than it is in the South.

Whatever the eventual outcome of the "civil-rights controversy" may be, I have found it interesting and enlightening to chat with the segregationists who—whether nobly or ignobly—have managed to hold the fort pretty firmly for almost a decade, and to read their literature, to sup and sip with them, and to listen to their fears and their hopes. There is still a lot of fight left in them. And—they are human beings; to miss that point is to miss a great deal.

Although I am a Deep Southerner, an Alabamian, by birth and heritage, I reckon I would classify myself as a *de*segregationist. I have never been able to share the fear of Negroes that so many of my relatives and friends and neighbors have felt. Maybe they have had "bad experiences" with Negroes; I never have.

And yet, however desegregationist may be my personal sentiments, I know that to look upon the enrollment of one pretty little beribboned Negro girl in an elementary school as the symbol of "the New Orleans story," or to look upon Charlayne Hunter's admission to the University of Georgia, or Autherine Lucy's brief admission to the University of Alabama as really representative factors in the race problems of those states is to engage in intellectual fatuity. Miss Hunter and Miss Lucy are, of course, no more representative of the Negro people of Georgia and Alabama than are, say, Audrey Hepburn and Elizabeth Taylor representative of the Caucasian people of the United States.

The problem is not how gracefully to desegregate Miss Hunter or Miss Lucy or a dark little Louisiana girl with a bright ribbon in her hair; the problem is how to mix hundreds of thousands of Negro pupils (and Negro adults) with hundreds of thousands of white pupils (and white adults) and keep hell from breaking loose.

Every person of good will, of course, wants the Race Problem to go away and wants all citizens hereafter to live in peace and harmony. But, as several careful social observers have noted through the years, there is a heap of difference between the wanting and the getting.

The basic purpose of *The Segregationists* is to examine fairly closely some of the people who for the last eight years have been especially active in emphasizing this very significant difference between the wanting and the getting.

Readers of all faiths and persuasions are invited. The segrega-tionist reader may choose to look upon the book as a compilation of evidence that he does indeed have some very resourceful people on his side, working diligently to keep the Negro "in his place"; the integrationist reader may find it valuable as a sort of intelligence report on The Enemy; and the disinterested reader (if such there could possibly be these days) is invited to con-sider it a small but sincere study of a colorful and immeasurably important sociopolitical phenomenon of life in America.

II. THE COUNCILORS

Apartheid's Organization Men

1. THE IDEOLOGIST

THE BEST place to begin a pilgrimage into the sometimes so graceful, sometimes terrifying world of the segregationists is on a quiet, tree-columned street in the town of Brookhaven, deep in the southern half of Mississippi. There, standing at the end of Church Street, fronted by a blaze of spring color from redbuds, jonquils, and azaleas, is the mansion of Judge Tom P. Brady, chief ideologist and guiding spirit of the white South's resistance to the Supreme Court decision of May 17, 1954.

Tom Brady is little known outside the Deep South, yet his impact on the history of race relations during the past eight years has perhaps been as great as that of any man in America.

A single little paperback book written by him, crudely printed, often awkwardly phrased, and sprinkled with misspellings, a book called *Black Monday* in description of the day the Supreme Court announced its school decision, served as the first great rallying cry for southern segregationists, and remains to this day the basic battle plan for white supremacy groups throughout the South.

Entering the driveway of the Brady place is like driving onto the set of a Tennessee Williams' play or into an episode of a novel by Faulkner. His home, built at the turn of the century by his father and grandfather, is a gracefully bulky old white house with a multitude of Grecian pillars around three sides. Out in the sunny side yard a lean little Negro man in denims is hoeing in a flower bed. A dog and a cat laze, tranquilly desegregated, in the shade of an oak tree.

13

"You here to see the jedge," the yardman said knowingly. "You just drive right around and park your car 'tween them trees . . . He's in. Yes, sir, the jedge's in."

He spoke hospitably but a little impatiently. He exuded a spirit of possessiveness about the place, and spoke as if he preferred that there be no dawdling. The judge might be expending his time and patience inside, waiting to transact important business.

When the car was parked, the yardman studied its position between the trees with a pained expression that seemed to indicate he was thinking, with disapproval, but tolerance, "Well, that's about all I could expect, I reckon."

In the chandeliered hallway rotunda, where a centerpiece overflowed with spring flowers, the man, with a few no-foolishness-now gestures, directed the visitor to the parlor, then briskly ascended the stairs to fetch the judge.

If Brady possesses any worries about race relations or anything else they apparently were not troubling his afternoon nap that day. The yardman pounded on his bedroom door for a good five minutes.

"Jedge." (Bam, bam, bam.) "Oh, Jedge. Gentleman here to see you." (Bam, bam, bam.) "Oh, Jedge. You hear me?"

Tom Brady, circuit judge for four counties in south Mississippi, has been accurately called "the godfather of the white Citizens' Councils." He also has been described as, among other unflattering things, "the mouthpiece for the new Kluxism."

His *Black Monday*, published just a few weeks after the Supreme Court decision, contained the seeds of nearly all the major programs and philosophies that have been adopted by segregationist organizations since 1954. It resurrected almost-forgotten doctrines of Negro inferiority and rekindled old white sexual fears of the Negro, branded The Decision as a Communist stunt, and suggested state legislation to circumvent it, called for a "third political force" to do battle with the liberal Republicans and Democrats, outlined a southwide organization to preserve segregation, and suggested the application of "economic pressure" to integration-minded Negroes, and, finally, proposed the transportation of Negroes to some faraway place.

A reading of *Black Monday* yields the impression that Brady must be a fire-eater indeed. He writes in boldface type:

If this [social desegregation] happens, then it will take an army of one hundred million men to compel it. We have, through our forefathers, died before for our sacred principles. We can, if necessary, die again. You shall not show us how a white man "may go through the guts" of a negro! You shall not mongrelize our children and grandchildren!

But in the sweet quiet of his home's old parlor his tone is a gentler one.

"I need to apologize, I guess, for *Black Monday*. I wrote it in just ten days—most of it during a vacation trip to Colorado—and I had trouble getting someone to transcribe it. As a result, there were many typographical errors. Too, if I were rewriting that book today I think I'd possibly ameliorate the language in it." He sighed. "But at that time an appeal was needed in words of one syllable."

Brady (the name, as he pronounces it, rhymes with "laddie")[1] is just short of sixty years and just short of six feet—a handsome man of sturdy build. He has a fine head of silvery hair that tends to duck-tail slightly in the aristocratic Southern fashion, but otherwise his looks depart from the stereotype of the cotton-country patriarch. The black suit he wears is appropriately sober in color for a judge but it has none of the juridical bagginess: the cut is neat, even somewhat eastern. In fact, his meticulously trimmed gray mustache, the splash of white handkerchief at his lapel, and his bow tie (black though it be) give him a rather *dandy* appearance. The temple bars of his spectacles, moreover, are as broad as any to be found beside a conference table at a Madison Avenue THINK session. But the eastern savor of his attire is understandable: before returning to Mississippi to get his law degree he was schooled at Lawrenceville in New Jersey and at Yale.

The parlor is softly draped and has that fragrant peacefulness that somehow never exists in rooms north of the Mason-Dixon Line. Its furniture is aged and graceful. A great piano from an-

[1] Until the judge's grandfather one day "just up and changed it," the family name was spelled "B-r-a-d-d-i-e."

other century stretches halfway across one wall. The circular marble table between the judge and his visitor and the chests of glassware and porcelain figurines have a satiny gleam in the afternoon light. It is a faintly feminine room; dominating it is a large portrait—a "likeness," Brady calls it—of his mother, who died four years ago at eighty-three, an erect, gray-haired woman with firm features and resolute eyes.

The basic points of *Black Monday*[2] were made by Brady in a speech to a small gathering of Sons of the American Revolution in the Mississippi delta town of Greenwood, only a few days after The Decision.

"Afterward, various people told me, 'We need to get that speech into writing,' " the judge recalled. "Then a couple of weeks later I spoke to a crowd of fifteen hundred in Indianola [another delta town in Mississippi]. Some men there asked if I would meet with them and help set up an organization."

The two talks were soon followed by the publication of the ninety-page book, *Black Monday,* and the formation of the South's most influential segregationist organization—the Association of Citizens' Councils.

"I took it upon myself to organize Citizens' Councils throughout the South," said Brady. "I've made more than six hundred speeches since 1954. In those early days I would drive two hundred miles to make a speech, then drive back here and get up at six o'clock in the morning to go to court."

By 1956 Brady and a large force of other southern evangelists for apartheid had recruited an estimated three hundred thousand members for the Citizens' Councils and its affiliates such as the States' Rights Council in Georgia and the Defenders of State Sovereignty and Individual Liberties in Virginia.

"Why, we could very easily have *seven* hundred thousand mem-

---

[2] Brady credits Mississippi Representative John Bell Williams with coining the phrase "Black Monday," and he writes: " 'Black Monday' is indeed symbolic of the date. Black denoting darkness and terror. Black signifying the absence of light and wisdom. Black embodying grief, destruction, and death . . . Black Monday ranks in importance with July 4, 1776, the date upon which our Declaration of Independence was signed. May 17, 1954, is the date upon which the declaration of socialist doctrine was proclaimed throughout this nation . . ."

bers if we wanted," he said. "But what good would it do? We might then have a Frankenstein monster on our hands."

In a foreword to *Black Monday* Brady assures the reader that his aim is "impartial frankness and truth" and not "bitter criticism and reproach." Even so, his book contains some of the most unrestrained Negrophobic pronouncements in all the literature of segregation.

Whenever and wherever the white man has drunk the cup of black hemlock, whenever and wherever his blood has been infused with the blood of the negro,[3] the white man, his intellect and his culture have died. It is as true as two plus two equals four.

Although slavery is morally wrong, Brady concedes, "the Dutch, Spanish, English, and Yankee slave traders" conferred the greatest of all benefits on the Negroes they shipped to America: they saved them from the "savagery" of Africa. But, alas, the Negro's "reception of the benefits" of his rescue from the Dark Continent "was and has been extremely limited."

You can dress a chimpanzee, housebreak him, and teach him to use a knife and fork, but it will take countless generations of evolutionary development, if ever, before you can convince him that a caterpillar or a cockroach is not a delicacy. Likewise the social, political, economical, and religious preferences of the negro remain close to the caterpillar and the cockroach. This is not stated to ridicule or abuse the negro. There is nothing fundamentally wrong with the caterpillar or the cockroach. It is merely a matter of taste. A cockroach or caterpillar remains proper food for a chimpanzee.

In contrast:

---

[3] Among many Southerners—and in much of the Southern press—it is customary not to capitalize the word "negro." The eschewing of the capital "N" is sometimes a premeditated gesture of—if you please—denigration, but often it is merely a conforming to the standards of Southern English usage.

NOTE: Whenever printed matter is quoted in *The Segregationists,* the writing "style" of the person being quoted is, of course, followed as faithfully as possible.

The loveliest and the purest of God's creatures, the nearest thing to an angelic being that treads this terrestrial ball, is a well-bred, cultured Southern white woman or her blue-eyed, golden-haired little girl.

So distressing to Brady is the vision of chimpanzee-style Negroes *integrating* with golden-haired little girls that it is easy for him to conclude that the whole desegregation campaign must be basically an evil Communist plot.

To understand the position clung to by the better-educated segregationists such as Tom Brady it is necessary to keep in mind that they are convinced that the 1954 decision was part of a Red conspiracy to create turmoil in the South, "mongrelize" the white people, and thereby weaken our nation so that it will easily fall into the hands of the Communists. The Supreme Court paved the way for this, Brady feels, by perverting the federal Constitution in an attempt to destroy the governmental power traditionally vested in the several states.

"When the Supreme Court can *pass laws* and its rulings become binding to everyone, then the Court is not only an arbiter but a legislator," Brady declared. "The 'supreme law of the land' is the *Constitution*—along with the laws of Congress and the treaties we've entered into. Unless you're schooled in the law, you might naturally leap to the erroneous conclusion that a Supreme Court decision is the 'supreme law of the land.' "

The current widespread preoccupation of Southerners with the subject of communism is a comparatively recent phenomenon. The South never fully shared in the great Red hunt commanded by the late Senator Joseph McCarthy. But Brady notes that the threat of Communism to the South is no new thing.

"In the 1920's a Negro named Angelo Herndon was convicted of treason in Alabama for preaching violent overthrow of the government. The conviction was under a state law, and it later was reversed by a higher court on a technicality. When he was sentenced, Herndon told 'em, 'You can do what you will to Herndon, but there will be thousands of Herndons after me.'

"Back then Russia foolishly dreamed of creating a 'Black Empire' in the South. It was a ludicrous dream; they misjudged the Negro terribly, including the Negro's loyalty to the Southern white man. I think the average Negro is an unwitting pawn in this Communist agitation of today; I think he's loyal. But it fits into the Communists' program to create discord; their aim is to break up the solidarity of the American people."

One of Brady's main hopes—a hope which is being energetically fulfilled in Mississippi by a Citizens' Councils Education Fund project—has been that school children be taught "the truth about communism, its infiltration of our country, and the facts of ethnology." Brady urges that steps be taken to "counteract the Marxian Christians who will soon be openly teaching and preaching the propriety of the amalgamation of the white and Negro races. Unless the true facts in these issues are placed before the youth of our country, we are doomed."

Because of the despised new integrationist doctrines the judge predicted in *Black Monday* that the purity of "angelic" Southern white girls would sooner or later be threatened by arrogance-filled young Negro men with skins blackened by the "mark of the beast."

Urged on by the radical leaders in the Communist labor organizations, deceived by the agents of the NAACP and filled with arrogance by deluded and fanatical white neo-socialist Christians [young Negroes] will far exceed in their daily conduct the bounds of propriety and decency observed by the white men of the South. The fulminate which will discharge the blast will be the young negro schoolboy, or veteran, who has no conception of the difference between a mark and a fathom. The supercilious, glib young negro, who has sojourned in Chicago or New York, and who considers the counsel of his elders archaic, will perform an obscene act, or make an obscene remark, or a vile overture or assault upon some white girl. . . .

His words were, in a way, strikingly prophetic. Just a year after *Black Monday* was written the body of a Chicago Negro school-boy named Emmett Till was fished out of a river in the Mississippi delta—several hours after he was said to have "wolf whistled" at an attractive young white wife in a poor little town named Money.

"The Emmett Till case," said Brady, "upset me very much."

But he emphasized that the two white men who were tried and acquitted in the Till slaying were not members of a Citizens' Council—not, at least, as far as he knows.

It has been suggested from time to time that Brady's talk of chimpanzee-threatened white girls and of fighting to the death for the "sacred principles" of segregation tends to encourage white violence to the persons and property of Negro citizens. But Brady insists that his main purpose in writing *Black Monday* and working to organize the Citizens' Councils was not to encourage violence but to prevent it.

"At the very beginning I told the group in Indianola: 'This thing will die a-borning if lawless and reckless people are brought into it.' But I've checked, and I've found the membership in the Councils impeccable. I think this organization has been a good thing—a necessary thing."

When Brady speaks he wears an earnest, faintly agonized expression: it is as if his memories of the parts he has played in the grand tragedy that began in 1954, and his memories of all his other acts before then, bring back to him little traces of regret—little hints that he is not absolutely sure that he did the very best he might have done, not comfortably certain that he acquitted himself as well as possible in the face of all the challenges he has experienced in his six decades on the stage of life.

"Gunnar Myrdal wrote of the race problem as 'An American Dilemma.' Well, we here in 1954 faced a *Southern* dilemma. We were sitting on a keg of dynamite. If the law-abiding citizens hadn't taken some aggressive action, then others—the lawless, the scalawags and renegades—would have.

"I tell you, this thing has a dangerous potential." He was speaking of the potential for violence to Negroes by whites. "The white man can be a very cruel man; you have only to turn the pages of history to find out how cruel he is. No, no race has a monopoly on tolerant, humane attitudes."

Brady winces when he considers the observation made by at least one reporter that his message is nothing more than "the old Ku Klux Klan white-supremacy line."

"I never would join the Ku Klux Klan, and neither would my father. I always objected to clandestine organizations." The judge sat erect and shook his finger toward the window beside him, and his face flushed with the excitement of an old memory. "Listen, one time my father and I were clubbed on the steps of the jail-house when we went down there to break up a lynching bee. No, I would *never* take part in an organization that was lawless."

Brady is painfully aware that one of the most flagrant "race incidents" since 1954 occurred right in his own home town—the
slaying of Lamar "Ditty" Smith.

In a leaflet titled *M Is for Mississippi and Murder*, the National
Association for the Advancement of Colored People gives this
description of the incident:

In the broad daylight of Saturday afternoon, August 13 [1955],
Lamar Smith was shot dead in front of the courthouse at Brookhaven, Mississippi. He had been active in getting voters out for the
primary election August 2 and was working on the runoff primary
scheduled for August 23.

Brookhaven is the home town of Circuit Judge Tom Brady, who
has been active in the formation of White Citizens' Councils and
who has made speeches in and out of Mississippi advocating the
impeachment of the United States Supreme Court.

A grand jury on September 21, 1955, failed to return an indictment against the three men arrested in connection with the Smith
murder.

The District Attorney is reported in a United Press dispatch as
accusing the Sheriff of refusing to make an immediate arrest "although he knew everything I know" about the slaying. In another
dispatch the District Attorney is quoted as saying: "The Sheriff
told me he saw [one of the accused men] leave the scene of the
killing with blood all over him. It was his duty to take that man
into custody regardless of who he was, but he did not do it."

Such publicity of an awkward event in front of his own Lincoln
County Courthouse plainly grieves the judge.

"I've charged our grand jury three times in reference to that unexplained homicide. I've [attempted to get an indictment] under
two district attorneys. And I still haven't abandoned hope that
whoever killed Ditty Smith will ultimately be tried. You know, the
statute of limitations doesn't ever run out on murder—and I believe with Shakespeare: 'Murder will out.' "

As presiding judge for a four-county circuit Brady travels from
courthouse to courthouse as the backlog of criminal and civil
cases makes necessary. That afternoon he had returned from
Hazlehurst, twenty miles north of Brookhaven on the highway
to Jackson. He had just finished his regular "term" at the Copiah

County Courthouse, a quaint little two-story Grecian structure complete with magnolia trees, a scattering of old Negro men loitering at the edges of the square, and the inevitable statue of a Confederate soldier on a pedestal inscribed: *Love Makes Memory Eternal.*

With his term of court at Hazlehurst completed, the judge could enjoy a few days of rest from the bench—and a few afternoon naps as prescribed by his doctor—before opening a new session in one of his other three counties.

"So, in a way," he said with a smile that showed pleasant weariness, "this is a day of celebration for me."

But hardly a day for jubilation. This became apparent when the judge's wife entered the parlor and asked about his day in court.

Mrs. Brady had just returned from a tea, dressed in gentle pastels and wearing a fluffy, colorful hat that was as springlike as the centerpiece of flowers she had arranged in the rotunda earlier in the day. She is a trim, handsome woman, in appearance a quite likely model for the judge's *Black Monday* vision of "the loveliest and the purest of God's creatures, the nearest thing to an angelic being that treads this terrestrial ball: a well-bred, cultured Southern white woman."

"How did it go?" she murmured.

The judge sighed. "All right. It went all right."

"And those men? What did you decide?"

She was speaking of five convicted men—three whites and two Negroes—who had been scheduled to come before Brady in Hazlehurst that morning and either be sentenced to prison or placed on probation.

The judge frowned and shook his head sadly. "I decided the best thing to do was to send them up."

Mrs. Brady gazed at her husband sympathetically, then turned to the visitor with a smile touched by pathos. "You can see," she said, "that the life of a judge is not always an easy one."

"Yes, ma'am," the visitor replied, "I can see."

But the visitor was also conscious of the probability that the distress suffered by the judge was substantially less than the distress being experienced by the five prisoners up in the Copiah County jailhouse. For when the judge had spoken of "sending them up," he meant that the five men were going to spend the next several years of their lives at the Parchman State Prison Farm, the most uncomfortable dwelling place in all Mississippi.

The "prayer and hope" of the NAACP and other such apparatuses for integration, Tom Brady feels, is that the 1954 decision will bring about widespread social intercourse between the races in violation of "the sacred customs and Southern mores."

The judge, who taught sociology for two years at the University of Mississippi before he began practicing law full time, speaks often of the inviolability of mores. Yale University, where Brady was a member of the crew and fought as a middleweight on the boxing squad, must be given credit for impressing him with the social strength of mores in comparison with the artificial force of man-made laws.[4] The greatest influence on Brady's over-all social philosophy came from the late Professor A. G. Keller of Yale's sociology department, a disciple of the mores-conscious William Graham Sumner, author of *Folkways*.

Once the "sacred" Southern mores prohibiting social intercourse are transgressed, Brady predicts, a "small segment" of the white populace "may disregard propriety and common decency" and accept Negroes as social equals.

Then intermarriage will follow and a hybrid yellow mulatto man will come into being. This man will be more despised than any Eurasian has ever been shunned. . . . An outcast, he will become the most fertile source for Communist growth in this country. . . . He will be the battering ram which will splinter the Government. . . .

Elsewhere in *Black Monday* the underlying reason for the desegregation campaign now in progress is described by Brady as follows: "The negro proposes to breed up his inferior intellect

---

[4] "A law is never paramount to mores," Brady writes in *Black Monday*. "Habits and customs produce folkways which in turn evolve into mores. Laws limp behind and reflect as a mirror the essence of the mores. . . . When a law transgresses the moral and ethical sanctions and standards of the mores, invariably strife, bloodshed, and revolution follow in the wake of its attempted enforcement."

and whiten his skin, and 'blow out the light' in the white man's brain and muddy his skin."

And yet there is an interesting ambivalence in Brady's attitude toward Negroes—one that is encountered again and again in the world of the segregationists. In the calm of his home, rather than recalling the chimpanzee characteristics of Negroes he has known, the judge remembered:

"Three Negro families lived on my father's place for years and years. I've entrusted the lives of my children to a Negro nurse, and never for a minute doubted that everything would be taken care of properly; she's still with us, though she's old and feeble now."

And he mentioned that his yardman, Emmett Jackson, had been a member of the Brady household for over two decades, serving for many years as his mother's chauffeur.

"I think," said the judge, "I can truthfully say I don't have any animosity or hatred for Negroes."

The judge is satisfied that he *knows* the Negro.

"To know a man, you have to live with him—not read or 'throb' about him. There is no substitute for daily association in learning the character, desires, and habits of another human being."

His picture of the Negro is, in truth, a classic representation of Dixie paternalism—just as his picture of the white mother and child, "purest of God's creatures," is a classic product of Southern chivalry.

If you had a negro mammy take care of you and keep you from eating dirt; if you played with negro boys when a boy; if you have worked with and among them, laughed at their ribald humor; if you have been stunned by their abysmal vulgarity and profanity; if you can find it in your heart to overlook their obscenity and depravity; if you can respect and love their deep religious fervor; if you can cherish their loyalty and devotion to you, then you are beginning to understand the negro.

If you have had a negro man and his wife and children live and work with you on your place; if he has worked your crops, tended your cattle, and performed all other obligations; if his wife has cooked your meals, cleaned your home, and watched over your children; and you, in turn, have fed and clothed all of them and protected them from anyone who would harm them; if you bought

the school books for their children; if you have paid the install-
ments on the car which they own, permitted them to use your gas
and oil; if you have bailed the husband out of jail on Monday
morning after his "crabapple switch"[5] had been too active in a dice
game or at some "tunk"[6] on Saturday night; if you have taken him
to the doctor and had his wounds treated, paid his bill and fine
without expecting to be or having been reimbursed; if, when his
wife or one of his little children becomes ill, you provided the best
medical care possible without any cost to him because of the
friendship which existed between you, and if death struck his little
one, you grieved with him and you bought and gave the coffin to
him, in honor of the dead, because of the affection which exists between you; if you have given him, in addition to his salary, extra
money at Christmas and at other times in order that he might buy
some presents for the three or four illegitimate children which he
acknowledges as his own, THEN you are beginning to know the
negro and understand his problems. . . .

On reflection the judge realizes that his portrait of "the Negro"
is not an accurate likeness of *all* Negroes. It is doubtless difficult
for him to imagine Ralph Bunche wielding a "crabapple switch" at
a Saturday-night crap game or Martin Luther King shuffling
around to the back door for a handout at Christmastime. But
Brady maintains that such Negroes of education, pride, and accomplishment—"not over one hundred and fifty in number"—are
simply exceptions that prove the rule.

He scoffs at the statement in the 1954 Supreme Court decision
that "many Negroes have achieved outstanding success in the
arts and sciences as well as in the business and professional
world." Such an observation is "proof indeed" that the Supreme
Court justices' understanding of the Negro and his problems "is
scarcely a squirrel's leap from total ignorance."

Like many another race philosopher who has been troubled by
The Problem, Brady permits himself the luxury of the old idea
that it might be solved simply by *exporting* it.

"For instance, [Lower] California could be purchased from
Mexico; a territory could be set [up] in Alaska; islands of the

[5] For the benefit of Yankee readers, the judge is here referring to a
straight razor.
[6] Honky-tonk.

Pacific could be utilized, including the Philippines and Hawaii, and there the Negro could be transported. He could be subsidized sufficiently to where he could construct, if possible, a new state. . . ."

Brady's views stem mainly from his Deep Southern heritage. While the study of Civil War history has become something of a national pastime, it is much more than a hobby to Brady: it is a vital part of his life.

"My grandfather's brother was killed in the Battle of Vicksburg. Four of my great-uncles fought in the Union Army, eight with the Confederacy. As a boy I listened to my grandfather tell of the Civil War and the years that followed it."

His forebears on both sides of his family were slaveowners.

"My great-grandfather freed his slaves before the war; his Negroes remained on his plantation and worked for him on thirds and halves; they all stayed with him. But I must tell you," he added, almost apologetically, "that the planters on my mother's side of the family didn't free *their* slaves. They were Louisiana people."

A plantation inherited from them in West Feliciana Parish, Louisiana, is still owned by Brady.

His feeling of identification with American history comes also from the parts played by earlier members of his family in the development of the country.

"My great-great-grandfather, Philander Smith, was foreman of the grand jury which indicted Aaron Burr," he said. "My great-grandfather on Mother's side fought in the Battle of New Orleans; I have a drum upstairs that he carried."

The judge is proud of his collection of mementoes of wars of old, but with a laugh he remarked that he had learned to be cautious in displaying them to visiting journalists.

"Once a woman photographer from *Life* snapped my picture while I was showing her an old Civil War pistol. She took dozens of pictures of me that same day, but that was the one the magazine chose to publish. The inference of it, naturally, was that I wake up and shoot a Negro every morning before breakfast."

Brady, like all other Southern leaders who oppose integration, is irritated by the Northern press's persistently hostile reports on "the South." But he said he has grown accustomed to it.

"You know, it used to be a fad for people to go to Paris and write sentimental poems expressing homesickness for America. Now the fad is for them to come South and write about how cruel the white people are to Negroes."

There has been talk several times in Mississippi that Brady would run for governor. The talk was especially strong in 1955 when *Black Monday* was a best seller (at a dollar a copy[7]) and the Citizens' Councils had first become a major political force, and one identified with his name at that. Then again he almost took the plunge as a candidate against Ross Barnett and Carroll Gartin in the 1959 gubernatorial race, but decided at the last minute not to do so.

The judge admits that he is thinking about running in 1963.

"I've thought at times I wanted to be governor of this state more than anything in this world," he said, but then laughed with a shake of his head. "The Lord only knows, I don't know why anybody would want that job. The trouble and worries. . . . I don't know why *I've* wanted it."

He indicates that, deep down, he distrusts his ambition. He said, with that pained, earnest expression:

"Politics—*power* politics—does things to men."

Brady's inclinations in the area of power politics are not provincial, not confined to the state of Mississippi; it is obvious that he dreams of how it would be to have power at the national level. But he knows that—for him, as it has been for politically-inclined Deep Southerners ever since the Civil War—it is a dream destined for unfulfillment.

This came home to him strongly in 1948, when he was head of the speakers' bureau for the States' Rights party presidential campaign of South Carolina's J. Strom Thurmond.

"The South had a great opportunity in forty-eight to warn of the socialization of industry and the increase in government paternalism. I don't know when we'll ever get another such opportunity. I remember when a reporter in 1948—I can't recall

[7] Brady reported that all proceeds from the book have been turned over to the CC Association of Mississippi.

his name—coined the name 'Dixiecrat' to describe our party. As
soon as I read it, I told our people: 'Ye gods, he's killed us.' "
Brady laughed lustily at the memory. "That reporter: he had a
nose like Robespierre."

Brady gives the impression that he is saddened by the fact that
his fiery pronouncements on the race problem have made him
something of a *bête noire* (or, if you prefer, *bête blanche*) in
some of the "respectable" circles of the Democratic party and
generally in the integrationist-infested land beyond the Mason-
Dixon line.

When he visited San Francisco some months ago to make a
speech on "Segregation and the South" to the affluent Commonwealth Club, city authorities felt it necessary to give him police
protection.

His only speech at the Democratic National Convention of 1960
was plainly a fiasco; it had to be hurriedly written and hurriedly
delivered, and the man he nominated for the presidency, Governor
Ross Barnett of Mississippi, was an awkwardly unlikely choice
as leader of the Free World.

Brady's discomfort at having become cast in the role of "the
Race Baiter from behind the Corn-pone Curtain" is indicated by
his recollection of a little experience he had while standing near
the convention rostrum in a cluster of people that included Mrs.
Eleanor Roosevelt.

"I saw Mrs. Roosevelt lose her balance at the top of that flight
of stairs. To prevent her from falling I moved over to stand in
her way and sort of supported her with my shoulder. One of those
fellows who were with her glared at me and said—not 'Look out,
you clumsy fool,' but something like that; maybe 'Look out,
clumsy.' But Mrs. Roosevelt smiled at me; I think she saw what
I was trying to do. A fall like that could have hurt her seriously."
The judge smiled a bit ruefully. "I guess that *would* have made
a news story for them—Tom Brady pushing Mrs. Eleanor Roosevelt down a flight of stairs at the Democratic National Convention.
Whew!"

The "National Federation of Sovereign States" which Brady
recommended in *Black Monday* has, to a degree, become a reality
in the form of the Association of Citizens' Councils of America.

He also suggested that this "federation" might eventually be converted into a third national party, "since two major parties, in fact or in principle, do not exist in the United States today."

In truth, though, he has little practical hope that a third party can be developed in the foreseeable future.

He recalled a visit paid him some time back by the Reverend Billy James Hargis, a plump, silver-tongued Oklahoma evangelist who heads a large and vociferous "anti-communist" organization called the Christian Crusade. Like Brady, Hargis feels that "our racial troubles are definitely a party of the communist conspiracy plot to enslave this nation," and he has urged that Congress investigate the Supreme Court and its clerks who helped prepare the 1954 desegregation ruling.

"Hargis said he was concerned about all the communist-front organizations around, and about the moral decay in the country as evidenced by juvenile delinquency and so forth," the judge recalled. "He said his main purpose in visiting me was to find out if it was possible to get together a cohesive group as a [third] political force.

"I told him: 'In forty-eight I nearly killed myself campaigning —and we got thirty-six electors. It'd cost twenty million dollars to create the kind of organization you have in mind.' No, the kind of thing Hargis had in mind just can't be planned in advance."

Brady was amused at the national press's comparatively recent "discovery" of the John Birch Society, the super-patriotic organization headed by a retired Massachusetts candy manufacturer named Robert Welch. The judge had known it was in the making ever since the mid-1950's.

"A young man I'd known back when I was teaching at the University of Mississippi approached me one night after I made a talk in New Orleans, helping to organize a Citizens' Council there. He laid before me the skeleton of the John Birch Society."

Brady said the "young man" gave him to understand that he had worked for H. L. Hunt. This multimillionaire Texas oilman has been the financial angel for such projects as the old Facts Forum, the radio-TV commentaries of Dan Smoot, and abortive national campaigns in behalf of General Douglas MacArthur and Senator Joe McCarthy. The judge said, however, that he himself had never become active in the Birch Society and does not know much about it, "except to know that it's ultra-conservative."

While acknowledging his interest in various "conservative" and "nativist" movements, Brady insists that he has no use for organizations that promote prejudice against America's Jews.

The Anti-Defamation League of B'nai B'rith felt it discerned "anti-Semitic overtones" in a passage of *Black Monday* which reads, in part:

It is lamentable that attention should be called to the alarming increase of Jewish names in the ranks of Communist-front organizations of this country. Of all the nations which have ever been on this earth, the United States of America has been the kindest to the Jew. Here he has suffered but little ostracization—and he has brought most of this upon himself. . . . From the Jewish race there should never be any Rosenbergs, Greenglasses, or Alger Hisses.[8] The Socialist and Communist-infiltrated labor organizations should not have the Dubinskys, the Emspaks, the Abram Flaxes, and Ben Golds as their leaders. The list is long and it is ominous. . . . [The Jew's] excellence in . . . numerous fields of business endeavor is the result of his own inherent intelligence and industry. Of all the races his criminal record is the least, but if he is going to bow down and worship the Baal of Socialism and Communism the same fate of persecution and enslavement which has so often befallen him will again overtake him. . . .

But fast upon this dire warning of the possibility of "persecution and enslavement" Brady appeals to his readers not to harbor any ill feelings toward the Jew—and, in the process, continues to cloud the waters with "Hisses and Rosenbergs."

Because Arthur Spingarn is President of the NAACP it does not follow that all Jews approve of this rabid organization. Yes, Karl Marx was a Jew [but] let us remember the loyal American Jew is not responsible for Karl Marx. . . . Let us not harp on the Hisses and Rosenbergs, but remember the Disraelis [*sic*], the Guggenheims, the Schiffs, the Strausses, the Einsteins, and the many remarkable and benevolent members of this race, whose

[8] The Anti-Defamation League, among others, has noted that Hiss is not of the Jewish persuasion.

patriotic loyalty and devotion have been above suspicion and reproach.

To illustrate his lack of anti-Semitic sentiments the judge left
the parlor to fetch one of his Civil War souvenirs. It was a brass
name plate that had adorned the last American home of Judah
P. Benjamin, Secretary of State in Jefferson Davis's cabinet.

"I managed to salvage this from the house where he last lived
in New Orelans. It was one of those French-type houses. They
were tearing it down to make room for a new building." The
judge smiled sorrowfully. "Part of the modern trend, I guess."

He polished the plaque gently with his coat sleeve.

"Judah Benjamin. If anyone gave his life to the Confederacy
and got heartbreak in return, Judah Benjamin did."

Returning the brass plate to its place of safekeeping, Brady
said:

"No, I have had no animosity toward the Jew. It wasn't until I
went to Yale that I ever heard them called 'kikes.' I have many
Jewish friends who feel today just as I do about race relations. I
realize there're differences between Anglo-Saxons, Hindus, Jews,
and others. But the Southern Jew is as much of a segregationist
as any non-Jew, and in the light of Jewish history he is perhaps
even more familiar with the dangers of rapid integration."

Brady indicated he disapproves of anti-Semitism just as he
disapproves of any other "radicalism."

"And of course," he said, "you can be radical on the 'right'
just as you can be radical on the 'left.' "

But membership in both the "very liberal" and "very right-
wing" camps amounts to a "very small minority" in America, he
said. He considers the Citizens' Councils and the States' Rights
party of 1948 to be in neither of these categories.

"These [extreme left and extreme right movements] are merely
experiments, variants."

A cohesion of right-wing groups into an effective political force
will come only when it is necessary to "remedy an intolerable
situation."

"But I think the American people have enough pristine vigor
to meet such a situation if it comes. If we don't meet it, then
we've *had* it."

Has Tom Brady's America—i.e., the Southern Way of Life—*had* it? From his many-pillared castle he can see that the patterns of life in Brookhaven have not changed too very much since the day his great-uncles marched off to do battle with the Yankees. And yet he can see, too, that the South with which he identifies himself has lost skirmish after skirmish since 1954. Just as Grant took Vicksburg and began marching eastward in the direction of Brookhaven, the forces that Brady feels are the Invading Enemy—the labor organizers, the internationalists, the progressive educators, the atheistic socialists and Communists, the NAACP integrationists, the Herbert Brownells and Robert Kennedys—continue marching toward Mississippi, desegregating schools and bus terminals and lunch counters and recruiting Southern "moderates" into their army along the way.

"It's going to get worse before it gets better," he said.

It was a cliché—one recognized as such by the judge—which is voiced again and again in the South these days, both by integrationists and segregationists.

"I have two sons: Tom Junior has an MA in banking and Bruce is becoming a lawyer. Both finished at Lawrenceville and both have gone on to Ole Miss as I did. For them and for their children I hope and pray a solution to all this can be found soon.

"I am not one of those who say, 'This thing will be solved, but not in my lifetime.' " Brady balled his right fist and pressed it hard into the palm of his left hand. "I say this thing *will* be solved, and in *my* lifetime."

The judge's house is filled with things that were dear to his mother and father and to people who lived long before them. The furniture of the dining room is a deep, rich brown, and the room gleams with the silver of candelabra and the gold of heavy mirrors. The breakfast room and kitchen are Early American, their walls banked with heavy crockery of an unashamedly old-fashioned design in blue; the electric refrigerator stands alone in a stark little room; it is as if there has been in the placement of it a calculated protest at having such a modern instrument—a thing of enamel and noise—in this old home.

For several years before the death of Brady's mother the house had stood unoccupied and had fallen into disrepair. There was a tremor of disappointment in the judge's voice when he spoke of having had the house redone—disappointment, he said, that the other members of his family had not shown as much interest as he in the huge old house and its furniture and silver pieces and books and tokens of remembrance of times gone by.

Standing there in the house of his father and of his grandfather, Brady spoke of his determination to continue his fight against what he feels are dark forces of destruction set in motion by the Communists and the Supreme Court.

"I act as I act because I must live where I live, and these issues are *here*. They can't be wished away."

And he added, "I will do *anything* to maintain the right of my children and the right of my grandchildren to educate their children the way they want and with whom they please." He paused, and thought. "I would *give* anything to see that that right is preserved. Anything. If necessary, I would *sell this house*."

It was perhaps the ultimate expression of Tom Brady's belief that his is a just cause.

2. AN EPISODE IN THE DELTA

JUDGE TOM BRADY had suggested that the Mississippi branch of his proposed "grass-roots" apartheid organization be called the Sons of the White Magnolia. But, he had genially added, " 'a rose by any name will smell as sweet.' "

The less flowery name that was eventually picked was simply the Citizens' Councils. The very pallor of the name probably helped to make it attractive to many Mississippians. A local Citizens' Council, often with bankers and lawyers and physicians and "big-mule" planters as its officers, seemed so unlike any "hate group" that had existed in the South before, so free of the thuggery and juvenile hocus-pocus of the Ku Klux Klans of years gone by.

Within a very short time after publication of *Black Monday* the organization's Mississippi membership was in the tens of thousands. The "CC" had become—as it has remained to this day—a force to be carefully thought about by every Mississippian before he acted or spoke on any matter that might be considered at all "controversial."

This ineluctable fact of Mississippi life was illustrated in a memorable manner by a series of occurrences in the delta county of Holmes. . . .

Sitting in a bright Memphis restaurant one recent afternoon, a former Holmes County planter named Eugene Cox recalled the September 1955 day that Preacher Marsh Calloway had driven out to his place to warn him of a gathering that some Citizens' Council members were planning to hold that night in the village of Tchula.

"Mr. Calloway, who was the Presbyterian minister over at Durant, had come hunting for me and my associate on the farm, Dr. David Minter. He said a mass meeting was being organized to hear a tape recording that concerned Dave and me. It wasn't officially called a Citizens' Council meeting, but I learned that J. P. Love, the head of the Council in Tchula, was going to preside."

The tape recording was of statements made to the county sheriff by four teen-age Negro boys, Cox was told. Some of the white citizens of Tchula seemed to figure that what the boys had said was proof that Cox and Minter favored racial integration.

Actually, Calloway's warning of the meeting did not come as a total surprise to Cox and Minter.

"For twenty years I had been talking to educators and business people in Mississippi, trying to get better schools for Negroes," said Cox. "Now that the 1954 decision had been handed down, we knew the extreme segregationists in the county were concerned about what might happen—that they were thinking: 'Who might cause us trouble'?"

Gene Cox looks like a Mississippi planter. He is a tall, strapping man in his fifties, with wavy gray hair and blue eyes. When he walks, he takes high, powerful strides, as if each step were carrying him over a cotton row. And when he sits reminiscing over a cup of coffee, he speaks in a soft drawl that is as soothingly slow as the Yazoo River.

But the plantation that he and Dr. David Minter operated near Tchula was an alien one to the delta. Even its name had an unfamiliar flavor: Providence Farm.

It was, in fact, a co-operative plantation, an outgrowth of an agricultural project sponsored back in the depression thirties by a group of ministers and professional do-gooders that included Reinhold Niebuhr, the theologian; Sherwood Eddy, the "Y" leader; and John Rust, the Memphis inventor of the Rust cotton picker. It was in part a religious missionary venture and in part an effort to help relocate some of the Arkansas sharecropper families who had been evicted during the attempt to organize the old Southern Tenant Farmers Union.

Cox had excellent qualifications for a job as one of the project's chief staff members. As a man "raised in the middle of a cotton patch in East Texas," he had some practical farming experience.

Too, he and his wife had the kind of missionary inclinations that the project called for. Cox had studied for the ministry for a time before choosing to take a degree in sociology at Texas Christian University. And his wife, who was born in Japan, was the daughter and granddaughter of Presbyterian missionaries.

The Delta Foundation project first located on a parcel of land in Bolivar County eighty miles or so northwest of Holmes. Jonathan Daniels, in *A Southerner Discovers the South,* described paying a 1937 visit there to Cox and the co-op's first manager, the Reverend Sam H. Franklin, and their helpers: "[A]ll the staff of the co-operative seemed to me like Robinson Crusoes washed up by good will on the delta of Mississippi where they were applying their city brains and missionary Christian enthusiasm energetically and ingeniously to the hard problems of the isolated land." And speaking of a donation that was being made to the project that year by some rich and philanthropic lady, Daniels remarked: "No better crop than such enthusiasm grows anywhere in the South and so long as such middle-aged Christians still bloom the members of the Delta can count on co-operative success. The boll weevil doesn't bite them."

In the beginning the co-op's participants were both white and Negro families. Then in the early 1940's the Foundation sold its land in Bolivar and moved the operation to a 2,600-acre farm in Holmes County. After that the great majority of the families served by the co-op were Negro.

The main pride of Providence Farm in Holmes County was its low-cost medical clinic, operated by Dr. Minter with the help of Cox's wife, who is a registered nurse. Minter, a former North Carolinian who is six years younger than Cox, had been with the project since 1938, except for a few years' tour of duty as an Air Corps medical officer during World War II. Like Cox, Minter had planned in his youth to become a minister; like Mrs. Cox, he came from a family of Presbyterian missionaries.

"In 1955 we had—in addition to the clinic—a small store and a credit union with about two hundred members, mostly Negroes," Cox recalled. "In years past we had had our own sawmill, dairy, and poultry unit, our own school, and a pretty extensive cotton-farming operation."

Then because of changes in the agricultural pattern of the delta

—the replacement of tenant farming by large-scale mechanized cotton cultivation—Providence Farm by 1955 had greatly reduced the size of its cotton crop. And improvements in the state's program of schooling for Negroes had made some of the farm's educational activities unnecessary.

"But we were still active in organizing 'institutes' for farmers, planning summer camps for Negro children, and raising money for scholarships for some of the kids. We had a program of crafts and a nondenominational Bible school, and in the summers we would bring in Negro college students to staff the camps and coach the kids in sports."

Five white families were living on the farm in 1955—Cox and his wife and three teen-age daughters, the Minters and their three children, and the families of the staff carpenter, tractor driver, and sawmiller.

These were the last of the "Robinson Crusoes" still dwelling on Providence Farm when the Reverend Marsh Calloway drove out to warn them that something more serious than the boll weevil might be just about to bite.

After hearing the minister out, Cox decided to telephone the Tchula Citizens' Council leader, J. P. Love, who only recently had been elected as Holmes County's next representative in the Mississippi Legislature.

"Love said he was sorry Dave and I hadn't been notified about the meeting earlier. I told him we wanted to go to it ourselves, that we'd rather do that than have somebody coming out to the farm at one o'clock in the morning to tell us what it was all about. I assumed then that it was something designed to discredit us."

Not until Cox and Minter arrived at the meeting did they come to realize that its design was a far more remarkable one: the purpose of the meeting was to excommunicate them from Holmes County.

The prelude to the extraordinary meeting that was being organized that September day of 1955 had begun one Saturday night away back in July 1954 which—coincidentally—was the very month that the first Citizens' Council was formed in Holmes County.

On that Saturday night a Negro named Henry Randale was

brought to Dr. Minter at the Providence Farm clinic with a bullet wound in the back of his thigh. He had been shot, he said, by the county sheriff, Richard Byrd.

Randale and several other Negroes had been standing beside a railroad crossing in Tchula, laughing and engaging in Saturday-night talk of this and that, when Sheriff Byrd drove up. The sheriff, a hefty fellow who had a reputation as a lawman who was "hard on niggers," ordered them to cut out their "whooping" and move on. Seizing on Randale, Byrd demanded to know what all the whooping was about.

Randale replied, " 'Twarn't none of me that whooped."

The sheriff, apparently considering this a not adequately respectful answer, beat him on the head, then, as Randale tried to run from him, fired a bullet into the back of his leg, and drove off. Randale's friends picked him up and carried him out to Dr. Minter at Providence Farm.

Many small-town Southern newspapers might have overlooked such an event as merely another routine incident in "The Law's" Saturday-night process of policing the Negroes. But the owner of two Holmes County newspapers, Mrs. Hazel Brannon Smith of Lexington, was a publisher with an outspokenness rare in rural Southern journalism.

An energetic, plumply attractive woman who was born and reared in Alabama, she had come to the delta in 1936 to publish the Durant *News*. She soon acquired a second paper, the Lexington *Advertiser,* and developed one of the more prosperous weekly publishing operations in Mississippi. Her success came largely because she was a skillful writer who seemed not to mind stepping on the toes of advertisers or elected officials when she felt it was in the public interest. She was especially noted for her editorial campaigns against the local bootlegging industry. This editorial straightforwardness—plus, perhaps, the fact that her husband was a Yankee, born in Philadelphia—naturally had won her a number of enemies in her circulation area.

In the editions of her Lexington *Advertiser* and Durant *News* immediately following the shooting of Henry Randale, Hazel Smith made it plain that she felt the incident proved Richard Byrd was not a fit man for the office of sheriff:

The laws in America are for everyone—rich and poor, strong and weak, white and black. . . . Laws were made to protect the weak from the strong. . . . This man was shot in the back. He was running only because he had been told to "get goin' " by the Sheriff. He had not violated any law. . . . He just made the one mistake of being around when the Sheriff drove up.

Sheriff Byrd promptly filed a $57,500 libel suit against Mrs. Smith.

Dr. Minter, who had treated Randale's wound and had heard his account of the shooting, was the main witness for the defense. The physician later remarked on the atmosphere that existed as he prepared to testify: "As part of the pre-trial campaign to discredit Mrs. Smith and also to discredit me as a witness there were many rumors spread all over the county that I was a Communist, that I was heading a spy ring and holding secret meetings, that I was distributing communist literature."

Cox said that he understood that Sheriff Byrd's attorney asked Minter just one cross-examination question: "Do you live in a community called Providence?"

It was felt by some spectators that the most valuable witness in Byrd's behalf was one who testified that Hazel Smith once had a Negro woman to dinner in her home. Mrs. Smith denied this.

Nevertheless, the jury brought in a verdict against her, awarding Sheriff Byrd $10,000 in damages.

Although no actual money payment was made pending Mrs. Smith's appeal of the case to the State Supreme Court, the verdict obviously renewed Sheriff Byrd's self-confidence as a guardian of the Southern Way of Life. With the belief that Hazel Smith had been permanently squelched, Byrd and other dedicated segregationists of the county focused their attention on Dr. Minter and his friend Cox.

Their chance finally came in September 1955, when Byrd arrested four Negro boys.

Byrd accused them of whistling at a white girl—a serious charge to be leveled at a Mississippi Negro at any time, and particularly grave just at that time; the Emmett Till slaying had occurred in an adjoining delta county only the previous month.

When it was learned that the four boys lived near Providence Farm and their families had taken part in some of the co-op's activities, the questioning of them was intensified. After interrogating the terrified youths through a weekend, a two-hour recording of their answers to questions was taped on Monday. It was later in that day that Preacher Calloway heard that the mass meeting was being organized.

When Cox and Minter, along with Calloway, drove in to Tchula that night, they found that a crowd of 700 white men from all over the county had gathered at the high-school auditorium.

"As I say, they didn't officially call it a Citizens' Council meeting," Cox recollected. "But J. P. Love was presiding. And there to play the tape recorder was William Moses, who was chairman of the Holmes County Citizens' Council."

Moses worked for the same auto sales firm in Lexington that had employed Richard Byrd before his election as sheriff.

Byrd was there, of course, and—according to a later United Press report—so was Holmes County Attorney Pat Barrett, head of the Lexington chapter of the Citizens' Council.

(Whether the gathering was really a "Citizens' Council meeting" is debatable, but not very pertinent, for by September 1955 the Council membership was so interwoven with the white community in general that it was practically impossible to distinguish the one from the other. As a Council leader later remarked, even as he was denying that Love's chairmanship of the Tchula gathering made it a CC meeting per se: "How could you have a meeting in this county without one of our members in the chair?")

Soon after Love called the meeting to order, said Cox, Moses switched on the tape recorder.

"The tape was two hours long," Cox remembers. "The boys who had been questioned lived on a place adjoining Providence Farm. Their families had come to the clinic, were members of our credit union, and had attended some of the institutes we'd held. The tape was full of loaded and leading questions. The answers the boys gave to them built up the image that Negroes and whites swam together in our pool at the farm, and that Dave Minter and I advocated school integration."

In a gesture of fair play Love invited Minter and Cox up to the auditorium stage to make their answers to the implications of the recording.

"So we went right up in front of the footlights," said Cox. "Dave told the crowd that to his knowledge there had been no interracial swimming at the farm. But a planter out in the audience stood up and said he had personally seen it taking place. I said they both might be right. I explained that my wife had hired a Negro girl as a maid to watch over our three daughters whenever they went into the pool, and she'd given the maid a swim suit to wear when she went with them. That fellow probably had seen the Negro maid with my children; that was probably it."

Both Cox and Minter denied that they had promoted any kind of social integration at Providence Farm.

"Since there's a Mississippi state law that says there must be no activities between Negroes and whites that might lead to inter-marriage, the trustees and staff of the project had decided long ago not to have any interracial activities on the farm at the social level."

After Cox and Minter had presented their "defense," there was a pause. Then one of the planters in the audience got up and made the motion for excommunication. The motion was that Cox and Minter be asked to move away "in the best interest of the county."

The Reverend Marsh Calloway rose to protest the motion. The whole evening's ceremony in the auditorium, he declared, was "un-American and un-Christian."

But when the vote was taken, all but two members of the audience stood up and were counted for excommunication and the Southern Way of Life.

"One of the two that voted for us was Marsh Calloway," Cox remembered. "The other was a fellow—a welder or machinist, I believe he was—who'd told the crowd, 'Gentlemen, I think we ought to pray about this.'"

Cox and Minter felt determined not to accept their neighbors' decision that they must leave the county. They vowed to stick it out.

But there were discouragements.

For one thing, the elders of Marsh Calloway's church in Durant met soon after the meeting and voted in favor of a resolution ask-ing him to resign his pulpit. A spokesman for the elders said Calloway's remarks had caused many of his church's members to "lose faith" in him. "His usefulness is at an end here," the elder spokesman said.

Cox said that the last he heard Calloway had been living in Louisiana, but he understood the minister had moved on from there since then.

Too, there were discomforts and inconveniences.

"We got a lot of anonymous telephone calls threatening us, and then they cut our telephone line," Cox remembered. "We heard rumors we were going to be burned out; the sheriff set up a road block for about a week and kept the deputies around the place. People were afraid to come to the clinic, and soon Dave's practice fell off to practically nothing.

"Another thing: Dave's insurance was canceled. The company said it was because he was considered an 'unusual risk.' Dave had to scout around a long time for a company that would sell him insurance. He finally found that Lloyd's of London was the only one that would insure him."

Ten months after the excommunication ceremony at the Tchula auditorium Dr. Minter packed up his family and moved to Tucson, Arizona. The move was made partly to benefit the health of one of his children. But the main reason, obviously, was that without a medical practice his usefulness in Holmes County—like Marsh Calloway's "usefulness" to his congregation—had come to an end.

Dave Minter commented later:

Most planters [had] stopped sending patients to me. There were a few exceptions, but there was evidently a concerted effort on the part of council members to boycott me. . . . One former patient [a white man] confided to me while drinking that he would have been to see me but that the council had told [people] to stay away. . . . There is very little which can be definitely blamed on the councils or rather the organized efforts of the councils. . . . It is hard to say if the council would have bothered about us if the Sheriff had not laid the groundwork, although eventually there would have been something done because of our opposition to them (not open but just the fact that we did not join). . . . Although no one admitted that the CC planned the [Tchula] meeting, it was certainly through their organization that word spread; also, at the meeting that night one prominent man from Goodman [another Holmes County town] recommended that a committee be appointed to investigate and report to the councils!

The Council organization clamped no "real boycott" on him and Cox, said Minter. They could still buy gasoline and groceries for the farm as usual.

The thing that the council did was to let loose "the winds of fear." . . .

A month after the Minter family's departure Cox and his wife and three daughters left. By then all the other white families had gone, too.

After twenty years the Providence Farm project was no more.

Gene Cox and his family have since lived in a suburb of Memphis. Sipping the last of his coffee in the restaurant there, he said, "You know, the problems we were trying to meet with the project back in the thirties still exist in the South. We still have the problem of the thousands of persons being displaced by mechanization in the rural areas. And the illiterates—the unskilled people who are physically and psychologically unfitted to make the transition from the farms to the industrial cities: they're still there as they were in the thirties. It's just that nowadays people don't seem to realize it."

Even after the Providence Farm project vanished, the 2,600 acres in Holmes County were still owned by the Delta Foundation.

"I go down there once every two or three months," Cox said. "We rent out some of the land for row crops, and the rest is in pasture. Four Negro families are living on the place, but no longer on any kind of cooperative basis. The credit union was liquidated long ago, and there's no clinic, of course; the house where Dave Minter and his family lived is empty."

But just before leaving the restaurant he added, "I wouldn't want another experience like the Tchula Meeting. But if I had to live over the past twenty years again, I really don't know what I'd have done differently. It's hard to determine what success we had. You never know what the results are of a thing like that."

In November 1955, just two months after the Tchula meeting, publisher Hazel Smith got some good news from the state capital. The Mississippi Supreme Court had reversed the Holmes County court verdict which had awarded the sheriff $10,000 in libel damages. However, this did not free her from the pressure of efforts by some of the more dedicated segregationists to force her and her husband to leave the county as Cox and Minter had been encouraged to do.

Her husband, Walter, was relieved from his job as administrator of the Holmes County Community Hospital in early 1956. Although all the physicians attached to the hospital had signed a petition urging that he be kept in the job, the hospital's trustees decided he was too "controversial."

In 1957 Mrs. Smith received two bits of "national recognition" which fit nicely into the segregationists' campaign to brand her as a radical integrationist.

The Fund for the Republic selected her for its annual American Traditions Award. In Mississippi this had disturbing implications. The CC Association's monthly newspaper, *The Citizens' Council,* had only recently proclaimed that the Fund for the Republic was a Red-infiltrated organization dedicated to forcing integration on the South.

That same year the Negro magazine, *Ebony,* printed Mrs. Smith's picture as an illustration for an article about Southern white women who were courageously crusading for integration. The picture had been obtained by *Ebony* from another magazine without Mrs. Smith's knowledge, and, in fact, the article which it helped to illustrate did not mention her.

But the *Ebony* article was circulated by her segregationist critics throughout Mississippi. Mrs. Sara McCorkle, who tours Mississippi high schools to speak in behalf of the Citizens' Council, found copies of the *Ebony* issue to be useful illustrations for her lectures on the dangers of creeping integrationism within the state.

The effort to rout Mrs. Smith took more concrete form in 1958 when thirty-five businessmen and planters of Holmes County launched a $30,000 stock sale to establish a new weekly to compete with her two newspapers. Among the thirty-five were many who had attended the meeting at which Cox and Minter had been "read out" of the county. And picked as editor of the new paper was

Chester Marshall, who had been Mrs. Smith's general manager for the past year.

William Moses, who had been the tape-recorder operator that night at the Tchula meeting, issued an interesting statement in behalf of this new entry into American journalism: "This is not against anybody. This is just to get a paper with an editor that thinks like we do. This paper will not take sides in controversial issues."

Or, as a United Press report explained, "Organizers of the new paper include lawyers and business people who contend that Mrs. Smith does not reflect the thinking of most of the white people of the county at a time when solidarity of opinion is needed to preserve the Southern Way of Life."

Ironically, Hazel Smith has never been an advocate of integration. As Hodding Carter III has noted, Mrs. Smith "is, in point of fact, a segregationist who rarely lets a column on the racial question go by without reaffirming that she is one."

But in view of her refusal to join the organized opposition to the Supreme Court school decision she might properly be considered a "moderate."

The world of the Southern "moderate" is a lonely one.

Even as she was being attacked by the Councils and by such rigid segregationists as Sheriff Byrd in her own community, her "moderation" earned her a considerable amount of condescendingly maudlin or simply insulting criticism from some of the nation's professional Liberals.

Typical was the report of Carl Rowan, the Minneapolis Negro journalist and State Department official, who is probably the most widely read commentator on "the Southern problem." In his book, *Go South to Sorrow,* Rowan made this analysis of Hazel Smith and the vacation she and her husband took shortly after he was fired from his hospital job:

Now this woman was deeply disturbed over what was taking place in her county. . . . How could outspoken Hazel Smith not say editorially what everyone knew was in her heart: that a Gestapo atmosphere lay over Holmes County covering it like the summer dew?

Sure, old Uncle Mose and Uncle Tom were timid and frightened; these black men were feared o' the white-man boss with his wealth and guns and book learning. But this was a white woman with bright blue eyes and brown wavy hair, a white woman with a lovely home up in the hills, two newspapers, a big Cadillac car —and a constitutional guarantee of freedom that she had never had reason to doubt. Yet when newspapermen from the North telephoned, or dropped in to chat, Hazel Brannon Smith admitted that *she* was afraid. . . . So this white woman did what few Delta Negroes could afford: she left Mississippi with her husband for two weeks of rest in the West, hoping the storm would blow over. . . .

You have traveled through Hazel Brannon Smith's Mississippi, and you have heard white people like her whisper that "this White Citizens' Council is the most vicious organization ever to arise in the United States." You have heard these white people whisper in woeful timidity that it is "akin to the Nazi Party in Germany." . . .

So we weep—and wish—wish these white whisperers would speak louder. Shout it out to the world! Shout in such a chorus that Hazel Brannon Smith can put her pen to work again. Yes, we wish, but we know that this white woman who loves liberty also loves that house up in the hills, that car out front, those newspapers, even as the black man down the Delta loves his fatback and molasses—and we know she will return to Mississippi and become so lost among the white whisperers that perhaps even Richard Byrd will forget her.

But in real life things are rarely so neat. Often there are loose ends which only death can tie together.

The truth is that Hazel Smith did not become "lost among the white whisperers." She continued to be Mississippi journalism's most outspoken opponent of the Citizens' Councils and the state's official apartheid agency, the Mississippi Sovereignty Commission.

In a typical editorial she wrote of the CC-Sovereignty Commission program in this fashion:

This monstrous thing will destroy us and our state as we know and love it if we do not summon the courage not only to lift our voices in protest but to fight it with every honorable means at our disposal.

Our freedom is being taken away from us here in Mississippi not by Communist Russia, Nazi Germany, or any other totalitarian country or philosophy—but by our own home-grown variety of fascism, Mississippi-born and nurtured.

It should also be destroyed here.

She has been in arguments a-plenty, but she usually has had the last word.

Back when the Holmes County crusaders for "solidarity of opinion" were organizing their paper to compete with hers, she wrote in an editorial:

For four years now your editor has been the subject and object of vilification and abuse conducted in a whispering campaign by a few misguided zealots. . . . Today, not only in Holmes County but in much of Mississippi, we live in an atmosphere of fear. It hangs like a dark cloud over us—dominating almost every facet of public and private life. No one speaks freely any more for fear of being misunderstood. . . . Almost every man and woman is afraid to try to do anything to promote good will and harmony between the races—afraid he or she will be taken as a mixer or an integrationist, or worse—if there is anything worse by Southern standards.

But she vowed to her opponents that she would not yield to their pressures and fold a newspaper which for so long had been a part of the life and thought of Holmes County:

This is not a lone woman editor you are fighting, it is not just a newspaper. . . . It is an institution interwoven into your life and the life of the community and county. It recorded . . . your triumphs and sorrows, the good and evil for 121 years. . . . And it will still be around to carry your obituary.

Her paper was still around, in fact, to carry the obituary of Sheriff Richard Byrd. The sheriff, who had lived so much of his life in an atmosphere of violence, died quietly of a heart ailment in 1960.

3. THE SECRETARY

WHILE Judge Tom Brady may be considered the chief architect of the Citizens' Council movement, its head construction foreman has been a former Mississippi State football player named Robert "Tut" Patterson.

As the prime organizer of the first CC, in Sunflower County, Patterson holds Citizens' Council membership card No. 1. And from the beginning he has served as the Confederacy-wide CC Association's executive secretary.

Until The Decision in 1954 Patterson had occupied himself with farming. When he abandoned most of his agricultural interests to become a full-time salaried executive of the Council Association some folks of a suspicious nature suggested that his devotion to the cause of segregation might have been stimulated by thoughts of the hundreds of thousands of dollars in annual dues being paid by CC members.

But if Patterson possesses anything more than a casual interest in money, he certainly does not reflect it with ostentatious living. He and his large family dwell in a little out-of-the-way delta hamlet called Itta Bena—in a rambling frame house that obviously has not been subjected to a paintbrush in some years.

And if the executive secretary of the Association of Citizens' Councils of America feels that a native black uprising is imminent there is no sign of this feeling around his house. When a stranger drives up, a spaniel in the yard merely gives him a bored gaze and nuzzles back to sleep on his crossed paws. A full five minutes of horn blowing and rapping on doors is needed to communicate the fact that a tourist has come to interview the official spokesman for the South's largest and most powerful segregationist organization.

Patterson's mother-in-law and aged grandmother-in-law are at home with two of his children, who are watching a morning television program beamed from the RCA Building in the enemy North. His wife and the other two of their four children are over at the schoolhouse (segregated), where Mrs. Patterson is helping with the decorations for a teen dance.

Fetched from the lake shore far behind his house, where he had been fertilizing his trees with a dibble stick, Patterson is wearing a rough plaid shirt and ancient green corduroy trousers. His field boots are caked with mud.

He is thirty-nine, a muscular bulk of a man with a blaze of wavy red hair. His eyes are blue, and innocent of that glint of cunning which is so often to be observed along the apartheid circuit: the expression in Patterson's changes back and forth between frank belligerence and crinkly good humor.

A measure of belligerent distrust is in the expression at first.

"I haven't interviewed anybody like this for four or five years," he said.

Patterson lamented that he had been "burned" over and over again by Yankee reporters who had been "all peaches and cream" while they were talking with him face to face but then had gone away and written uncomplimentary things about him.

"Now that I'm interviewing you," he said with a sigh of resignation, "I guess you can write anything you want and I couldn't deny it because there's just you and me here talking."

Leading the way into his "study" in a little one-room sleeping cottage behind his house, Patterson shook his head with despair as he reflected on his attempts to make the reasons for the CC's position on race relations clear to people outside the South.

"I've explained and explained and explained." He stabbed open a couple of cans of beer for his visitor and himself, and dropped heavily into an easy chair. "A long time ago I finally decided that logic has got nothing to do with this thing. We're through explaining."

But if anything is obvious it is the fact that the big, rather boyish-looking CC secretary loves nothing better than to discuss The Problem and tell how he feels it should be solved.

As a temporary solution Patterson recommends that people up North cease "meddling in the affairs" of Mississippi and the South. Left to themselves, Patterson knows, white Southerners will "solve" the race problem by reconstructing the traditional barricades against integration. To let the barriers down, Patterson feels, would be to welcome interracial familiarity and ultimately the "mongrelization" of the white race.

"Of course the threat of mongrelization won't really be eliminated until the two races are *geographically* separated," he said.

Legal segregation, even as it has functioned in Mississippi, has not been very effective in preventing reproductive contacts between whites and Negroes, Patterson recognizes.

"You know that outfit called the Black Muslims wants a few of our states to be set aside just for Negroes. It might be a good idea to go along with their program and give 'em three or four states. I'd suggest"—he laughed, relishing the thought—"I'd suggest New York, and Illinois, and Michigan, and—let's see—maybe California."

In fact, the development of one all-Negro state in this country has virtually been accomplished, he said. He was speaking of the District of Columbia, where the population is now upward of 60 per cent Negro.

"Before long they'll give 'em self-government in Washington, and soon after that they'll elect a Negro[1] police chief and a Negro school superintendent—and then the last of the white people still living there will leave.

"Then one day the Capital will be moved—out to the Ozarks or somewhere. Of course the Negroes will be told that it's being moved

[1] Patterson pronounces the word "Negro" the same way that civil-rights campaigners pronounce it: *Nē'grō* (rhyming with "free throw")."

Actually, it is not lingually comfortable for most Southerners—black or white—to give the word that pronunciation. Most Southerners—those who do not have occasion to make public speeches about The Problem as does Patterson—naturally pronounce it *Ni'grə*—just as they pronounce Toledo, Toronto, and Colorado in such a way that they rhyme with Nevada.

Many Yankee authors, when quoting the speech of a Southerner, think his pronunciation of the word "Negro" as *Ni'grə* illustrates bigotry, and they (the said Yankees) render it phonetically in their manuscripts as "Nigra." Such a rendition is interesting but is, I think, misleading.

Of course almost all Southerners who employ the word "nigger" employ it consciously as a disparaging word.

because Washington is too vulnerable to enemy attack or something."

The CC Association's official newspaper, *The Citizens' Council,* reported a few months ago that Patterson, "after thinking about the question at length and discussing it with a number of his associates," had drafted a long-range "platform" for the organization. Designed, in pseudo-paraphrase of the Golden Rule, "to prevent the NAACP from doing unto us as it hath done unto others," the main planks of Patterson's platform are these:

We advocate: . . .
The recognition of racial differences as fact . . .
The migration of Negroes and white people who seek integration to states whose customs and laws sanction it . . .
The movement of Negroes and white people who desire to live among their own kind to communities populated exclusively by members of their own race. We advocate laws insuring the future racial integrity of these communities . . .
The strict enforcement of state voter qualification laws . . .
Separate public schools and other facilities for the black and white races where they are required to maintain peace and order . . .
The use of public-welfare programs to help the unfortunate to rehabilitate themselves. We deplore the use of these funds to encourage immorality and indolence . . .
The establishment of a Federal Commission with advisory groups in each state to study and advance plans for geographical separation of the black and white races.

Patterson majored in animal husbandry when he was in college, but he speaks with pride of the amount of reading he has done in recent years on human racial matters. His philosophy of race is probably fairly well summarized in a comment made by him a few years ago:

"As a race the Negro is definitely inferior to the white. The only fields in which they are superior are in their physical strength and their natural capacity as entertainers, making fun of themselves for the benefit of others."

It is a philosophy that really does not require the reading of heavy books. Practically all white men of the Mississippi delta are equipped with it from infancy.

And Tut Patterson's past, his present, and his hopes for the future are intimately identified with that fertile stretch of cotton land that spreads eastward from the Mississippi River.

He grew up in the delta town of Clarksdale, the son of a cotton trader, the great-grandson of a Confederate general.

The past is meaningful to him. In his cottage study he has a collection of old documents and keepsakes that recall the days of slavery and the Civil War and the hard years that followed it. His grandmother-in-law, a woman of ninety, has spoken often to Patterson of her memories of living through Black Reconstruction at another delta town, Friar's Point.

"That old lady can remember when there was a Negro sheriff in her town. She can remember the Negroes coming down the sidewalk and forcing the whites to walk in the gutter. . . . Sometimes she'll wake up at night and be nervous, thinking she hears something; it's just that she's remembering some of the bad things that happened way back then."

Patterson was a star end and captain of the Mississippi State Maroons. When his visitor recalled seeing the Maroons defeat the Alabama Crimson Tide in 1942, Patterson proudly remembered he caught a pass for the winning touchdown in that game.

Right after college he became a major in the Army paratroops and served twenty-seven months in Europe, fighting with the 82nd Airborne Division in the Battle of the Bulge.

His years after the war were not so dramatic as his seasons as a football hero and paratroop officer. He was married in 1945—to a petite, attractive blonde from Mississippi—and settled down for a few years on a dairy farm in Tennessee. In 1951 he returned with his wife to Sunflower County in the delta, the home county of Senator Jim Eastland. There, in partnership with two men who had been his fraternity brothers in college, he went to work managing a plantation.

Then came the Supreme Court decision of May 17, 1954. It was for Patterson a summons to combat—a new kind of combat with very nearly as much excitement as a homecoming game or a parachute drop.

Judge Tom Brady's stirring *Black Monday* message convinced him that the great hour of crisis was at hand.

"I became obsessed with the thing. I started agitating around town [Indianola, the county seat of Sunflower]. One day down at the compress [the warehouse where cotton is compressed into tight bales for storing] I talked to Mr. Hawkins [D. H. Hawkins, manager of the compress], and said we ought to get ourselves a little organization to see if we can't do something."

Patterson, Hawkins, and a dozen other men of Sunflower County—planters and businessmen and local political officials—met the night of July 11, 1954, and set up the Indianola Citizens' Council, the first of the hundreds of CC's that soon would blossom throughout Dixie.

"We didn't consider ourselves hatemongers and racists and bigots," Patterson recalled. "We were faced with integration in a town where there were twenty-one hundred Negro students and seven hundred white. . . . We just felt like integration would utterly destroy everything that we valued."

Within six weeks after the Indianola meeting Citizens' Councils had cropped up in seventeen Mississippi counties. And by October 1954 an Association of Citizens' Councils of Mississippi had been formed—with Tom Brady among its executive committee members and Tut Patterson as its executive secretary.

The great secret of the Council movement's success was the very simplicity of the organization. There were no fancy titles as in the Klans of old—no "imperial wizards" or "grand dragons"—no uniforms, passwords, blood oaths, or other mumbo jumbo.

Each Council simply had a board of directors and four committees: an information and education committee to "educate our citizens, black and white, to the advantages of segregation and the dangers of integration"; a membership and finance committee to "seek white patriotic voters for membership"; a legal committee to "anticipate moves by agitators [and] recommend application of economic pressure to troublemakers"; and a political committee to "screen all candidates [and] discourage Negro registration by every legal means."

Later the reference to "economic pressure" was dropped as a part of the official CC program, and Council spokesmen made a point of denying that the Councils—as organizations—advocated the application of such pressure to anyone.

"The idea of solid and unified backing of circuit clerks, sheriffs, and local and state officials in the proper discharge of sworn duties was worked out," Patterson commented in the CC Association's first annual report. "It was acknowledged that the impending threat was of such magnitude that our elected officials would be unable to deal with it without the unyielding and organized support of thousands of responsible white citizens to counter the steadily mounting pressure and unceasing attacks from left-wing groups [which are] irrevocably dedicated to our destruction."

In the early days, as Patterson and other missionaries from the original CC spread their gospel through Mississippi and collected new members at five dollars a head, they moved quietly.

"There has been no publicity and we suggest to each group that they keep it out of the papers and off the air," one of Patterson's fellow founders of the movement, Herman Moore, an Indianola banker, was quoted as saying at a 1954 organizational meeting. "The news has trickled out, just as we had expected it would. The Negro knows that we are organizing, but he does not know what we plan to do. The best thing, we think, is to put him where he has stayed for forty years and keep him guessing. . . ."

In 1955, just as the council movement was flowering all over the old Confederacy, several notorious incidents of violence occurred in Mississippi. They were cited by many writers as evidence that the Councils were promoting bloodshed.

In its statement titled *M Is for Mississippi and Murder,* the New York headquarters of the National Association for the Advancement of Colored People bitterly referred to a remark that Patterson had made to Homer Bigart, then a reporter for the New York *Herald Tribune:* "Sir, this is not the United States. This is Sunflower County, Mississippi."

"In this climate of opinion which derides the courts and the rule of law, which harps on violence, sometimes nakedly and sometimes through the device of repeated disavowal," the NAACP commented, "three persons were murdered in Mississippi between May 7 and August 28, 1955."

The Reverend George W. Lee, head of the NAACP in Belzoni, a town that advertises itself as "the heart of the delta," was killed by two shotgun blasts May 7.

Then came the shooting of Lamar Smith on August 13 after he insisted on voting in Judge Brady's home town, Brookhaven.

And, finally, there was the kidnap-slaying of Emmett Till in the delta county of Tallahatchie on August 28.

"These were not murders of passion, or for profit, but futile, cold, brutal murders to bolster a theory of superiority based upon skin color," the NAACP statement said.

The NAACP issued a pamphlet containing a simplified map with five towns of Mississippi marked in red: "BELZONI, site of assassination of Reverend George W. Lee; BROOKHAVEN, where Lamar Smith was shot down in broad daylight in front of the courthouse; MONEY, site of [the] kidnaping of fourteen-year-old Emmett Till whose body was recovered three days later from the Tallahatchie River across the county line; SUMNER, where the accused slayers of the boy [J. W. Milam, thirty-six, and his half-brother, Roy Bryant, twenty-four, whose wife was whistled at by young Till] were tried and acquitted; WINONA, state headquarters of the White Citizens' Councils."

The Mississippi State president of the NAACP, Dr. A. P. McCoy of Jackson, said publicly: "I directly blame the Citizens' Council for Lee's murder."

Moreover, the NAACP filed a formal petition with the Justice Department blaming the Citizens' Councils for creating an "atmosphere of violence" which led to the deaths of Lee, Smith, and Till. The petition urged the government to act immediately to halt the "state of jungle fury" existing in Mississippi.

But no noteworthy action was taken by the Justice Department. And, in fact, no concrete evidence was produced that the CCs had anything to do with the deaths.

Tut Patterson called the death of the Till boy "regrettable" but insisted that the Council organization was not responsible for it.

"This is absolutely not so," he said, "no more than the boy's death can be attributed to the church he belonged to."

In a letter to Council members some time later Patterson declared:

"Our members know that our Councils have prevented violence, and will continue to do so, here in Mississippi. . . . That is why we organized against integration; to prevent violence."

In retrospect the theory might well be advanced that the existence of the Citizens' Councils *has* tended to reduce rather than increase the killing and maiming of Negroes by white men in Mississippi.

With the very notable exception of the brutal Poplarville lynching,[2] the years since 1955 in Mississippi have been remarkedly free of "race incidents"—considered in the light of the state's long history of lynchings and Negro killings.

In truth, violence has not been necessary. The organization that Patterson and his friends had launched possessed a weapon just as effective as direct violence—economic pressure.

One of Patterson's fellow charter members of the CC, Attorney Arthur Clark of Indianola, was quoted in 1954: "It is the thought of our group that the solution of this problem may become easier if various agitators and the like could be removed from the communities in which they now operate. We propose to accomplish this through the careful application of economic pressure upon those men who cannot be controlled otherwise."[3]

Patterson has taken pains on several occasions to deny that the Councils have promoted the "economic-pressure" technique, but has made it plain that he does not disapprove if Council members practice it—as long as it is not done in the name of the Council organization.

"The Association of Citizens' Councils of Mississippi has never advocated economic pressure. Of course we don't denounce indi-

[2] A Negro named Mack Charles Parker, who had been accused of assaulting a white woman, was dragged from his cell in the Poplarville jail and lynched by a band of white men on the night of April 24, 1959. Evidence gathered by the FBI in the case was presented to two grand juries in Mississippi, one state and one federal, but neither returned an indictment.

[3] In his 1954 book *Black Monday* Judge Tom Brady had suggested that "as a last resort" the white South could declare "a cold war and an economic boycott" against any Negro who chose to follow the "communist-inspired program" of the National Association for the Advancement of Colored People.

"A large percentage, over a third, of the negro women in the South are domestic servants," he wrote. "When this source of revenue is cut off, and they are no longer employed, a deplorable situation will arise for the negro. . . . It will be inconvenience upon the white women of the South to discharge their maids and cooks, but this can be done, if necessary. . . .

viduals who use freedom of choice in their business arrangement. . . . The only boycott we have heard of lately is that used by
the NAACP, the CIO, and our federal government. . . . This is the
dagger, the cannon, and the atomic bomb of the mongrelizers. Must
we use peeled bananas, water pistols, and cream puffs against
these weapons?"

Typical of this *individual* (rather than *organizational*) pressure
was the move made against a group of Negroes who signed a
school-desegregation petition in the delta town of Yazoo City.
Shortly after the petition was filed with school officials, the Yazoo
City Citizens' Council ran an advertisement in the local paper
listing the names of the fifty-three Negroes who had signed it. The
ad urged that the readers "look them over carefully." Within a few
days all but six of the original signers had asked that their names
be removed from the petition. And to date there has been no
further attempt to integrate the schools of Yazoo City.

"Again the Council could and did claim that it was not responsible for whatever forced or persuaded the signers to withdraw their names, and again there is no provable connection
between the two events," remarked the keen student of the CC
movement, Hodding Carter III. "Nevertheless," Carter added in
a nice understatement, "it seems obvious that the two had some
relationship."

Similar school-integration petitions were wrecked in the Mississippi cities of Jackson, Clarksdale, Vicksburg, and Natchez—
again not by the Councils, according to Council spokesmen, but by
members "acting as individuals."

The success of the economic-pressure technique at the local
level led to several interesting attempts to apply it on a much
broader scale.

A great many negro employees will be discharged, and, though it will
work a grave hardship on many white employers, still it is better 'if our
right eye offend us to pluck it out' . . . The negro of the South should be
forewarned, and WHEN THE NEXT CASE [desegregation court case]
IS BROUGHT IN ANY OF THE REMAINING THIRTEEN STATES,
THE ECONOMIC BOYCOTT SHOULD BEGIN. The irony of the African
proverb, 'Full belly boy says to empty belly boy, be of good cheer,'
should be explained to the Southern negro."

In late 1955 white segregationists in Mississippi and neighboring states had "boycotts" of one sort or another going against the Falstaff Brewing Company, the Philip Morris Tobacco Company, and the Ford Motor Company.

The attempted boycotts of Falstaff beer and Philip Morris cigarettes were inspired by stories published in *The White Sentinel,* a Negrophobic and anti-Jewish newsletter published in St. Louis by one John W. Hamilton, a former lieutenant of the veteran Jew baiter, Gerald L. K. Smith.

The White Sentinel, in editions that were widely circulated by CC members and other Mississippians of segregationist persuasion, reported that Philip Morris had contributed to the Urban League (the "State Department of the NAACP"), and that Falstaff had paid for a life membership in the NAACP for one of its Negro salesmen. It was suggested that white people could show their disapproval of this by purchasing other brands of beer and smokes.

The attempt to boycott the Ford company was prompted by master of ceremonies Ed Sullivan's employment of Negro entertainers on his Mercury television show. The Ford boycott never made much headway, perhaps partly because so many automobile dealers in the Magnolia State were influential members of the Citizens' Councils.

But there is evidence that the Falstaff and Philip Morris boycotts were considerably more effective.

The Citizens' Council Association's monthly newspaper, while denying that the organization was behind the boycotts, reported with apparent satisfaction that Philip Morris sales had fallen off 17 per cent in 1955.

And officials of Falstaff simply decided prudence might be the better part of racial valor.

"At the height of the controversy," *The Wall Street Journal* reported in March 1956, "Falstaff Brewing Corporation flew a vice president to Jackson, Mississippi, to explain publicly the company's position—and to confer with officials of the segregationist Citizens' Council."

Of this visit Hodding Carter III reports in *The South Strikes Back*:

The Falstaff official also came with a check in his pocket for $50,000, so related Judge Brady, to "buy off" the alleged Council boycott. The executive committee [of the Mississippi CC] rejected the check and disclaimed all responsibility for the boycott, but suggested that perhaps a public statement disavowing any support for the NAACP might do more to calm the situation. Falstaff Corporation followed this suggestion and the boycott began to lift, with much crowing from John Hamilton in St. Louis.

In the end, the influence of John W. Hamilton and his Citizens' Protective Association of St. Louis declined in the Deep South. His racism recipe was rather too peppery for the taste of all but the most unappeasable white-supremacy devotees. Typical of the propaganda disseminated by Hamilton's association in the South with Council members' assistance was this essay, entitled "The Kiss of Death," and illustrated by a gorilla-featured Negro man kissing a fair Caucasian woman:

We look frantically around for Russian spies, believing that Russia will attack us with armies. . . . In the meantime, Russia is laughing. She has a more deadly weapon than the atomic bomb. She knows our strength is in our white stock and that when she has mixed our blood with Negro that we are licked forever. . . .

Negro blood destroyed the civilization of Egypt, India, Phoenicia, Carthage, Greece, and Rome. . . .

Remember, mixing white children with Negroes is a form of insanity. It takes the form of religion, democracy, brotherhood, etc. It is a pollution complex directed from Moscow. Remember discrimination is not a sin. It is a sign of Mind or God working through man to protect what is good. . . .

The heavy larding of anti-Semitism that some of the Council-promoted editions of *The White Sentinel* contained caused many observers—Jewish members of the CCs among them—to fear that the new Dixieland apartheid organization was launching a crusade against Jews as well as against integration-minded Negroes.

Patterson expresses amusement at recalling a visit paid him by two representatives of the Anti-Defamation League of B'nai B'rith soon after he had written a letter to CC members recommending that they read *The White Sentinel* and several other Jew-baiting as well as Negro-baiting publications.

"One of them warned me, 'If you're not careful, we'll say you're anti-Semitic.' 'All right, you can say what you want to,' I told 'em. 'But I'll tell you this: if you do call me that, *I won't* deny it.' " He laughed with satisfaction. "That was the last I heard from 'em."

The secretary obviously related this incident to illustrate his adeptness at verbal one-upmanship.

But, as a matter of record, Patterson and his fellow officials of the parent CC organization have since 1955 kept their official propaganda quite free of anti-Jewish material—although Patterson has made no notable attempt to stem the southward flow of anti-Semitic propaganda which he helped to start in 1954 and 1955.[4]

In his second annual report in 1956 Patterson looked back with pride at two major accomplishments of the Mississippi CC organization. One was the successful promotion of an amendment to the state constitution giving the Mississippi Legislature authority to abolish the public-school system "as a last resort in order to prevent racial integration in the schools." The other was the passage of a constitutional amendment "to raise voter qualifications in Mississippi."

Under the new voting law each person who wants to register as a voter must fill out a lengthy questionnaire with answers satisfactory to the local registration officials. The questionnaire demands of the registrant, among other things, the ability to write a "reasonable interpretation" of any section of the Mississippi constitution chosen by the registrar. The applicant must also satisfy the registrar with a statement setting forth his "understanding of the duties and obligations of citizenship under a constitutional form of government."

Before the amendment was enacted as many as twenty thousand to thirty thousand Negroes had voted in statewide Mississippi elections; since the amendment their number had been reduced by about half—since it is a fact that Negroes rarely answer the questionnaire to the registrar's satisfaction.

Speaking of the new law that "raised voter qualifications," Patterson commented:

[4] See Chapter IV (1).

"It is impossible to estimate the value of this amendment to the future peace and domestic tranquillity of this state."

In the grand tradition of what the NAACP calls "the deceptive disavowal," Patterson has declared that the Citizens' Councils are "not opposed" to Negro voting. This statement prompted one Mississippi Negro editor to suggest, with singular optimism, that CC officials should patrol the polls to protect Mississippi Negroes who wished to vote. "Mr. Patterson," he said, "warrants the hearty thanks and congratulations from all intelligent Negroes of the state for his statement."

But of course Patterson's statement was merely a part of the Citizens' Council cant designed to pacify those who might suspect that the organization is involved in the obviously systematic denial to Negroes of the opportunity to vote in Mississippi. In truth, he has considerable scorn for the notion that the mass of Negroes of Mississippi should be given the vote.

He indicated this when a tiny tow-haired boy, the youngest of Patterson's four children, invaded the backyard cottage to exhibit his cowboy getup and speak of doing in the Bad Guys with his plastic pistol.

"Why, it'd be like giving the vote to these children of mine," Patterson protested. "You give the vote to my children, and you know who they'd elect for president? *Elvis Presley!*"

In 1956 an assembly of the South's most influential white supremacists—including such luminaries as Tom Brady of Mississippi, Roy Harris of Georgia, and Leander Perez of Louisiana— voted to create the present master organization for the region's multitude of segregationist groups: the Association of Citizens' Councils of America. It links the CC organizations of Mississippi, Alabama, Arkansas, Florida, Louisiana, South Carolina, and Texas with the States Rights Council of Georgia, the North Carolina Defenders of States Rights, the Tennessee Federation for Constitutional Government, and the Virginia Defenders of State Sovereignty and Individual Liberties.[5]

[5] These had largely replaced the earlier organizations formed in reaction to the Supreme Court decision: the American Society for the Preservation of State Government and Racial Integrity (New Orleans); Caucasian League (Miami); Citizens' Segregation Committee (Birmingham); Florida States

Patterson, picked as executive secretary of the master organization as well as of the Mississippi association, moved his office from Winona to new quarters in the larger delta town of Greenwood.

Since then the Association of Citizens' Councils of America has claimed—with very debatable accuracy, of course—a total membership of 300,000, including 80,000 members in Mississippi.

As it has grown in size and influence the Association has acquired more and more up-to-the-minute publicity techniques—most notably manifested by the Citizens' Council Radio-TV Forum. The Forum is managed from Jackson by a retired banker's son named William J. Simmons, who also publishes the Association's official monthly magazine, *The Citizen,* which until recently was published in newspaper form and called *The Citizens' Council.*

It is difficult to determine whether Patterson realizes the extent to which the CC movement has changed from a "grass-roots" rural movement to a Madison Avenue-type operation manned by city folks.

But Patterson seems sincerely disinterested in becoming citified himself. He spoke of his preference for living in little Itta Bena rather than in Greenwood where his office is.

"I like to get as far away from town as I can," he said. *"This* is too close to town to suit me."

Unlike some of the South's milder segregationists Patterson does not suggest that Negroes in his state eventually will be desegregated —after a few more generations of education, training in the responsibilities of citizenship, et cetera.

"There won't be any integration in Mississippi. Not now, not one-hundred years from now, maybe not six-thousand years from now —maybe never."

True, the enemy Liberals are busy nibbling away at the barriers

---

Rights, Inc. (Miami;) Grass Roots League (Charleston); Knights of the White Christians (New Orleans); National Association for the Advancement of White People (Washington); National Association for the Preservation of the Races (Memphis); National Association for the Preservation of the White Race (Augusta); North Carolina Association for the Preservation of the White Race (Durham); Patriots of North Carolina (Greensboro); Pro-Southerners (Memphis); Pro-Southerners League (Fort Pierce); The Southerners (Mobile); Southern Gentlemen's Organization (Baton Rouge); White America, Inc. (Pine Bluff); White Brotherhood (Atlanta), et cetera.

of apartheid just now. But national public opinion can change rapidly, he said.

"I remember—just in my time, I remember—seeing newsreels with pictures of planes flying down over black Ethiopians, machine-gunning 'em. That was in my time."

The hope for preservation of the Southern Way of Life rests with national public opinion, not—as some of his fellow white suprem-acists feel—with future political developments.

"The solution to this problem will come when the North gets just four or five million more Negroes. And at the rate they're migrating up there now, that won't take many years. Then when the Northern whites get a bellyful of 'em, they'll decide the South ought to be left alone to solve the problem our own way."

He displayed a letter he had recently written to a segregation-minded Jackson columnist, analyzing the 1960 census report for Mississippi. He noted that while the Negro population in the country as a whole had risen 25.5 per cent between 1950 and 1960, Mississippi's Negro population had decreased by 70,751. The letter explained:

Assuming that Mississippi's negro population equals the na-tional average in fertility and longevity, our 25.5 per cent increase over our 1950 negro population of 986,494 would be 251,555 negroes. Evidently these 251,555 negroes have left the state, and when you add our decrease in negro population of 70,751, accord-ing to our 1960 census, we arrive at the astounding figure of 322,306.

We find that most old negroes and school-age negroes remain in Mississippi.

In other words, in the past ten years Mississippi has contributed 322,306 breeding-age negroes to the economic and social struc-ture of northern and border states. This contribution will do more to create an understanding of our negro problem than all the written logic and dramatic presentation of facts would have ever done. We trust that this migration will increase in the next decade.

Patterson said it has been his observation that Negroes prefer city life to rural life.

"Negroes like to live in urban places. You know how dogs like to sleep all piled up? Negroes are the same," he said, laughing heartily. "They like to live in a pile."

On weekdays Patterson drives the ten miles from Itta Bena into Greenwood to the "national headquarters" of the Association of Citizens' Councils of America. There, in a street-level office—a long room in a run-down little office building, a room decorated with a large Confederate flag—Patterson, aided by a few office clerks, carries on his propaganda battle against the "mongrelizers."

A representative packet of material from him contains such pamphlets as James F. Byrnes' *The Supreme Court Must Be Curbed;* the Reverend G. T. Gillespie's *A Christian View on Segregation;* an anonymous *Jewish View on Segregation;* James O. Eastland's *We've Reached the Era of Judicial Tyranny;* Herbert Ravenel Sass's *Mixed Schools and Mixed Blood;* Georgia Attorney General Eugene Cook's *The Ugly Truth about the* NAACP; a few segregationist tracts from the Black Muslims; and a collection of reprints of Washington news stories about sundry rapes, muggings, and "barbecuings" of white women by Negroes in the nation's capital.

The packet of "educational material" also contains a few blotters imprinted with "famous quotations." One of them—a favorite among segregationists with a bent for history—is a quotation attributed to a president who is often championed by civil-rights campaigners: Abraham Lincoln.

I will say, then, that I am not, nor ever have been, in favor of bringing about in any way the social and political equality of the white and black races; that I am not, nor ever have been, in favor of making voters or jurors of negroes, nor of qualifying them to hold office, nor to intermarry with white people, and I will say in addition to this that there is a physical difference between the white and black races which I believe will forever forbid the two races living together on terms of social and political equality, and inasmuch as they cannot so live, while they do remain together there must be a position of superior and inferior, and I, as much as any other man, am in favor of having the superior position assigned to the white race.

Day after day from Patterson's office flow the message of the inferiority of Negroes, the message of their lustful and violent nature, the message of their desire to corrupt the blood of the South's innocent white children in the interest of atheistic Communism.

It is perhaps a job that few men would relish. But Patterson seems to thrive on it. For he sees the race problem in simple black-and-white, right-and-wrong terms, and there is no evidence that he ever is afflicted with doubts.

"The fate of this nation may rest in the hands of the Southern white people today," he believes. 'If we white southerners submit to this unconstitutional judge-made law of nine political appointees [the Decision of 1954], the malignant powers of mongrelization, communism, and atheism will surely destroy this nation from within. Racial intermarriage has already begun in the North and unless stopped will spread to the South.

"Integration represents darkness, regimentation, totalitarianism, communism, and destruction. Segregation represents the freedom to choose one's associates, Americanism, state sovereignty, and the survival of the white race. These two ideologies are now engaged in mortal conflict and only one can survive. They cannot be fused any more than day can exist in night. The twilight of this great white nation would certainly follow. There is no middle ground."

4. THE CAPITAL OF THE COUNCIL COUNTRY

IN RECENT YEARS the nucleus of power in the huge Citizens' Council organism has gradually shifted from Tut Patterson's little headquarters up in the delta to a sleek suite of offices in the capital city of Jackson.

It is from the Plaza Building on Congress Street that a well-tailored man named William J. Simmons directs the nation's largest propaganda apparatus in the service of segregation.

As editor of the organization's official newspaper and as president of the Citizens' Council forum, which produces films and taped programs for broadcasting on hundreds of radio and television stations, Simmons has become the most influential figure in the Association of Citizens' Councils of America. Many Mississippians say he has more political power than any other man in the state. Indeed, it is just possible that Bill Simmons is the single most significant obstacle to the realization of that dream of racial equality which was expressed in the 1954 Supreme Court decision.

It would be hard to pick a more appropriate location for the organization's command post. The Council Association's office suite in Jackson looks right down into the rooms of the governor's mansion across the street—and a few blocks to the north the street dead-ends at the front steps of the capital of Mississippi.

For several years now no governor of Mississippi—or, for that matter, any other man of high office or ambition in the state—has acted or spoken on anything related to The Problem without having given meticulous consideration to the reaction it might produce up in the Plaza Building.

In contrast to the sleepy pace that characterizes many of the white South's other field headquarters in the current war for segregation there is an efficient hum of activity in the Jackson CC suite. In the reception office a visitor finds a pair of attractive stenographers intensely busy at paper work—under militant gazes from large portraits of Stonewall Jackson and Robert E. Lee.[1] From a middle office the stout, middle-aged secretary of the newspaper and CC forum corporations, Louis W. Hollis, escorts a printing salesman, explaining to him the families of type he wants used in a new publicity brochure. Richard Morphew, a much younger and stouter man whose task it is to arrange the forum's radio and TV programs and serve on mike as interviewer, bulges toward his office with a fistful of copy for a verbal assault on integration. A Mississippi state trooper, his hip weighted with pistol and holster, arrives with a large brown envelope, specially delivered by hand from the office of Governor Ross Barnett (who is himself a CC member and a man with a widely recognized talent for listening very closely to the words of wisdom that flow down from the heights of the Plaza Building). There is a frequent ringing of telephones; when the stenographers answer, their voices have that expected magnolia sweetness. And yet the girls seem expertly guarded in their words in the presence of a stranger: 'Secrecy is our strength"; that is one of the key slogans of the Association of Citizens' Councils.

It becomes plain after only a few minutes in Bill Simmons' office that he is a man very different from Tut Patterson.

He is well over six feet tall but, unlike the former football captain, Simmons is rather soft in appearance—not fat but not at all athletic-looking. A small-chinned, rather pale man in his middle forties, wearing a blue tie and a gray suit of excellent stripe and cut, it is obvious that his are tastes born of the city rather than of the cotton country.

His brown hair has thinned only slightly, and he wears it in a

[1] The hard-eyed portrait of defiant Lee the victorious warrior is more commonly seen on Dixieland walls these days than is the traditionally more popular portrait of the defeated Lee of benign expression.

boy part well to the left side. By far his most distinguishing feature is his mustache. Simmons' adversaries speak of it as a Hitlerian mustache, but it is, in fact, much more abundant than Adolf's and is not nearly so intimidatingly dark. His eyes are large and of an indefinite blue-gray color, and communicate little or nothing at all.

In contrast with many lesser segregationists, Simmons almost never permits himself the luxury of using the word "nigger" or speaking in insulting terms of Negroes. His speech is slow and his movements somewhat ponderous, yet there is never any indication that his wits lack quickness.

"Taking a long range view, there are two steps that will eventually win for us," he said. "These are, first, the organization of the whites in the South, and, second, the migration of Negroes to the North."

Simmons' office is comfortable but not pretentious. The wall that he faces when sitting at his wide desk is covered by a full-size flag of the sovereign state of Mississippi. Scattered over the wall to his right are four framed photographs of Mississippi scenes, one of them a picture of his handsome wife, son, and daughter and their large pet dog at their suburban home.

"In no place has there been integration—even so-called 'token integration'—without the active support of white people in the community. As long as people are strongly organized on the local level—as long, in other words, as the 'die-easys' are not in control —a community can withstand pressure from Washington regardless of what kind it is.

"The other thing we know is that as Negro migration from the South steps up, pro-segregation feeling outside the South increases rapidly. We see signs of this every day."

Simmons' slim fingers riffled one of the high stacks of correspondence on his desk. The letter on top of it was from Senator J. Strom Thurmond of South Carolina, but Simmons was not thinking of correspondence from persons long committed to the Southern Way of Life.

"From the letters we get we see segregationist sentiment growing in many Northern cities—in Detroit, in the Jewish sections of Brooklyn, in many other places. It develops whenever Negroes move out of the areas they've been restricted to in the past."

Simmons noted that while the over-all Negro population in the United States increased by one-fourth in the decade from 1950 to

1960, the number of Negroes in most Southern states increased only slightly, and two states—Mississippi and Arkansas—reported a drop in Negro population.[2]

Indeed the figures indicate that "the Negro problem" has become national as well as Southern. The 1940 census showed that 69 per cent of the Negroes in the United States lived in the eleven "Confederate states"—Alabama, Arkansas, Florida,, Georgia, Louisiana, Mississippi, North Carolina, South Carolina, Tennessee, Texas, and Virginia; by 1950 the proportion had fallen to 60 per cent; today only 52 per cent of them live in the eleven states—and indications are that their migration northward continues at a swift pace.

"This migration of Negroes will have profound implications," said Simmons. "Resistance to integration is, of course, in direct proportion to the number of Negroes in a community.

"This talk of 'integration' in the North—it has been ridiculous to call a school 'integrated' when it has only two or three Negroes in it.

"The North is just now beginning to experience integration, and I feel sure that white parents of the North don't want to submit their children to it any more than we in the South do."

Simmons' attitudes toward Negroes come partly from his Deep Southern heritage. Like most of the organization men in the battle for white supremacy, he can point with pride to a number of forebears who wore the uniform of the Confederacy.

"My father's father, George W. Simmons, fought with the Mississippi Infantry at Vicksburg and Port Hudson. My maternal great-grandfather, William Alexander Noble, also was in the Mississippi Infantry, in Hardee's Division; he was killed at Shiloh in April 1862."

The occasion for Simmons' reflections on the Civil War was the

[2] Of the eleven states of the old Confederacy, only Florida and Texas had substantial gains in Negro population: 277,085 more in Florida and 209,667 in Texas. Mississippi's Negro population dropped 70,751 and Arkansas' dropped 37,852. Alabama gained only 654, Georgia, 59,934; Louisiana, 156,799; North Carolina, 68,668; South Carolina, 7,214; Tennessee, 56,273; and Virginia, 82,047.

In comparison, California gained 421,689, Illinois, 391,490; Michigan, 275,285; New Jersey, 196,310; New York, 499,320; Ohio, 273,025; and Pennsylvania 214,265.

arrival at his office of Paul Faulkner, a lean, handsome, silver-haired insurance executive who is a director and former president of the Jackson Citizens' Council. Faulkner had come to map final plans with Simmons for their participation in a dress-uniform ball that was to be held a few nights later as part of the Civil War Centennial Celebration. Faulkner is commanding officer and Simmons is an honorary colonel of a unit of an organization called the Confederate Grays. The time had come when a decision had to be made on what name to give their unit.

Simmons expressed regret that some of the city's Grays had been displaying an inappropriately flippant attitude. It seems that the men at one of the insurance companies had named their unit the "Guaranty Grenadiers" and, alas, the boys down at the gas company had decided to call their unit the "Blue Flame Rebels." Faulkner agreed this was deplorable.

A telephone call interrupted their somber meditations. The call was from Representative John Bell Williams who has been acclaimed by Judge Tom Brady as the coiner of the phrase "Black Monday." Williams was in town to make a speech to the Mississippi Teachers Association urging that public schools be abolished rather than suffer desegregation. There has been much talk that Williams, with Citizens' Council backing, might run for governor before long. Simmons consulted his desk calendar and suggested a time when he and Williams could get together for dinner.

Then he turned back to the problem of a name for his and Faulkner's Confederate unit. He had been doing a bit of research, said Simmons, and had decided they might name it in honor of the gallant Southern unit, the Burt Rifles. Referring to some notes he had made at the library, Simmons listed half-a-dozen battles in which the Rifles had fought.

Faulkner was very enthusiastic about the suggestion.

"But you don't list the Battle of Sharpsburg there." Faulkner frowned thoughtfully. "I'll do some research of my own on this. Bill, I feel sure they were at Sharpsburg."

The gathering they were planning to attend was to include a re-enactment of the 1861 ceremony in which Mississippi officials signed the historic document of secession from the Union. As Faulkner was leaving the office, he remarked with a laugh:

"While we're going through the secession ceremony, Bill, maybe we could just get somebody from the state capitol in on it and make it *official*. Why, then, if the federal government tried anything funny, we could appeal to the United Nations for protection against an imperialist power."

Simmons laughed, too, but hardly boisterously. In six years as editor of *The Citizens' Council* he has heard and/or written just about all the states' rights-segregationist jokes in the book.

Simmons was born in 1916 in the little town of Utica, thirty miles southwest of the capital, but his family moved to Jackson when he was eight. His father, now very advanced in years, was a banker in Jackson; there has always been a good deal of wealth in the Simmons family.

He finished high school at Central in Jackson, then got a bachelor's degree with honors in English at Mississippi College in the little town of Clinton.

"I'd say that while I was growing up in Jackson, my attitudes toward Negroes were typical for a young Southerner," Simmons said.

But beyond that the pattern of the development of his racial philosophy is not at all typical. It was formed—as he remembers it now—not so much in Mississippi as in Europe and the West Indies.

"During my college years I'd taken several trips on freighters south from New Orleans," he recalled. "I covered the Greater and Lesser Antilles and the adjacent coasts of South and Central America."

Then after graduating from Mississippi College in 1937 he traveled extensively in Europe for a couple of years. For a time he studied at the Institute of Touraine in France.

Simmons seems rather cautious when he recounts his past in Europe. Popular among his critics in Mississippi is the rumor that he was an admirer of Hitler and "a Nazi." Simmons has characterized such reports as gossip produced by the malice of his opponents.

He said he was aware of the talk that he runs the CCs as a "Gestapo" organization. "But does this look like Gestapo to you?" he asked with a shrug and a smile. "Do *I* look like that?" In truth, neither it, nor he, did.

He left school on the Continent and went to England after the outbreak of World War II.

"And in 1940 I became a civilian employee of the Royal Engineers of the British Army. I served for a time in England, then was transferred to the West Indies. Most of my work for the British was in Trinidad. I came back here to Jackson near the end of the war."

Later during the war he also was briefly in the United States Navy, until discharged for medical reasons, and he was employed for a time by the State Department.

Simmons went into business after the war, but without notable success. For four years he and a group of associates operated a non-sked airline out of New Orleans, but never quite managed to establish it as a regular feeder line and its operations eventually ceased. He then lived in Lake Charles, Louisiana, where he had an interest in a natural-gas company and served as its chief accountant, but after four or five years a larger corporation gained control of the firm, and Simmons came home to Jackson.

When the Supreme Court announced its school decision on May 17, 1954, Simmons had at his disposal plenty of time to review the philosophy of race which he says was developed during his years of overseas service with the British Army.

"My strong feeling on the ethnic question had arisen in large part from the time I'd spent in the West Indies—from the vivid experience of living with the fruits of a hundred and fifty years of integration," he said. "Not many people here have had such an opportunity to see the effects that racial integration has on the moral, social, and economic standards of a country. I'm speaking of the caste system that exists after 'integration' has taken place. There is an almost unceasing hostility between people of different shades. I reached the solution that integration is not a solution to the race problem; it merely compounds the problem."

Every issue of Simmons' newspaper and magazine have denounced the 1954 decision. Even so, he feels that at least one "good" thing has resulted from it.

"One of the controlling attitudes of Southern white people through the years had been their sense of responsibility for taking care of Negroes. Now, because of all the agitation for civil rights and privileges, this attitude has just about gone with the wind. So there's a good chance that in future decades there'll be less actual fraternizing of the races than there was before The Decision."

The short-range goal of most Council members is to maintain the system of legal apartheid which existed relatively unchallenged before May 17, 1954. This goal is—as that charter CC member of Indianola expressed it—"to put [the Negro] where he has stayed for forty years and keep him guessing. . . ."

But Simmons makes it clear that he would not be satisfied simply with maintaining the Southern Way of Life as it has existed in Mississippi since the end of Reconstruction.

"Segregation is at best a temporary palliative," he said. "The only real solution is to establish a Negro state. Nothing less than physical separation of the races will really solve the problem."

Of course Simmons does not feel that Mississippi would be suitable for such a conversion into an all-Negro state.

Can he really imagine such a South African-type "solution" to the race problem ever coming to pass in the United States?

"I don't know; I don't know what public opinion will be willing to support in the years to come." He smiled, and then made a remark which seems like a non sequitur only at first glance. "I hate to think what would happen if a bunch of whites did what Muhammad[3] is doing."

"As long as there are large numbers of whites and coloreds living in the same area, there will be tension; this is one of the facts of life," said Simmons. "The period when there was the least tension was that from 1876 [when Reconstruction ended]—from the time when the North and South arrived at a settlement of the problem and federal troops were withdrawn from the South—to a few years previous to the Supreme Court decision in 1954."

Does he foresee that the same thing that occurred in 1876 will happen again—that federal pressure for abolition of segregation in the South will be removed as it was in 1876?

"No." He smiled. "No, things are never the same as they were in the past."

Simmons has said that if the CCs were outlawed and mass integration were imposed on Mississippi by the federal courts, "great violence will be inevitable, of a kind to make the present stuff look

[3] Elijah Muhammad, head of a sect called the Black Muslims, proposes that several of these United States be cleansed of "white devils" and turned over to "so-called Negroes." See Chapter IX (2).

like child's play. Any violence that has occurred so far has been spasmodic and unorganized, but I could not speak for the future course of events in such a condition."

Hodding Carter III, in his judicious study of the Citizens' Council movement in Mississippi, *The South Strikes Back,* predicts that the organization will experience a dramatic crisis if the integrationists choose to mount a direct attack on the Mississippi Way of Life.

Actually this is the biggest problem for that section of the Citizens' Council leadership which wishes to continue as a "respectable" organization in the fight to prevent integration. Any wide-scale integration attempts whatsoever, in the immediate future in Mississippi, are sure to bring violence. . . .

If such violence occurs, the Council will have to decide which side of the street to work—that of violence or that of nonviolence. If it chooses the former, the movement as it is now constituted would disappear, because a large portion of its members from the upper and middle classes would not stand for such activity under their own auspicies no matter how ardent they might be in the defense of segregation. On the other hand, if it chooses the latter, the Council stands to lose an even larger portion of its membership to whatever rabble-rouser comes along to promise a last-ditch fight, with blood in the streets and all the other features that the Council's leaders have promised and warned of so forebodingly in the past.

To this writer, at least, it seems clear that in the event of attempted mass integration "respectability" would go to the wall and the old Ku Klux Klan approach would emerge triumphant. The Council's motto, "Dedicated to the maintenance of peace, good order, and domestic tranquility in our community and in our state and to the preservation of our States' Rights," would soon enough boil down to "Segregation at Any Price," and it would be a motto a large minority of white Mississippians would rally around with a vengeance. The sifting off of the more conservative members because of disapproval of the new methods could in time isolate the Council from the rest of the white community, but the trail it might leave before this isolation was completed could well be a bloody one.

Carter hopefully adds that "this is the blackest picture of the future, however, and one which is not actually expected to materialize. . . ." He feels that when integration is attempted in Mississippi, it will come in token form—and even that not for many years to come.

So far having succeeded in preventing integration except in a few scattered instances, the white South has not been put to the agonizing test. Simmons, while he so far has held mostly winning hands, realizes that the stakes of the game might get higher.

"I think the people of the South will use whatever means are necessary to defend themselves," he said. "I think we've practiced great forbearance and great patience considering the incitations. But," he added, "patience and restraint shouldn't be confused with timidity."

With that nigh Pavlovian reflex to the subject of "economic pressure" Simmons denies that the CC organization has utilized any such thing to accomplish its ends.

"No, there never has been any economic pressure by the Councils as such," he has said. "There never has been any organized attempt or recommendations to that effect by any Council. . . . As for economic pressure on Negroes themselves, when the petition for integrated schools was presented here in Jackson [in 1955] by forty-three Negroes, all of them lost their jobs except those in public employ, but to my knowledge only one of their employers was a Citizens' Council member. When people are annoyed by anything," he added, "You can just expect them to react against the source of their annoyance. So it is with Negroes who persist in acting against what their employers think is correct."

The Anti-Defamation League of B'nai B'rith reported back in 1956 that "there is growing evidence that anti-Semites have infiltrated the [Citizens' Council] organization and that anti-Jewish literature is an accepted part of the materials being recommended and distributed by Citizens' Council units. . . . Moreover, some of their membership have established correspondence with leading American professional anti-Semites. This is a matter of increasing concern to American Jews in general and to Southern Jews in particular."

But Simmons has taken care to emphasize that the Negro citizenry is the only group his organization wants to "physically separate" from the white people of Mississippi.

"The Council is definitely not anti-Semitic or anti-Catholic, since we obviously have members from both groups," he has said. "If you ask me, if there were no anti-Semitism, some of those Jewish money-raising outfits would manufacture it out of whole cloth. It would make about as much sense for us to be anti-Semitic as to be anti-snow in Alaska. It has nothing to do with our problem. For that matter, Methodists have had more to do with promoting integration than have Jews, and there is even a Baptist on the board of the NAACP."

In a reminiscence curiously remindful of an anecdote told by Tut Patterson,[4] Simmons said that three men who said they had been sent by the Anti-Defamation League had once visited his office and expressed disapproval of the CC organization. "They threatened me by saying that if I didn't watch my step, they would call the Councils anti-Semitic. I said, 'All right, you may do that. But if you do, I won't deny it.' "

In truth, Simmons' publications have avoided the anti-Semitism that accompanies the anti-Negro propaganda of so many other organs dedicated to "racial integrity."

Privately, Simmons has said that he considers the tirelessly anti-Jewish Southern organization, the National States Rights party, "a little nutty." But, on the record, he prefers not to voice criticism of any group—no matter how extreme—that combines its particular obsession with a campaign for segregation of Negroes.

"Lenin always told his party people: 'Never attack the Left.' " He smiled. "I never attack the Right."

The Citizens' Council organization, which had budded in the delta, was in fairly full flower before Simmons became active in selling it to the South. He first became familiar with Robert Patterson's name through the letters-to-the-editor column of the Jackson newspapers; they exchanged a bit of segregationist mail in the weeks following The Decision. But it was not until late in 1954 that Simmons attended a CC meeting, and not until the first Council was organized in Jackson in the spring of 1955 that he became a card-carrying CC member. In October of that year he published the first issue of *The Citizens' Council* as the official newspaper of the Mississippi Citizens' Council Association.

[4] See page 60.

A 1961 circulation of 45,000 was claimed for the four-page monthly newspaper—and on certain special occasions, as during the Little Rock crisis, extra batches of 10,000 or 20,000 copies have sometimes been ordered by the Councils of an embattled area.

The 45,000 circulation figure may well serve as a revealing index to the size of Citizens' Council membership in the South. Since late 1955 it has been customary for the membership fees of Citizens' councilors to include the price of a subscription to *The Citizens' Council;* when ordered in bulk by a local Council, the price has been a mere dollar a year. This would seem to hint that the Council leaders' repeated claims of 80,000 to 85,000 members in Mississippi and 300,000 to 350,000 throughout the South represent dreams rather than realities. It hints, indeed, that the number of paid-up, active members in the Councils at any given time is hardly more than, and possibly less than, 45,000.

But to pick at the figures claimed by the Council leaders is an unfruitful occupation. For the strength of the CC structure lies less in the size of its faithful membership than in its potential for expansion in a climate of trouble.

Louis W. Hollis, secretary of the CC Association and of its radio-TV forum as well as executive director of the Jackson Council, concedes that local Councils are inclined to lose members and become dormant when the Negroes of their communities are peacefully "keeping their place."

"But during the Little Rock crisis a thousand new members came in in just one month," said Hollis. "And take Harrison County down on the Gulf Coast. For years we had never been able to establish a Council there. Then came the wade-ins in the Gulfport-Biloxi area in 1960. Now at Gulfport and Biloxi we have the second and third largest Councils in Mississippi."

The largest in the state is the Jackson Council, thanks mainly to the efficient organizational efforts of Hollis.

Hollis is a neat, sandy-haired, gray-suited, bespectacled man of about sixty, with that ready smile and that soft indoor quality of physique that seem fitting for a veteran merchandising executive, a Lion, a Mason, a deacon of the First Baptist Church, and a member of the John Birch Society.

He had joined the Jackson Citizens' Council not long after it was

organized in the spring of 1955 but had not been an active partici-
pant until Simmons invited him to become a full-time member of
his staff in late 1957.

"When I first came up with Bill, we had 2,200 members in
Jackson," he recalled. "Now we have between 5,000 and 6,000."

Hollis' most noteworthy stunt to increase membership in the
Jackson Council was the organization of a block-by-block survey
"to learn the feelings of Jackson citizens on racial segregation in
schools and residential areas." Hollis called it a "freedom of
choice" survey.

It surprised nobody that the Council interviewers found hardly
anyone opposed to segregation—hardly anyone willing to voice
such an opinion in the presence of a Council representative, at any
rate.

Typical of the survey questions were these:

"Will you cooperate with your Citizens' Council to protect property values in your neighborhood from attempted residential integration?" Ninety-nine per cent answered "Yes."

"When attempts are made to integrate the school in your neighborhood do you intend to keep your children or grandchildren out
of school until the attempted integration fails?" Ninety-nine per
cent answered "Yes."

"Do you intend to allow your children or grandchildren to be
integrated?" Ninety-nine per cent answered "No."

"As an indication of the high public regard for the Jackson
Citizens' Council and its leadership," reported *The Citizens' Council,* "more than two out of three of the non-members surveyed (including ladies) signed up for membership."

Aside from the questionable quality of the questions, an explanation of the method of the survey indicated it was not quite as objective in approach as, say, a Gallup Poll.

A block leader is selected from the [Council] members living
in the block. The leader and other Council members meet at the
leader's home, where Hollis explains the program in detail.

At the same time, the Council office mails a letter to each resident of the block, explaining the purposes of the survey, and nam-
ing the block leader. [The letter warns that white Jacksonians are
"going to be faced with three very serious attacks from the NAACP

and other pressure groups: . . . 1. School integration. 2. Mass voting by Negroes as a bloc. 3. Residential integration."]

The office furnishes survey cards, membership invitations, information pamphlets, and other material, with each resident's name typed on the cards. The Council members conducting the survey first complete their own cards, then call on their neighbors to obtain the needed information. About a week later the block leader collects the completed cards and returns them to the Council office for tabulation and analysis. . . .

Hollis says that as the survey is completed in each of Jackson's wards the block leaders will hold a ward meeting to select a ward leader and concentrate on follow-up calls encouraging non-members to join.

In an editorial in *The Citizens' Council* Bill Simmons proudly commented: "Has any other grass-roots movement ever registered a 99 per cent vote of public confidence? We know of none. . . ."

Like Simmons, Hollis' "strong feeling on the ethnic question" is not the home-grown variety common among most Dixie segregationists.

True, his grandfather was a Confederate soldier, and his father, a sawmiller, was reared in Gadsden, Alabama. But Hollis' mother was from Eastport, Maine, and—Hollis recalled in a tone of gentle affection—"she was never much of a Southerner." Hollis was born in Chattanooga and spent his youth in the "Upper South" cities of Knoxville, Memphis, and Little Rock.

His strong segregationist feelings were acquired not in the South but in Harlem, said Hollis.

"For ten months during World War II I managed the largest store in Harlem, the Kress store on 125th Street. I had three hundred employees at one time; it was the biggest store in the chain then."

It was the store where the great Harlem race riot had begun a few years before Hollis became its manager, he said.

"Until the riot, only white girls had worked in the store, but then it became unsafe for them to go up there. By the time I became manager the only whites in the store were the assistant manager and myself."

When the company first placed him in charge of the store, it was being picketed by a union. The labor dispute was settled three weeks after his arrival, but he remembers it was an uncomfortable period.

"As I walked to and from the store, the nigger pickets [Although he does not speak with a Southern accent, Hollis chooses frequently to pronounce the word Negro as "nigger"] would curse me as a 'white s.o.b.,' " he said. "I had a nigger bodyguard assigned to escort me to the subway and back every day. . . . This sort of thing eventually meant economic destruction. Soon after I left the store closed."

During twenty-one years with the S. H. Kress Company Hollis managed stores in seven states on both sides of the Mason-Dixon line. He returned in 1946 to Jackson, where one of his jobs as a Kress manager had been, and went into business for himself, as an appliance wholesaler and investment counselor until Simmons induced him to make the Citizens' Council crusade his career.

"If integration were to come to Jackson, the same sort of thing that happened in Harlem would happen here," Hollis said. "I keep telling our Council leaders that they must accept responsibility for the social order, for if the social order goes, then they can expect the economic order to go.

"Mississippi went through the thing I'm talking about to some extent during Reconstruction. At one time we had a nigger lieutenant governor, a nigger senator, nigger sheriffs, and many nigger legislators—and they threw the state into such a debt that not till 1934 was it paid off. Today the same thing is happening in several Northern states—in Michigan, for instance."

But Hollis says he feels no animosity toward Negroes who are campaigning for equality. "You can't blame a nigger for wanting to be white any more than you can blame a poor man for wanting to divide the wealth."

Since Hollis identifies himself as a "member of the business community" and sees himself as a defender of the "economic order," it is understandable that he would take pride in belonging to the super-conservative John Birch Society.

"Our present project in the Birch Society," he said matter-of-factly, "is the impeachment of Earl Warren as chief justice of the

Supreme Court. We have some two hundred other patriotic societies joining us in this."

Noting the Kennedy administration's appointment of many integrationist Liberals to high office, Hollis has resigned himself to the probability that things are going to get worse for the Birchers and Councilors before they get better.

"We're going to be in a state of siege for several years," he said. Yet he sees a silver lining in the clouds. "There is going to be a tremendous upsurge of conservatism during the next four, eight, and twelve years. And as this moves like a tidal wave, we will be carried to victory. Conservatism is on the march now for the first time in thirty years—and we [the Association of Citizens' Councils] are part of the conservative movement."

He also is encouraged by the success that the government of South Africa has had in maintaining segregation in a land where Negroes outnumber whites far more heavily than in Mississippi.

"We [of the CCs] have a close association with the white leadership in South Africa." Hollis smiled. "In South Africa the whites would die before they surrender. I think we would, too."

Since 1958 the CC Association's most important propaganda vehicle has been its radio-TV "forum." The Association recently reported that the CC forum's fifteen-minute taped and filmed interviews with congressmen and other notables were being supplied free to 478 radio and television stations. The series has featured about one out of four members of the Senate and House of Representatives. During 1961, a total of 11,619 radio and TV programs were broadcast.

Predictably, most of the programs present Southern senators and representatives making arguments in behalf of segregation and states' rights and denouncing "outside agitation" and the "judicial tyranny" of the Supreme Court.

But the scope of the Citizens' Council forum series goes far beyond the race issue. Many of the speakers are from states beyond the Mason-Dixon line, and the subjects of their talks illustrate the fact that the CC movement is very interested in promoting "conservatism" in the nation as well as maintaining white supremacy in the South.

In one filmed interview, Republican Senator Barry Goldwater

of Arizona speaks on the "political power of corrupt labor leaders." In another, South Dakota Senator Karl Mundt calls for a "reform" of the electoral college system to reduce the power of minority bloc voting in states more populous than his own. Republican Representative Ralph Gwinn of New York warns of the "rapid trend toward a Labor-Socialist government." Representative August Johansen, Michigan Republican, joins Democratic Representative John Dowdy of Texas in describing "how United States foreign aid helps communism." Republican Representative Wint Smith of Kansas speaks on "communism in the churches." Democratic Representative Dale Alford of Arkansas discusses with the president of the American Medical Association the inadvisability of federal participation in health care for the aged. And Republican Representative Noah Mason of Illinois explains "why federal aid to education is not needed."

Some of the programs are prepared as serials. The House Un-American Activities Committee's much-disputed film account of the 1960 riot of students and police at San Francisco City Hall, "Operation Abolition," is presented in a five-part series. A discussion between Mississippi Representative Arthur Winstead and the Reverend D. F. B. DeBeer of the Union of South Africa of the comparative "progress in race relations" made in their respective sovereign states is distributed in four parts.

A great many of the films and tapes have been prepared, through arrangements made by Mississippi's Senator James Eastland and Representative John Bell Williams, in the government recording studios at the Capitol in Washington. Eastland and Williams are billed for them at the regular rates available to members of Congress. The films and tapes are then shipped to Jackson where the CC has them duplicated and distributed.

The show-business publication, *Variety,* commented that this arrangement means, in effect, that "the American taxpayer is subsidizing segregationist propaganda."

"Through the 'sponsorship' [by Eastland and Williams] the White Citizens' Council Forum of Jackson, Mississippi—the 'educational' arm of the segregation-buff organization, the White Citizens' Council—is able to get Congressional rates on tv films and radio tape," said *Variety.* "It's all accomplished within the Congressional rules which limit the recording studios (equipment and staff are maintained by government funds) to members of Con-

gress only. The studios were established to give Congressmen and
Senators a convenient and inexpensive way to send radio-tv reports back to their Congressional districts. The member is billed at
cost."

Variety mentioned as an example a forum interview of Representative Williams and Arkansas Governor Orval Faubus one day
when Faubus was visiting Washington to appear on the Westinghouse Broadcasting Company's syndicated TV show, "Youth
Wants to Know."

The fifteen-minute Williams-Faubus interview for the Citizens'
Council forum cost the "sponsor"—*i.e.,* Williams—something between $30 and $55, *Variety* reported. In comparison, said *Variety,*
the charge to the producer of the thirty-minute "Youth Wants to
Know" program, filmed at commercial rates in Westinghouse's
studios, was $2,000.

The man who is probably most familiar to the public as a spokesman for the CC Association is young Richard Morphew, executive
director and moderator of the Citizens' Council forum.

Well over six feet tall and generously fleshed, Morphew has fine
features—quick, dark eyes, and an abundance of wavy, black hair.
He is in his twenties and has five children. In contrast with Simmons' almost languorous speech, Morphew talks swiftly. He prefers
"I am" to "I'm," and in other ways speaks in that diaphrag-
matic, studiedly mellifluent manner characteristic of radio-video
performers.

He was raised in Birmingham and Kansas City, and is a graduate
of the University of Missouri School of Journalism. After college
he spent a hungry year in Los Angeles trying to make his mark as a
free-lance writer, then worked briefly for TV stations in Kansas
City and Jackson before going to work for Simmons when the CC
forum was launched.

At lunch with Simmons and a visitor at a private key club
restaurant downtown, while being served by trimly uniformed
Negro waiters (who of course will have to be replaced if Simmons'
desire to establish a separate state for the darker race is ever fulfilled), Dick Morphew advanced the theory that the NAACP's only
motivation in the current civil-rights controversy is simply greed
for money.

Speaking of Mississippi's NAACP leaders, he asked with a good measure of bellicosity: "If they think integration is right, why don't they try to enroll their own children in the white schools here in Mississippi?"

He scoffed at the suggestion that they might be reluctant to do so because they felt that reprisals against them would be swift and certain. Dismissing the idea that leaders of the NAACP sincerely desire an end to the present system of segregation, he said:

"They don't believe in integrating the schools any more than we do. They raise all this furor just to raise money for their treasury."

It was Morphew's contention that those Negro parents who have enrolled their children in previously white schools in other Southern states have done it solely for the pay they received from the NAACP.

Of the pressure of Northern public opinion in favor of giving equality to Negroes, Morphew said he feels this is motivated by spite as much as anything else: "They have had to integrate with them. So now they look at us in the South and think: 'You have got to take the same medicine.' "

During the gracefully served luncheon numerous greetings of "Hey, Bill," were cast at Simmons. There was only one slightly strained moment—when a high official of the University of Mississippi was encountered at the cloakroom. There was a light, seemingly jovial exchange of conversation, but it also seemed obvious that both Simmons and the Ole Miss official were touched by a thought or two of the Billy Barton case, which that day was the banner story in all three Jackson daily newspapers.

Although Simmons had no on-the-record comment to make about the "Barton incident," he did indicate that it had been one of the more nettling events that had taken place during his career as Dixieland apartheid's number-one organization man.

The singular story of the Barton case provides a nice insight into the kind of behind-the-scenes activity that many dedicated Southern segregationists have been engaged in these last eight years.

It began when a never-officially-identified Mississippian received an unusual telephone call from Atlanta on August 17, 1960. After hanging up, the said Mississippian wrote a remarkable letter to Albert Jones, director of the Mississippi Sovereignty Commission, a state agency that has subsidized the Citizens' Council Association in the amount of $5,000 a month. According to the Jackson *State-Times*, the letter was written on Citizens' Council stationery and, according to Hazel Brannon Smith's *Northside Reporter*, its author was "a spokesman for the Citizens' Council reported to be W. J. Simmons. . . ." Simmons himself has staunchly refrained from acknowledging or denying authorship of the letter, saying, "I have made no comment about the incident, and I intend to make none."

At any rate, the letter addressed to Sovereignty Commission Director Jones was quoted by Hazel Smith's newspaper as follows:

This is a confidential report on a matter I think will be of considerable interest to the Sovereignty Commission.

Today Mr. Lufburrow, executive secretary of the States' Rights Council of Georgia, one of our affiliated state-wide organizations, phoned me from Atlanta the following information:

A young man named Billy Barton of Pontotoc, Mississippi, was actively involved in several lunch-counter "sit-in" demonstrations in Atlanta, including the one at Rich's department store which caused quite a disturbance.

Barton has been employed this summer on the staff of the Atlanta Journal. He will be a senior student at the University of Mississippi this fall. He wants to be editor of the student newspaper at Ole Miss. . . .

Barton is a close friend of P. D. East, publisher of the *Petal Paper* at Petal, Mississippi. We have a full file on East's activities, which are intended to be extremely harmful to the best interests of Mississippi, to put it mildly.[5] Barton plans to leave Atlanta next

[5] East for several years had been the gadfly of Mississippi journalism; a persistent annoyance to the Citizens' Councils. A husky, prematurely gray-haired man, he has been a sort of Mississippi version of Harry Golden, publisher of the *Carolina Israelite*.

When CC officials advertised they were going to hold an organizational meeting in his home county in south Mississippi, East ran a full-page advertisement in his own paper headlined: "Yes, YOU, too, can be SUPERIOR . . . Join The CITIZENS' CLAN and BE SAFE From SOCIAL WORRIES." New members, he said, would automatically acquire ten freedoms, among them: "Freedom to wonder who is pocketing the five dollars you pay to join. . . . Freedom to take a profitable part in the South's fastest growing business: Bigotry. . . . Freedom to be superior without brain, character, or principle."

It was inevitable that economic pressure would soon be applied to East

week and visit East at Petal or Hattiesburg before school opens.

Ralph McGill, editor of the Atlanta Journal, has taken Barton under his wing and has offered him a permanent position on the Atlanta Journal after graduation from Ole Miss. All those who are familiar with the key position occupied by Ralph McGill in the left-wing apparatus will recognize the significance of this fact. It means that Barton is well regarded in left-wing circles as a promising young man and has been selected for advanced training.

The information contained herein was transmitted to Lufburrow this morning by an informant planted on the staff of the Atlanta Journal who has had Barton under observation for some time. Lt. Poole of the Georgia Bureau of Investigation vouches that all information received from the informant, who is a student at Tulane University, is absolutely accurate. I have been in contact with Lt. Poole from time to time in the past on other matters, and have full confidence in him. . . .

Lufburrow says the informant describes Barton as "very dangerous."

I regard this information as important, and very revealing. It indicates the painstaking efforts of the pro-integration people to plant sympathizers in key positions on our college campuses, where they can exert a maximum influence on student opinion. This process has been going on for many years, as we all know, but I believe this is the first time we have been fortunate enough to gain knowledge of their detailed plans in advance.

Please assure the members of the Sovereignty Commission of our wish to be of assistance at all times. The full facilities of our office and organization are available to you whenever needed.

This extraordinary letter rested in the dark files of the State Sovereignty Commission until December. Then a letter came to the old CC favorite, Governor Ross Barnett, from one Mac Dale, who

---

and his little paper, but when it came, East declared in his column: "We have only six words to say to those who would attempt to put economic pressure on us; the words are: GO TO HELL IN A BUCKET!"

The *Petal Paper* lost practically all of its local circulation, but East's singular nonconformism in the face of the general Mississippi trend brought him enough subscriptions from different parts of the country to keep him in business for several years despite the pressure. And he continued to sound off on what he considers to be the excesses of the South's segregationist leadership: "It appears to be something of a rat race in the South today," he has written, "to see which state can first attain complete and total assdom."

was then editor of the Ole Miss student newspaper. Dale noted that Barton was working as his managing editor and said he had been disturbed to hear rumors that Barton was a member of the National Association for the Advancement of Colored People. Dale wondered if the governor had any information on this.

Governor Barnett forwarded the letter to the Sovereignty Commission, and Commission Director Albert Jones—in a maneuver right out of the Keystone Cops—simply sent editor Dale the letter he had received from the never-officially-identified Mississippian, taking the "precaution" only to ink out the letterhead and the signature.

Awkwardly for Jones and the governor Dale turned the letter over to Barton—and the feathers promptly hit the fan.

Barton threatened to sue all concerned for defamation of his character.

The twenty-year-old student said it was true that he had attended one "sit-in" demonstration in Atlanta, but as a reporter for the Atlanta *Journal* and not as one of the demonstrators. He said he had never met P. D. East or Ralph McGill (and noted that McGill is not editor of the Atlanta *Journal* but is an executive of the Atlanta *Constitution*). And he demanded a lie-detector test to prove that he was not a "very dangerous" trainee of any "left-wing apparatus" and was not a member of the NAACP.

Moreover, such a lie-detector test actually was performed on young Barton and duly reported under a banner headline by the Jackson *State-Times*.

The polygraph expert who interrogated Barton solemnly reported that the test "indicates that he exercised no deception whatever in his answers" when he denied that he was an NAACP member, that he had led a sit-in demonstration in Atlanta, that he knew either McGill or East, or that he had been "selected for advanced training" by persons in "left-wing circles."

Editor Hazel Brannon Smith ran editorials in her weekly newspapers denouncing what she called the Sovereignty Commission's "alignment" with the Citizens' Councils "in a cheap game of character assassination involving a defenseless University of Mississippi student."

What little confidence Mississippians had left in the State Sovereignty Commission after it started making $5,000 per month donations to the private Citizens' Council in defiance of state constitutional authority has now vanished and the time has come for the Commission to be abolished.

If the privately-financed Citizens' Councils want to hire spies to go around checking on people, that is their affair as long as they can get away with it. . . . We doubt the majority of Citizens' Council members want their $5.00 per year dues used to hire snoopers to go around spying on their fellow Mississippians in "state police" style like in the Communist countries.

But when the State Sovereignty Commission, supported with all of our tax money to the tune of a $350,000 budget, starts cooperating with these spy activities of the Citizens' Councils, then it is time to call an immediate halt. No state agency should be allowed to unduly harass any of its citizens at any time, certainly when there has been no crime committed—and even if the student had been guilty as accused, he still would not have been violating state laws.

[T]he time is here when the freedom of all Mississippi people is threatened by the Citizens' Councils and the State Sovereignty Commission—and there are few people who will deny it. It is time for everyone to speak out and oppose this violation of our basic rights and freedom as American citizens. . . .

Governor Barnett, saying he had not personally taken part in the correspondence regarding Barton, passed the buck to hapless Jones of the Sovereignty Commission. The governor issued a public statement of assurance that "there is no desire on my part or on the part of the Sovereignty Commission to meddle into student affairs."

Jones, a middle-aged former sheriff and tax collector, could only offer the limp excuse that he had forwarded the letter to Dale as a "confidential report" not meant for publication.

"[The State Sovereignty Commission] has no intention of hurting Mr. Barton in his campaign for editor of the paper or otherwise," said Jones.

As was expected by Jackson newspaper readers, two of the three dailies then being published in the city, the *Clarion-Ledger* and the *Daily News,* sided with the Citizens' Council and the governor and his Sovereignty Commission.

Politics "gets quite ruthless at times," the *Daily News* piously philosophized in an editorial, and "as to the young Mr. Barton's claim that he has been slandered, it is hoped his hide is tough enough to take it in a measure of degree that Barnett and personnel of the Sovereignty Commission and Citizens' Council are doing. For these people, too, are getting pretty soaked in the thunderstorm of ugly adjectives. . . . We wish Mr. Barton continued success in his intriguing campaign for the editorship of the Ole Miss paper[6] . . . Now let's all get off the emotional gag in the Barton-Barnett-Sovereignty Commission dime novel and go fishing."

But this time Hazel Smith was not nearly so lonely in her battle against the Citizens' Council Association and its bankrolling bedfellow, the State Sovereignty Commission.

State Representative Phillip Bryant of Oxford, for example, denounced the Sovereignty Commission as a "private Gestapo" and deplored its shelling out of tax money for "cloak-and-dagger investigations that develop into character assassinations." Bryant declared: "When one man or group controls the Commission and develops it into a private Gestapo, it then is obvious what can happen to our democratic process."

Even before the Barton episode, several other newspaper editors in Mississippi had joined Hazel Smith in damning the State Sovereignty Commission for giving the CC Association $20,000 down and $5,000 a month in tax money to use in telling "the Mississippi story" to the nation.

There was a considerable amount of reflection on the fact that in 1960 the CC Association had campaigned tirelessly—and successfully—to get Mississippians to vote for a slate of unpledged presidential electors rather than for Kennedy or Nixon. The independents won with 112,000 votes, while the combined total of votes for Kennedy and Nixon was 181,000.

"Since the Citizens' Council was the principal architect of the campaign of the unpledged electors," wondered Oliver Emmerich, editor of the Jackson *State Times* and the McComb *Enterprise-Journal,* "was any of the $20,000 down payment or the $5,000-per-month allowance of the State Sovereignty Commission used as expenses of the unpledged electors?"

[6] In the spring election at Ole Miss, Barton was defeated by a vote of 986 to 807.

"Surely," wrote Hal DeCell, editor of the Deer Creek *Pilot*, "sanity and sensibility have deserted us if we continue to submit meekly to such public scalpings."

It was no surprise at all that the Council-Sovereignty Commission partnership was roundly denounced by Hodding Carter, publisher of the Greenville *Delta Democrat-Times*, a perennial foe of the state's extreme segregationists. Yet Carter felt it was probable that not many citizens of the state would voice their objections to it, since "most Mississippians have learned that you publicly oppose the Council only at your own peril."[7]

In the normal Mississippi course of events, it might be expected that criticism of the Citizens' Council-Sovereignty Commission combine would be limited to a few newspaper editorials, mostly written by such "controversial" publishers as Hazel Smith and Hodding Carter, and that the rest of the Mississippi citizenry would, as usual, remain silent.

But two men of Jackson, a young white lawyer and a Negro grocer, chose instead to do a surprising thing: they sued.

In a brief filed in Federal District Court at Jackson, Attorney William Higgs and Grocer Robert L. T. Smith asked for an injunction stopping "the enforcement, operation, and execution" of the state legislative act which created the Sovereignty Commission. The suit, which is dormant just at this writing, appealed especially for an order restraining the Sovereignty Commission from handing over any more money to the Citizens' Councils.

The suit was not only against the Sovereignty Commission. Also named as defendants were the Citizens' Council Forum, the Citizens' Councils of America, the Jackson Citizens' Council, Governor Barnett, State Treasurer Evelyn Gandy, and State Auditor W. D. Neal.

"The defendants Citizens' Councils," the brief declared pessimistically, "have acted, do act, and will act jointly and indiscriminately in advocating and compelling resistance and subversion of

[7] On April 1, 1955, shortly after *Look* magazine had published an article by Carter describing the Citizens' Council movement, the Mississippi House of Representatives, by a vote of 89 to 19, passed a resolution censuring him for "lying about the state and the activities of the Councils, and for 'selling out the state for Yankee gold.'"

the law of the land as embodied in the 14th Amendment to the Constitution of the United States of America, in particular, the Equal Protection and Due Process Clauses of Section One thereof in so far as they secure equal treatment and facilities to Negro citizens and taxpayers under state law of all the respective States and of the United States."

The young white attorney, Bill Higgs, is a rare specimen to have flourished in the recent climate of Mississippi.

It is well to take a second look at him, for it is from such young Southern liberals that the Citizens' Councils expect most of their troubles to develop in the years ahead.

Born just twenty-seven years ago in Greenville on the Mississippi, a little town which for some unexplained reason produces most of the state's intellectuals and dissidents, Higgs was graduated from the University of Mississippi in 1955 and from Harvard Law School in 1958.

He chose to practice law in Jackson, and, because of his excellent scholastic record at Harvard, he soon had a promising list of clients. But unlike most young men fresh from law school and searching for a toehold in the legal profession of Mississippi's capital, Higgs chose not to go along with the existing order of things and "play the game."

In 1960 he not only campaigned for fellow Harvardman John F. Kennedy against the Citizens' Council's slate of unpledged electors, but even dared to run for the House of Representatives against John Bell Williams.

Against his politically conservative, militantly segregationist— and very personable and popular—opponent, Higgs ran a campaign the likes of which had not been seen in Mississippi in many years: his platform included greatly increased expenditures for federal housing and medical care for the aged, diversion of farm-support payments from big planters to small farmers, federal aid to education, and a long string of other "liberal" proposals.

As he expected, Higgs received hardly 10 per cent of the votes.

"But the campaign gave me the opportunity to make four thirty-minute speeches on television, and they were *real liberal* speeches —the only ones like them heard in Mississippi during the sixty campaign."

Not so very long ago Higgs had his office in the Barnett Building, a multistoried structure named after Mississippi's present governor. However, following his entry into the political arena on the losing side, Higgs soon lost almost all of his clients and lost his office in the Barnett Building.

Recently, while preparing his suit against the powers-that-be of Mississippi, he was keeping shop in a couple of rear rooms in an old frame house a few blocks north of the capitol. In the front room a symmetrically constructed girl of nineteen or twenty was typing away on one of the briefs Higgs was submitting in his case against the CCs, the Sovereignty Commission, Governor Barnett, *et al.* Higgs himself had been reduced to using a card table for his desk.

"It's been an interesting experience, but, financially, I don't know how much longer I can make it." He laughed. "My main problem right at the moment is trying to figure out how I can get together enough money to pay my secretary her salary for last week."

Higgs is blond and fraily handsome, with rosy cheeks and eyes that sparkle with enthusiasm as he speaks; he looks even more boyish than his years. A young Daniel going forth to sling legal phrases at Mississippi's Goliaths, Higgs is well aware of the size and strength of his adversaries.

"I'm only one lawyer, but *three firms* represent one part or another of the Citizens' Council organization; those three are the first, third, and fifth largest law firms in Jackson."

And of course the elected officials whom Higgs was suing have a fairly formidable array of state-paid legal talent to call upon.

Higgs is an obviously bright, personable young man with a soothing delta drawl; if he had kept quiet and not insisted on fighting against institutions of conformity that have existed in his state under one name or another for more than a century, he doubtless now would be getting ahead. Doesn't he think it has been awfully impractical of him to take the course he has taken?

"I've thought about that, of course." He smiled. "And I decided it isn't impractical at all. My observation is that the person who does the right thing most often comes out best in the long run."

Oddly—in view of his gallant assault on the fortresses of segregation—Higgs officially classifies himself as a segregationist.

"I am a staunch Segregationist," he declared during his campaign against Representative Williams, capitalizing the word in a mimeographed speech transcript. "I believe in our way of life and it must be preserved."

He added in the same speech, however, that he felt "we can best preserve segregation by an intelligent and unemotional approach to the problem," and that he believed in "reason, wisdom, and intelligence rather than incompetent emotionalism and demagoguery which has been characteristic of my opponent."

Perhaps his segregationist pronouncements during the campaign were, as much as anything, merely a bit of realistic politicking, for it is well known that any candidate for public office in the Deep South automatically eliminates the possibility of victory if he fails to speak out for "our way of life."

Beside the card-table desk in his office, away from the political hustings, his opinions on segregation seem less "staunch." He speaks of the need for more Negro policemen in Mississippi, and he advocates that Negroes be given the right to vote in his state.

"I'd favor some form of token integration," he said. "I've become convinced that the white people of Mississippi are going to have to get their feet wet sooner or later."

Higgs is one of the few white Mississippians who have made bold to attend meetings with Negro leaders in the state to discuss present problems, and to examine with them the possibility that someday in the future cracks might appear in the dike of segregation.

In a little second-story office in west Jackson the Negro most feared by the segregationists of Mississippi—Medgar Evers, field secretary of the state NAACP—spoke of those few interracial meetings as hopeful signs in his organization's fight to end apartheid.

Evers is in his middle thirties, a brown, muscular man with a close-clipped brush of hair and a narrow mustache. He habitually scatters quick little fragments of laughter among his words, but there is about his dark eyes a fairly constant expression of quiet anger.

"Oh, of course years ago there were meetings attended by both whites and Negroes, but always there was a master-servant relationship between them," he said. "Now we're having some genuine, down-to-earth interracial meetings where people sit down and talk about real issues and Negroes are respected for what they can contribute to the discussion. Contrary to the statements of segregationists that the 1954 decision caused a deterioration of race relations in Mississippi, I would say there is now an increasing respect between the races. I know of instances where we've gained respect in areas where we never thought it was possible."

He did not specify, however. And he added with a few stitches of humorless laughter: "I'm not saying this is widespread. Yes, we have in Mississippi many white people who're 'interested in the problem' but who don't have the courage to speak out against evil."

Mississippi is the only state in which no grade-school integration suit had been filed by 1961. But Evers pointed to other actions which have been taken through federal authorities to gain equal rights for Mississippi Negroes: a few cases involving the right to vote, and, most notably, a suit to gain the right for Negroes to swim at public beaches on Mississippi's Gulf Coast.

"We've only spoken out mildly, but we're beginning to get results. Not the end results, which will be total integration and first-class citizenship." Again his humorless laugh. "It will be some time before we achieve that."

Through his years in the campaign for integration Evers has occasionally expressed himself in terms considerably more violent than those voiced by such "passive resisters" as Martin Luther King. In the November 1958 issue of *The Citizens' Council* Editor William Simmons tingled the spines of his white readers with an assortment of quotes from an article on Evers which he reported had appeared that month in the Negro magazine, *Ebony*.

The CC article, printed under a front-page cartoon headed "The Mau Maus Are Coming!" read:

A brief collection of related facts:
"Ebony" is a magazine published by Negroes for Negroes.
Medgar Evers is a Mississippi Negro, the state's field secretary for the NAACP.
The November issue of "Ebony" contains an article by Medgar Evers, "Why I Live in Mississippi."

Some quotes from that article:

"He read extensively of Jomo Kenyatta's Mau Mau reign of terror in Africa, and dreamed of arming his own band of black-shirts and extracting an 'eye for an eye' from whites who mistreated their black brothers."

". . . his dream of an American 'Mau Mau' band, roaming the Delta in search of blood."

"I'll be damned if I'm going to let the white man lick me."

Evers' first child is named Darrell Kenyatta Evers.

Although the quotes were taken out of context, they no doubt are an accurate measure of the bitterness Evers has felt toward white Mississippi in the past—and still feels at times.

"Yes, at one time," he said, speaking of the months when he was in the segregated army of World War II, "I planned to come back and take 'an eye for an eye.' "

He sighed, and moved restlessly in the chair behind his desk.

"But I changed my mind. Violence creates more problems than it solves. No, that's not the answer—although," he added with his sketchy laugh, "sometimes you might feel like it. But, no, I don't have bitterness in my heart as I once did."

Evers grew up in the Negro "quarters" of the tiny town of Decatur in east Mississippi, one of seven children of a sawmill laborer. His father was an illiterate but—Evers proudly remembers—"a quiet and resolute man." His mother had gone as far as the eighth grade in school.

"Growing up in east Decatur gave me a number of experiences which have always lived with me," he said quietly. "Particularly clear to me is the memory of a very good friend of my family—and the thing that happened to him. That was about 1939.

"A white woman accused him of 'sassing' her. Actually, he worked for her, and he had merely said something she didn't like." Evers gazed out the window. "A bunch of white men took him to the fairgrounds and lynched him. They beat him to death."

On a wall beside Evers' desk, above a framed photograph of his pretty wife and two of their three children, there is a placard which reads: *Don't Talk Politics in Here UNTIL YOU'RE A REGISTERED VOTER.*

Evers recalled that he first registered as a voter in Decatur shortly after he got his army discharge at the close of World War II. But he did not get to vote when election time came.

"Theodore Bilbo was running for the Senate that year," Evers said. "I remember standing across the street, listening to him speak to a white crowd in Decatur a few days before the election. I remember that red tie and stickpin of his, and how he popped his suspenders and said: 'The best way to deal with the nigger is to visit him the night before the polls open.'

"And some white fellows did come out to our house the night before the election. They said to my father: 'Tell the boys not to come to town tomorrow.' "

Despite the advice of the moonlight delegation Evers and his brother and four other young Negro veterans who had registered went down to cast their votes next day, but, said Evers, a group of white men armed with pistols turned them away from the polling place.

In more recent years "fairly nice numbers of Negroes" have managed to vote in Decatur, he said. But of Mississippi's total Negro population of almost a million only 20,000 or so have ever voted in any one election. And as a result of the state's stringent voter registration law that was passed after the 1954 decision, probably no more than 10,000 Negroes voted in the past couple of elections.

"Getting our people registered as voters remains a problem all over the state," said Evers. "If we could get the ballot we could weed out many of the injustices that Negroes suffer."

Evers' name first became familiar in Mississippi after his graduation from Alcorn A. and M. College in 1952. With his diploma from the Negro college in hand, he did a most singular thing for a Mississippi Negro: he applied for admission to the Ole Miss Law School. His application was rejected, of course, but the audacity of the gesture brought him to the attention of national leaders of the NAACP. He was hired as Mississippi field secretary for the organization in 1954.

As a full-time paid employee of the NAACP, Evers has enjoyed a measure of security from the type of "economic pressure" which has been so successful in quelling many other leaders of the Mississippi Negro protest. Even so, the path of an NAACP spokesman in the most segregated state in the country has its pitfalls.

In 1961 Evers was sentenced to thirty days in jail on a contempt-of-court charge after he criticized a Forrest County decision in the case of a Negro named Clyde Kennard, who had been given a seven-year prison sentence for theft.

The long sentence given Kennard was all the more notable for the fact that only a short time previously he had attempted—without success, of course—to enroll at all-white Mississippi Southern College in Hattiesburg. The sentencing climaxed a series of bizarre happenings to Kennard that inspired the British *New Statesman* to comment:

It is not, after all, much good declaring the public schools open to all races if, in Mississippi at least, a Negro student who tries to enrol in the Southern Mississippi College is first of all carted off to the lunatic asylum, then heavily fined for driving without a license and possessing whisky, and finally—to crown the edifice and complete the warning—sentenced to the maximum of seven years' imprisonment for 'arranging' the theft of five bags of chicken feed.

Evers described Kennard's conviction as a "mockery to judicial justice [in] a courtroom of segregationists apparently resolved to put Kennard legally away." It was this statement that prompted Forrest County Judge Stanton Hall to fine Evers $100 and sentence him to thirty days in jail. A few months afterward, however, the contempt conviction of Evers was reversed by the Mississippi State Supreme Court.

Surrounded by a white community that possesses the economic and police power of the state and—with the exception of a handful of nonconformists like Hazel Smith and young Higgs—is either dedicated to maintaining segregation or dedicated to maintaining silence, Evers recognizes the obstacles that stand in the way of any effective protest by Mississippi's Negroes.

"The Negroes are not satisfied—not by a long shot. I'd say 95 per cent of them are dissatisfied to the point of doing something. But to be candid, we realize that almost all Mississippi Negroes are subjected to their employers, and it is economically expedient for them to acquiesce."

Evers described the Citizens' Council-Sovereignty Commission combine as "a secret police with huge sums of public money to spend on going around and spying on private citizens."

"This has a tendency to intimidate Negroes—either economically or by causing a fear of violence."

But time is working on the side of the desegregationists, Evers maintains. And he says he believes the CC-Sovereignty Commission alliance is in for hard days.

"I believe a few more Barton cases will send it to its doom," he said. And with that slight laugh of his he added: "Yes, their days are numbered."

It has been suggested that it is part of the NAACP's over-all strategy to hold off grade-school integration attempts in Mississippi until the barriers have been broken down in other, less militantly segregationist states. Evers says this is not so.

"We aren't holding anybody off. Whenever Negroes here are ready to move against school segregation and request us to assist them, we'll lend them assistance. And, you know, it only takes one individual to institute a lawsuit—and there are many individuals who are dissatisfied to the point of taking action. Some incident might take place to catapult them into action immediately."

Only a few days earlier Judge Tom Brady of Brookhaven had voiced the opinion that the defeat of the integrationists was inevitable, and he had predicted: *It will come in OUR lifetime.* Medgar Evers now used the same phrase, voiced it with just as much vigor as the judge did, and meant exactly the opposite thing.

"We're going to attack the laws they [white Mississippians] have on their books, and then let the federal government do our fighting for us—or at least," he amended quickly, "let them assist us in the fighting.

"Integration is going to come to the schools of Mississippi," Evers said, biting the words determinedly, *"and it will come in OUR lifetime."*

The future of segregation in Mississippi depends, of course, not only on the course of events within the state but on the course of events throughout the South and, indeed, throughout the nation and the world.

At this writing (and this phrase must be emphasized, for Evers is quite probably correct in his remark that "some incident might take place to catapult" the integrationists into action), it is necessary to report that nothing of significance in Mississippi has been desegregated—not a thing.

In fact, the campaign for first-class citizenship for Mississippi Negroes has experienced some serious setbacks since 1954. The number of Negro voters in the state has been sharply reduced. NAACP chapters which had existed more or less openly before The Decision have been shattered or driven underground in several Mississippi communities. And that public tolerance for an occasional Liberal among the white populace has rather completely disappeared—and along with it the tolerance for those interracial conferences of the past, master-servant as the relationships at them might have been.

Elsewhere in the South, Citizens' Councils and CC-type groups have occasionally yielded ground, but in Mississippi the Councils so far have been triumphant. Eight years after the Supreme Court decision was handed down it would be inaccurate to suggest that the Negroes of Mississippi have really budged an inch in the struggle for equality.

Nor does it seem justifiable to predict of the Citizens' Councils and their governmental affiliate in apartheid, the Mississippi State Sovereignty Commission, that "their days are numbered." It seems much more likely that the Councils' membership will tend to increase with each new serious assault on the Mississippi Way of Life—as was the case after the "wade-ins" on the Gulf Coast.

The loss of funds from the Sovereignty Commission undoubtedly would be an economic blow to the Council organization—but hardly a fatal one.

Not so long ago a Salt Lake City oilman named B. C. Campbell presented the Citizens' Council Association with a gift of deeds to thirty acres of oil lands in Utah. A few weeks later the CC announced it had received another ten-acre tract of mineral-rich land as an anonymous gift from another oilman.

In accepting the deeds CC Treasurer Marvin Collum said such gifts marked the beginning of an endowment program which "will enable Council leaders to plan intelligently for the future."

Collum, who is senior vice president of the First National Bank of Jackson as well as treasurer of the CC, noted that "many individuals" are including bequests to the Citizens' Council Association in their wills. The Council Association, said Collum, "would welcome contributions in the form of real estate, securities, mineral lands, and insurance policies."

To understand the potential of the Citizens' Council movement it is necessary to recognize that numerous "members of the business community" have a vested interest in segregation and are willing to pony up a few dollars now and then to protect their investment. And it must be recognized, too, that there are quite a few white people who believe in the cause of segregation enough to fight for it not only *unto* death, but—through wills and insurance policies—to fight for it *beyond* death.

5. THE HOBBYIST

"STAY RIGHT THERE at the inn and I'll come meet you out front," the man who is known as "Mr. Segregation of the South" told the tourist over the phone. "No, you won't have any trouble recognizing me. I'm short and gray-headed, and I'll be wearing an old plaid shirt and slacks and driving a beat-up Chevrolet."

He was right. The visitor had no difficulty at all spotting Roy V. Harris, the sixty-five-year-old Georgia political figure who publishes the tirelessly white supremacist weekly Augusta *Courier* and is national president of the Association of Citizens' Councils of America.

He came wheeling up out of the Sunday morning in a weather-worn 1954 Chevvy, a short man with time-thinned hair. His trousers and plaid flannel shirt were rather bunchy at the waist; he had, he explained, lost quite a few pounds in recent months, yet he still had retained the tenpin shape that is familiar to his thousands of political friends and foes throughout Georgia.

Over a get-acquainted cup of coffee in the inn's restaurant he seasoned the conversation with a generous amount of bonhomie and laughter.

No, he said, the fact that he is president of the segregationist Georgia States' Rights Council and head of the white Citizens' Councils should not be taken to imply that he feels any ill-will toward Negroes.

"I was born and reared in Wrens [a tiny community not far from Augusta in northeast Georgia], and I came up working out in the field with Negroes," he said. "My daddy ran a country store. He bought cotton and sold fertilizer—sold everything, in fact,

101

but coffins. And he had a farm, mostly as something to keep us children of his busy.

"Many times I've sat under a cotton-patch tree with Negroes and eaten together with them."

Even so, he said, he and his fellow cotton pickers, the Negroes, never did quite mix—not in the manner recommended by the NAACP, anyway.

"This thing they're trying to do now is to mix us socially." He winced and shook his head. "If that happened, we'd wind up with a new race of people in this country."

To alert the people of Georgia to the "danger" of this is the main purpose of his remarkable little newspaper, the Augusta *Courier.*

The task of writing and editing the four-page tabloid weekly with only the help of a woman stenographer takes a lot of time away from his prosperous law practice and his business as a real-estate developer. And since the paper does not accept advertising, the publishing of it most likely takes a few dollars out of Harris' pocket now and then.

"Putting it out is a lot of work. But," he cheerfully shrugged, "it's my hobby."

The *Courier,* which is devoted almost entirely to white supremacist polemic, has a circulation of "six or seven thousand," Harris said. Often quite a few hundred extra copies are distributed in the Atlanta restaurant owned by Lester Maddox, who was runner-up in the 1961 race for mayor of Atlanta and is the peppery leader of a segregationist organization called GUTS ("Georgians Unwilling To Surrender").

Harris said that certain Mississippians—presumably including William J. Simmons of Jackson—had approached him with the idea of merging the Augusta *Courier* with the CC's official monthly publication in order to create a single, more powerful segregationist organ.

"But I didn't want to," said Harris. "I decided I could do more good by remaining independent."

In truth, Harris takes pains to emphasize that the *Courier* does not speak for any organization or anyone except Harris himself. The motto on the *Courier*'s masthead reads: *He who spares no class of men is angry at no person, but the vices of all.*

In contrast with the conviviality of Harris in person his newspaper is superbly splenetic. His headlines, which are printed in red ink, breathe fire.

He pictures the desegregation movement as part of a plan to overthrow the United States—a plan devised by Socialists and Communists and aided and abetted by Jack and Robert Kennedy:

> Kennedys Wage War on White People
> of South, While Commies Rip the U.S.

He reminds *Courier* readers that Nikita Khrushchev said only a few months before his visit to the United States: "We cannot expect Americans to jump from capitalism to communism, but we can assist their elected leaders in giving Americans small doses of socialism, until they suddenly awake to find they have communism." And he has dozens of times reprinted Nikolai Lenin's long-ago prediction: "First we will take eastern Europe, then the masses of Asia, then we will encircle the United States, which will be the last bastion of capitalism. We will not have to attack. It will fall like an overripe fruit into our own hands."

Many of the *Courier*'s columns are employed to quote the writings of those biologists and psychologists who have concluded that Negroes are genetically and mentally inferior to Caucasians:

> Equalitarian Dogma Is the Scientific Hoax of the Century[,]
> University of Virginia Professor of Psychology Charges

He frequently reprints editorials from the South's outstanding segregationist newspapers, especially the Charleston *News and Courier* and the Richmond *News Leader*. And, as might be expected, he gives a considerable amount of space in his paper to reports of racial strife in Africa and the North—atrocities to whites in Angola and the Congo, muggings and rapes by Negroes in the District of Columbia, murders by Negroes in New York, and such:

> Power-Drunk, Vote-Hunting Politicians In Washington
> Go on Rampage While Crime Runs Amuck in U.S. Capital

and

Law, Order Breaking Down in New York's Negro Jungles

Harris also seems to take special delight in expressing a lively disapproval of the national Protestant "establishment's" let's-all-be-friends campaign for peaceful integration:

National Council of Churches Said One of Most Dangerous Organizations in United States to Liberty and Religion

About once a month the *Courier* prints a column under the by-line of Senator Herman Talmadge, a column which is prepared in Washington for publication in divers Georgia papers as an on-the-spot interpretation of significant events in our nation's capital. "Herman Talmadge Reports" it is called.

Through Harris' four decades as a formidable politician in Georgia he has been an intimate—a friendly intimate, for the most part—of both Talmadge *père* and Talmadge *fils*. Yet Harris does not quail at criticizing Herman when he feels that the junior senator is engaging in legislative folly on Capitol Hill. Recently, when Senator Talmadge introduced four Senate bills which were designed to curb the power of the United States Supreme Court and which were plainly doomed to defeat, Harris headlined and sub-headlined as follows:

Talmadge Indulging Again in "An Exercise of Futility"
Jackie and Lyndon,
Old Sam, Will Kill
Bills Like Shooting
Ducks in Bathtub

Since the *Courier*'s circulation in the main is confined to Georgia, Harris directs much of his fire at the "moderates" of the state who advocate (or, at least, are resigned to) desegregation. His favorite targets are those intellectual and pseudo-intellectual residents of Atlanta who would like to eliminate Georgia's unique county-unit system of voting, which would of course tend to reduce the control of the rural "wool-hat" votes by such men as Talmadge and Harris, and tend to increase the power of those men who can swing the urban vote (particularly the Negro bloc in the big city of Atlanta).

The main threat to the political power of the so-called "wool hats"—as Harris sees it—is embodied in Atlanta's two dailies, the

Journal and the *Constitution,* both of which are parts of the Ohio-based Cox newspaper chain. He recently headlined:

> Ohio-Owned Newspapers in Atlanta
> Seek to Kill County Unit System
> Politically Hungry
> Cox Gang Would Get
> Complete Control of
> State Government

And his very favorite whipping boy is Ralph McGill, publisher-columnist of the Atlanta *Constitution* and perhaps the nation's best-known "white Southern liberal." A recent typical review by Harris of a McGill column began:

> McGill and King See Eye-to-Eye About Disobeying Laws;
> Their Disapproval Based on Ground That Laws Are "Unjust"
> Negro Muslims'
> Riot at United
> Nations Upheld
> by Newspaper Head

Ralph McGill and Martin Luther King, Jr., are both advocating that Negroes violate any law which doesn't meet with their approval.

Martin Luther King, Jr., told a group of Negroes at Warren Memorial Methodist Church in Atlanta . . . that the Negro students and ministers in Atlanta were right to violate any law they believe is unjust.

This was on the night of the same day when followers of Elijah Muhammad staged a riot in the gallery at the meeting of the United Nations.

The next morning, in his column, Ralph McGill defended the followers of Elijah Muhammad for staging their riot. . . .

Harris the "die-hard" said he and McGill the "do-gooder" had been good friends in years past—especially back in the days when McGill's writing was devoted to the analysis of football and baseball plays rather than to pronouncements on the South's social problems.

"He was one of the best sports writers there ever was," said Harris.

The opposing positions they have taken on The Problem have

made it necessary to shelve their old chumship in more recent years—at least in public.

"Ralph and I run into each other now and then at meetings. And we speak—and maybe rib one another a little. But, oh, you know, we don't act very friendly." Harris laughed. "We have to keep up appearances."

Harris took his visitor on a long drive all through the little city of Augusta and its outlying neighborhoods. He expressed special pride in showing a new subdivision of neat little brick homes which he and his real-estate business associates had had constructed for occupancy by Negroes. Throughout the drive he made it unmistakable that he has a tender feeling for Augusta; he speaks of the city as if it were a beloved person.

Aside from its interest value as a guided tour of a charming municipality, the drive with Harris was memorably exciting as a sheer automotive adventure.

The national president of the Association of Citizens' Councils of America drove as if he were pleasantly unaware that any vehicles save his own were on the roadways of Augusta. As he wheeled his 1954 Chevvy along he talked fairly constantly, pointing out sites of interest, executing left and right turns without deigning to give signals—driving, in fine, in the merry manner of Mister Magoo.

While driving past the National Golf Club in a long line of automobiles, as Harris was pointing out its beautiful tees and greens, his car kept bearing toward a policeman who was standing in the middle of the road directing traffic. It seemed inevitable that the cop would be clobbered, and this apparently crossed the cop's mind, for he waved Harris to a halt.

"Boss," the policeman said, rather sadly resignedly, "how 'bout watching me instead of the golf course. You're holding up traffic way on back."

Moving on, Harris nodded and said, "He's right, you know." Then he laughed brightly. "Course, he doesn't know who I am." And he added, without any belligerence, "I know him, though."

And he drove on in pretty much his own fashion. Once the car got stuck in the mud as Harris was exhibiting an area down by the

Savannah River levee which he felt was ripe for a housing development. At an intersection a few minutes later two cars traveling in opposite directions barely escaped Harris' Chevrolet.

"Hm," he lightly said, "I believe I might get us killed yet."

And he shifted into another gear and began speaking of the effect that the 1954 Supreme Court integration decision is having on Augusta's housing situation.

In the Southern tradition, a large portion of the houses for Augusta's Negroes had always been built quite close to the houses occupied by white people. The reason for this housing pattern was obvious: it placed Negroes conveniently close to the white homes in which they worked as domestic servants.

The result was that much, perhaps most, of Augusta's housing had never been segregated—that is, not *geographically* segregated.

The white officials of some Southern cities feel that they can blunt the effect of the 1954 decision through their geographical school zoning laws—just as many a Northern city maintains *de-facto* segregation by requiring the children who live in its Negro housing ghetto to attend a school within their residential zone (*i.e.,* a school within the Negro ghetto which just happens to have an all-Negro enrollment).

But in the likely event of a federal school integration order in Augusta, such a Northern-style "solution" would seem to be impracticable in Harris' home city. Because of the crazy-quilt pattern of housing (racially speaking) in Augusta, it would be difficult indeed for the city's white officials to maintain segregation by the old Yankee yes-we're-integrated-in-theory-but-not-in-practice zoning technique.

Now in Augusta, said Harris, efforts are being made to plan new housing developments exclusively for the occupancy of Negroes or exclusively for the occupancy of whites. This way, it is felt that public-school segregation can be maintained in the manner that New York City and Chicago, say, are able (with varying degrees of success) to maintain it—through segregated housing.

"So you see," said Harris, "the 1954 decision, so far, is actually resulting here in more segregation rather than less segregation."

Meanwhile, as the federal judiciary prepares to decide how deliberate the speed of social change in Georgia must be, segregated schooling in Augusta continues apace. Howsoever the little city's Negro schools might be "intangibly" inadequate and "inherently unequal" (to borrow the phraseology of the 1954 decision), it is only fair to report that they look better than the older schools now attended by white pupils. So many of them are new and trim; they give bright, modern touches to the graceful old city.

Augusta, too, is a place of many churches. Harris estimated that more Augustans belong to the Catholic Church than to any other, followed by the Baptists, Methodists, and Episcopalians, in that order. There is in Augusta, as a matter of fact, an imposing temple for the Negro followers of the late Sweet Daddy Grace.

Although Harris devotes many columns of his *Courier* to the perfidies—as he interprets them—of such integrationist "Liberal" religious apparatuses as the National Council of Churches, he himself gives the impression that he is neither especially hopeful nor especially gloomy about the hereafter.

"When I was running for a political office some years ago," Harris said, "somebody asked an old friend of mine what my religion was. And my friend said, 'Roy's a Methodist—but not enough to hurt.' "

Roy Harris has had a strong voice in the governing of Georgia for almost forty years.

His only noteworthy official political position at this writing is membership on the State Board of Regents, a body which (with the aid and abetment of the federal judiciary, to be sure) formulates Georgia's policies for higher education.

But in years past he was an even bigger man in Georgia politics. It seemed very likely that he would one day become at least governor of the state—and perhaps go even higher than that.

Not long after he had graduated from the University of Georgia and had begun practicing law in 1919 in Jefferson County he was elected to the State House of Representatives and, in time, to the State Senate. In 1932, a year after moving to Augusta (in Richmond County), he was again elected to the State Legislature; he served there until 1946, eight of those years as Speaker of the Georgia House of Representatives.

In those days, of course, the political history of the sovereign state of Georgia was being predetermined—to a considerable extent—by the father of the present junior senator from Georgia, the late and (in retrospect) extremely improbable Governor Eugene Talmadge. For quite a few years Harris and the elder Talmadge cooperated politically.

"But in the New Deal days our group—the group I'd always been with in the Legislature—split with Gene," Harris recalled. "Gene was so violently opposed to Roosevelt—and to his programs for child welfare, old-age benefits, and so forth."

Harris emphasized that in most sociopolitical provinces he has never considered himself a "Conservative."

"I went along with FDR's domestic and social legislation. All along I've scrapped for a foreign-aid program and for federal aid to schools. I guess I'm a stand-patter on the race issue, but I guess you could call me an ultra-Liberal on some things."

Having split with Gene Talmadge, Harris managed the successful gubernatorial campaign of Ed Rivers in 1936. Gene came back into the governorship in 1940 and, said Harris, "I kept my mouth shut during that campaign."

"Then in 1942[1] I managed Ellis Arnall's campaign and got him elected governor," Harris said.

An interesting alliance—for Arnall was ostensibly a Ralph McGill-type "Liberal" who, while he was Georgia's chief executive, won much Northern recognition for his benignly "un-Southern" expressions. An intelligent, articulate, soothingly charming man, Arnall seemed to delight the sophisticates of the North. He appeared on the fine old radio program, *Information, Please,* and acquitted himself nicely in repartee with Fadiman, Adams, Levant, *et al.* It seemed not at all inconceivable that he would become vice president of the United States.

The alliance of Harris and Arnall ruptured in 1945.

It was commonly believed in Georgia that the parting of the ways came about because Harris wanted to become governor and Arnall refused to help him fulfill that ambition. But that is not true, says Harris.

"Arnall wanted me to run for governor. He would manage my campaign. Then," said Harris, "when I got elected governor, I could manage his campaign for vice president.

[1]Until 1942 governors of Georgia were elected to two-year terms. Since then they have been elected to four-year terms. But now, as in the past, Georgia governors are not permitted to succeed themselves in office.

"For him to become vice president, he said we would have to line up with the CIO and the Negroes.

"He asked me, 'Willing to play ball?'

"And I said, 'I'm sho' not.'

"The next morning," as Harris recalls it, "one of his friends asked for legislation that would let a governor succeed himself. . . . Later he called a special session of the Legislature and attempted to get through an amendment [to the State Constitution] that would let him run again [for reelection as governor of Georgia]. I whipped him in the House.

"He and I are now very friendly personally," Harris said of Arnall, "but we weren't for a long time."

Soon after his political divorcement from Arnall (who went forthwith into a political eclipse) Harris "got back with" Gene Talmadge and his son Herman. He helped Herman manage his father's successful campaign for governor in 1946, then, fast upon the elder Talmadge's death just before the oath of office could be administered, Harris helped get the young Talmadge (Herman) installed in office as governor—and, some few years later, as a United States senator.

In the 1958 election Harris supported Ernest Vandiver for governor, and Vandiver won. It would be inaccurate, though, to describe Harris as a "Talmadge man" or a "Vandiver man." He seems to be pretty much his own man.

Although the Augusta *Courier* has, by and large, been a supporter of Vandiver, Harris roasted the governor most searingly in January 1961, when the first two Negroes were admitted to the University of Georgia at Athens. He ran a cartoon which pictured the governor as a two-faced "Janus II" and was captioned "NO NOT ONE—BUT TWO OR MORE." And Harris raged in red headlines:

> Vandiver . . . Has Surrendered Fight to
> Preserve Segregation in State
> Governor's Pledge
> To People of State
> During His Race
> Was "No Not One!"

. . . Governor Ernest Vandiver has thrown in the towel and surrendered in the fight to preserve segregation in the schools of Georgia.

On Tuesday, January 10, 1961, Governor Ernest Vandiver wired [Federal] Judge W. A. Bootle that he would not defy his order [to admit the two Negroes to the State University] and . . . a spokesman for the Governor said:

"It means there is nothing anybody can do about it."

In Every Speech

This certainly is a different position from that taken by Governor Vandiver when he was a candidate for election.

In every speech he made, he said:

"When I am your governor, neither my three children, nor any child of yours, will ever attend a racially-mixed school in the State of Georgia."

And then he wound up that statement—on almost every occasion—by saying:

"No not one."

No Not One

"No not one" was the theme song of his campaign.

In his speeches for election to governor and in his speeches to the Legislature, he also said . . . [etc., etc.].

As for Herman Talmadge, Harris indicated he is not at all sure that Georgia's junior senator is more interested in maintaining segregation than he is in retaining residency in metropolitan Washington.

"I'm afraid," Harris sighed, "that Herman has 'Potomac fever.' "

After the long excursion through Augusta, over richly resuscitating bourbons in the vast living room of Harris' home, there was talk of music and poetry.

Harris' wife, a signally pretty woman with delicate features, dark eyes, and raven hair with only a few nice brush strokes of gray, was discussing seventeenth-century verse with a lean, fair, graceful-voiced young schoolmistress. Mrs. Harris is a music teacher. The clean, well-lighted living room was dominated by a grand piano. Playing on the phonograph was an Ormandy rendition of a composition by Johann Sebastian Bach.

Of which poet is Mrs. Harris reminded when she hears the music of Bach? the fair schoolmistress asked.

"You'll shoot me," said Mrs. Harris, "but I think of Shakespeare."

"Why would I shoot you for thinking that?" the schoolmistress replied. "But rather than Shakespeare, I think of Milton."

There was a slim volume of verse by Dylan Thomas on the coffee table.

"Are you a Dylan-tante?" the schoolmistress murmured to the visitor, applying the bastinado, of course, but with a really rather delicate touch that somehow is never ever quite equaled for grace north of Georgia.

The visitor replied something, something surely forgettable, the while feeling with dead Dylan:

> *Time held me green and dying*
> *Though I sang in my chains like the sea.*

Later, there was talk, too, of Faulkner (William) and Wolfe (Thomas), and of which was the better writer. This phase of the literary discussion was, again, inconclusive. Yet Harris did volunteer that he had never read anything written by Wolfe; he had read a bit of Faulkner and, he said, if Wolfe was no better than Faulkner then he wanted none of him.

"My favorite writer," Harris said (as Evelyn Waugh said some few years back), "is Erle Stanley Gardner."

It would seem, in truth, that Harris prefers non-fiction to fiction. He had just been reading Will Durant's *Our Oriental Heritage,* and the book had given him (especially Durant's discussion of ancient Egypt), he indicated, some valuable ethnological insights.

"The more you read about Egypt the more you see that they had a civilization unrivaled—until they brought in Negro slaves and finally had a new race of people. Go back to Egypt when its people were white and it was developing a civilization, and then go over the desert [the Sahara Desert] and see what the Negroes accomplished in the same time," Harris suggested. "The white Egyptians developed the greatest civilization on earth, and the Negroes of Africa developed two things: the institution of slavery, and cannibalism—nothing else.

"They [the Negroes south of the Sahara] had the same opportunity the Egyptians had. Why didn't they develop the same cultural atmosphere the Egyptians did? It was the same on the Amazon; the people there had the same opportunity and still didn't develop a civilization.

"Myrdal [Gunnar Myrdal, author of the influential 'Liberal' analysis of race relations in the U. S., *An American Dilemma*] proceeds on the theory that if we let Negroes associate with white people, our civilization will rub off on them but that they can't develop a culture of their own. And the tragic thing is, he may be right. All the civilization the Negroes have has been aped from white people.

"Take the Negroes in Africa today," Harris proposed. "The minute you turn them loose [as in the Congo] they go back to their old tribal customs of eating the enemy."

In these less literally carnivorous United States, Harris recognizes, the problem is less one of who might ingest whom. He concedes that the "race problem" is, in considerable measure, a problem of color. But:

"I'm one of those persons who has a preference for a certain color," he said. "I think color alone is important. I just prefer white over either mulatto or black. And I think I have a right to prefer it."

In an editorial a few weeks ago Harris nicely articulated the feeling that lies so near, perhaps, to the roots of the flower of American patriotism which somehow has recently withered so.

Something has happened to this nation.

We seem to have lost the great emotion which was possessed by those who carved this country out of a wilderness, fought the Indians, endured the hardships, and laid the foundation for a great nation and a great people.

Everywhere we turn, we seem to be up against an impossible barrier.

In western Berlin today we seem to have a tiger by the tail. We can't turn loose and we don't know what to do with what we have.

We witnessed the same thing in Cuba.

We had the same experience in South Korea.

We are up against the same situation in Laos.

At home, we have problems that seem almost insolvable.

Khrushchev threatens to bury us and talks about his big bombs that will destroy millions of people at a time.

People are beginning to wonder how we got this way. They are asking what happened to us, where did we miss the boat. . . .

There is only one answer to our situation and that is that the termites have been gradually eating away at the very soul of a people and today we seem to have lost confidence in our mission. . . .

Outside, strolling in the yard beside his house, the national president of the Association of Citizens' Councils of America talked of his shrubbery and of his flowers.

Growing flowers is also his hobby, he said.

Harris was eliminating his little cedars, deadly robbers of the earth's nutriments, as his front-lawn's hedge growth. He was replacing them with tender-leaved shrubs that remain ever green and are bright with spring yellow all the year round.

He had been carefully developing new root systems for his azalea bushes, of which he was (very justifiably) proud. He directed attention to a couple of them.

"I planted that one about two and a half years ago. And this one I planted just last year. I'll be planting some more—along." He smiled. "It's good to have things ahead of you to do."

An untimely frost had cruelly browned his white camellias.

"But I think our azaleas this year," he said, "are the prettiest we ever had."

And Harris, very gently, meticulously, plucked one azalea whose petals looked of life and lavender. Harris—"Mr. Segregation of the South"—held it out to his visitor, and said:

"It's like an orchid, isn't it?"

III. THE KLANSMEN

Inside the Invisible Empire

1. THE BED-SHEET RENAISSANCE

THE Ku Klux Klan, which had lain so drably dormant in the South since its great bed-sheet boom time in the 1920's, was prodded suddenly awake by the Supreme Court's 1954 integration ruling.

Its growth since The Decision, although substantial, cannot in truth be described as spectacular. And yet in this season of discontent—as in certain painful seasons of the past—the Klan just might prove to be the segregationist South's most formidable weapon in the battle for white supremacy.

The size of the Klan's membership—75,000, give or take a few thousand—is perhaps less than half that of the Citizens' Council-type organizations.

But it is probably accurate to say that a man's membership in the Klan implies a stronger commitment to action than does a membership in a Citizens' Council. Many a Southerner has joined the "socially acceptable" Council in his home town simply as a gesture of half-hearted willingness to drift along with the segregationist mood of the community; but for a man to be willing to dude himself up in KKK bed linen and take a blood oath beside a flaming cross he probably must possess a rather more intense degree of interest in defending the Southern Way of Life.

Speaking very generally, Citizens' Councils (and their CC-type affiliate organizations) draw most of their leadership from business and professional men and politicians whose families by and large are safe from the "dangers" of racial integration. That is to say: if a Negro family moves next door to the average Council leader, he can afford to move to a white suburb; or if Negro pupils are admitted to the public school attended by his daughter and son, he can afford to transfer his children to a segregated private school.

The Ku Klux Klan, on the other hand, is made up mainly of people of low income—people who cannot afford to send their children to private segregated schools, who cannot afford to flee to racially pure suburbs to escape Negro neighbors, and whose jobs might seem to them to be most immediately threatened by the institution of "fair-employment" laws.

Too, Klansmen and their families are likely to be the least educated and the least "sociologically sophisticated" citizens of a community—the least well equipped to accept Negroes as their equals. For them (again, of course, speaking in general) the race problem is not "an American dilemma" (within Gunnar Myrdal's context); in this segment of white society there is a strong and really sincere feeling that Negroes are not quite human and therefore are not entitled to the rights and privileges enjoyed by men (i.e., white men). It follows, therefore, that Negroes must be "kept in their place."

For quite a few members of the Klan the effective response to an integration threat is not an injunction or a referendum or a melodiously worded pamphlet. It is, instead, a whip, or a length of metal pipe, or a stick of dynamite.

To speak of *the* Klan is, to be sure, erroneous. There are several Klans functioning in the South, and they vary considerably in purpose and procedure.

The general public's "image" of the Klan is as a mob of men, in masks, pointed dunce caps, and flowing white robes, who dash about at night, flogging Negroes and white Liberals. There is a measure of truth in this notion, and, understandably, integrationist organizations do not much trouble themselves to dispel it.

One of the most carefully prepared studies of Southern racial difficulties which have been published since the 1954 decision is a booklet titled *Intimidation, Reprisal and Violence in the South's Racial Crisis,* edited by the pacifist American Friends Service Committee with the aid of the liberal National Council of Churches and the liberal Southern Regional Council. It is enlightening to examine some of the projects undertaken by members of—or men who have chosen to identify themselves as members of—the Klan. A few fairly typical 1957 activities reported in the Alabama and South Carolina domains of the Invisible Empire were these:

Maplesville, Ala.: Six Negroes were beaten in what a newspaper account said appeared to be a senseless outrage. The six men, one a soldier on leave, were watching television in the home of one of them when Ku Klux Klansmen arrived. The masked men beat the Negroes from the rear, using rubber hoses or blackjacks. . . . Earlier in the evening twenty-two carloads of Klansmen pulled up in front of the town hall, donned robes, and marched through town. After the beatings two of the Negroes left town. . . .

Evergreen, Ala.: Four Negroes were beaten by a mob in Klan regalia. The victims said the robed men accused them of NAACP membership. Two of those beaten were ministers. . . .

Centreville, Ala.: White men horsewhipped a Negro preacher north of here. Bibb County Sheriff Carl A. Griffin said the Rev. T. D. Wesley gave this account: After preaching at a Negro church, he was driving along a country road when men in two or three cars stopped him, handcuffed him and tied him with a rope. They drove him up a side road and beat him with a horsewhip, then left him, still bound, in the unlocked trunk of his car. He managed to free himself and drove to Centreville, where he was taken to a Selma hospital. Wesley said one of his assailants wore a kind of hat or hood which came over his face. The sheriff said no explanation for the beating had been uncovered. . . .

Gaffney, S.C.: Five men identified as members of the KKK were charged with bombing the home of a white physician whose wife wrote an article urging a "moderate" approach to the racial integration crisis. . . .

Greenville, S.C.: Four admitted members of the Ku Klux Klan were convicted for conspiring to flog a Negro, Claud Cruell, at his home July 21, 1957. Two also were convicted for flogging the 58-year-old Negro landowner and Baptist deacon because of his association with a white family who rented a house on his 100-acre farm. Cruell and his wife were caring for the seven white children of the white tenant when a group of white men stormed into the house. They wrapped a chain around Cruell's arm, dragged him to another room, and beat him. The white tenant had left the children with the Negro couple while he visited his wife in a hospital. . . .

Camden, S.C.: Guy Hutchins, director of the Camden High School band, was beaten by hooded men. Hutchins said he was surrounded by four or five men while he was changing a tire, that they pulled a sack over his head, drove him around, and then tied him to a tree while each hit him a half-dozen times with a board. . . . Hutchins was hospitalized with severe bruises. He said the attackers falsely accused him of making a pro-integration speech to a civic club. . . .

While the Klan's well-known tradition of violence gives it a significant measure of power—the power to intimidate people by inflicting physical pain or, at least, generating fear by threatening to do so—it is also a significant weakness of the institution. Often sadistic men in hoods and sheets commit senseless outrages, and often personal grudges which are quite unrelated to the Klan's campaign for "racial purity" are settled in an ungraceful manner with clubs or horsewhips: frequently the result of such unseemly occurrences in a Klan group is that all but the most disreputable elements of the membership (the thugs, if you please) drop out of the organization.

In recent years the central leadership of the Klan, headquartered in Georgia, has made a continual effort to present the Invisible Empire to the public as an organization sufficiently "respectable" to attract an effectively large number of dues-paying members—as in the "good old days" of the 1920's.

At Home With the Wizard

The Imperial Wizard of the largest Klan group in the country—the United Klans, Knights of the Ku Klux Klan of America—spoke to a visitor a few months ago about his organization's desire for "respectability."

"The majority of our members want to give the Klan more nationwide appeal," said Robert Lee "Wild Bill" Davidson of Macon, Georgia. "I'm trying to bring it out of the darkness and make it a progressive movement, not just a protest movement."

Davidson, who had been Grand Dragon of the Klan in Georgia since 1957, was elevated to the highest office of the Invisible Empire when longtime Imperial Wizard Eldon Edwards, an Atlanta auto plant worker, died in August 1960.[1]

It would, of course, be fatuous to expect a Klan chieftain to have any particular appearance; even so, the boyish looks of Wild Bill Davidson somehow seem congenially alien to such an imposing title as Imperial Wizard.

He is still in his early thirties, a tall, sapling-slender fellow with cheerful brown eyes and tidily parted black hair. He and his wife (who calls the Wizard "Bobby") and their four children live in a box-shaped two-story house in the back yard of his mother's little old frame home in Macon. Its living room is no bigger than a medium-size hallway; when the long-legged Imperial Wizard sits in a chair on the north side of it, his feet reach almost to the south wall.

An especially gentle touch in the room is a whatnot lined with rows of tiny porcelain dogs.

"Every time I make one of my out-of-town trips for the Klan," Davidson said, "I bring my wife back one of these dogs."

The Davidsons have three real dogs in addition to the porcelain ones.

When at home the Imperial Wizard wears a polo shirt and slacks and off-beatnik slippers, and puffs restively at a dark cigar.

It had been a bad season for Davidson. His father as well as his old friend, Eldon Edwards, had passed away within a year. A fire had severely damaged the bag-savalging plant which he had inherited from his father. His truck had just broken down. His home freezer had just conked out and a good part of the meat stored in it had spoiled.

All this, together with his heavy schedule of work in behalf of the Invisible Empire, had caused him high blood pressure and nervousness, the Wizard said. He thought it might soon be neces-

---

[1] Until a few months after Edwards died and was succeeded by Davidson, this largest of the country's Klan groups had as its official title "U. S. Klans, Knights of the Ku Klux Klan." Both the titles "United Klans" and "U. S. Klans" are used in this chapter to refer to the Edwards-Davidson organization.

sary for him to reduce his Klan activity for the sake of his health.

But while his strength remains, he said, he will work diligently to achieve the decades-old KKK goal of bringing all the country's klaverns into one Klan organization—"or at least," he said, "into a single association with one policy."

A Klan organization of the type that gained such power in the 1920's would be the white South's best vehicle for "consolidating all the forces that believe in preserving segregation," Davidson maintains.

"The Citizens' Councils can't survive in the long run because they're controlled by politicians," he said. "I'm not kicking the Councils, you understand. But we've got to take [the leadership of the segregation battle] away from politicians and put it in the hands of the *people.*"

In contrast with the Councils and Council-style groups, Davidson said, the Klan is run by its members and is a throroughly "democratic" organization.

"Of course a Catholic can't belong to the Klan; that's because his own religion won't let him join any fraternal order but the Knights of Columbus," he said, and added: "The nigger is kept out for the simple reason that we're fighting for segregation and he's not. I'm not anti-Semitic and the Klan's not anti-Semitic, but Jews don't belong to the Klan because the Jewish faith doesn't accept Christ as the Saviour."

Davidson brought out a stack of Klan pamphlets which he said details the philosophy of his Invisible Empire and explains why Negroes, Jews, Catholics, and persons of foreign birth may not belong.

"THIS IS A WHITE MAN'S ORGANIZATION, exalting the Caucasian Race and teaching the doctrine of White Supremacy," says a booklet on the "ideals" of the Klan. "This does not mean that we are enemies of the colored and mongrel races. But it does mean that we are organized to establish the solidarity and to realize the mission of the White Race. . . .

"THIS IS A GENTILE ORGANIZATION, [although] we sing no hymns of hate against the Jew. He is interested in his own things and we are exercising the same privilege of banding our own kind together. . . .

"IT IS AN AMERICAN ORGANIZATION, and we do restrict membership to native-born American citizens. . . . [Aliens in America] obey the mandates of governments of which they are still the subjects even to the extent of endeavoring to break down the government under which they find protection while seeking their nefarious ends. . . . They do not easily readjust themselves. Thus we find the groups: Irish-Americans, German-Americans, and all kinds of hyphenated Americans. What pleasure would they find or what service could they render in this organization which is distinctively an American-American organization? . . .

"IT IS A PROTESTANT ORGANIZATION. . . . We can say to the world without apology, and say truly, that our forefathers founded this as a Protestant country and that it is our purpose to re-establish and maintain it as such. . . .

"WE MUST KEEP THIS A WHITE MAN'S COUNTRY. . . . Our forefathers never intended that [this Republic] should fall into the hands of an inferior race. . . . Every effort to wrest from White Men the management of its affairs in order to transfer it to the control of blacks or any other color, or to permit them to share in its control, is an invasion of our sacred constitutional prerogatives and a violation of divinely established laws. . . . One of the sad facts in American political life is the readiness of so many politicians to sell their noble white birthright for a mess of black pottage. . . . Purity of the White blood must be maintained. One of the crying evils of the times is the mixture of White blood with that of Negro. This evil has gone on since colonial days until perhaps more than half of the Negroes in the United States have some degree of White blood flowing in their veins. This condition is not only biologically disastrous but is giving rise to grave social problems. Mulatto leaders who, under present social conditions, are forced to remain members of the negro group and who aspire to white association because of their white blood are boldly preaching racial equality in all of its phases. The guilt for this state of affairs rests upon those members of the White Race who for a moment of sexual pleasure have betrayed [their] own kind and bartered their own blood. It has become necessary to devise some means for the preservation of the white blood in its purity, because, despite prohibitive laws, racial intermixture is continuing and the problem of mixed blood is becoming more and more acute."

In a booklet, *Principles,* the Klan's racial creed is summarized this way: "Let the white man remain white, the black man black, the yellow man yellow, the brown man brown, and the red man red."

It is a bit ironic that Davidson distributes the Klan's *Principles* with an unqualified endorsement, since it is a fact that he himself is, in the oversimplified terminology of the Klan, a "red man"— and is proud of it.

"I'm half Cherokee Indian," he said. "No, not half, I guess. My grandfather on my mother's side was a full-blooded Cherokee; he was a blacksmith—one of the best."

Davidson chooses to trace his "klannishness" even further back in history than the early post-Civil War days when the first KKK was organized in Pulaski, Tennessee.

"We originated in the Scottish Klans," he said. "We go back to the days of Rob Roy."

His great-grandfather was a Confederate soldier in the War Between the States and is buried in the family plot in Wilkinson County, Georgia, where the Imperial Wizard spent most of his youth. After high school Davidson served a hitch in the Navy, then returned to Georgia and—after a time as a common laborer and then ironworker—he worked as an insurance salesman until he joined his father's bag business in 1949.

While recalling his days as a salesman Davidson dug into the living-room closet and brought out a fancy suède jacket decorated with Wild Bill Hickok-style fringes.

"I took to wearing this when I was selling insurance," he said. "Everybody started calling me 'Wild Bill' back then, and the name sort of stuck—even after I quit wearing it and went to work at the bag company for my dad.

"When you're selling something," he added, "you've got to do something that gets attention. Wearing this jacket got a lot of it."

Davidson's talent for selling the Klan took him progressively higher in the Invisible Empire. He joined the Klan when he was nineteen, served as a Kludd (chaplain), an Exalted Cyclops (head of a local Klavern), then as Grand Dragon (state president) of

Georgia, and finally as Imperial Wizard (above which there is no other in the KKK).[2]

While exploring the closet, Davidson mentioned that the golden Klan robe he wears as Imperial Wizard was just then at the cleaners. But he did display the satiny green robe which he wore back in the days when he was merely a Grand Dragon, and his wife's Klanswoman's robe, a white one daintily trimmed with red and blue.

"I'd say the women of our ladies' auxiliary have taken more interest in the Klan than their men have." The Imperial Wizard laughed. "The men'd rather hunt and fish."

One of Davidson's four children, a sandy-haired, wide-eyed little fellow of seven or eight, brought in a sofa pillow to make the visitor comfortable. It was a bright yellow pillow stitched with the blue lettering, "KKKK" (for Knights of the Ku Klux Klan).

The Imperial Wizard, smiling proudly at his son, said the Klan has high hopes for its junior division.

"The children in the Junior Klan have their own regalia and their own ceremony of initiation," said Davidson. "We have a baseball and football program for them."

The Imperial Wizard displayed a large Klan charter which he had just prepared for a Junior Klavern.

"It's more or less something to keep them off the streets," he said; "something like the Boy Scouts."

Davidson said the most dedicated Klansmen today are young men with children of elementary-school age. The Imperial Wizard himself has long been active in youth work; he is, for example, a director of a Baptist Training Union in Macon.

"The youth of today, you know," he said, "are the leaders of tomorrow."

For the kiddies as well as the grownups the traditional Klan mask is optional, said Davidson.

"It's now illegal in Georgia to wear a mask on public property,"

[2] The Anti-Defamation League recently estimated that the Klan organization headed by Davidson has between 15,000 and 20,000 members. Despite losses as a result of schisms and defections, the group guided by Davidson's wizardry had an over-all gain of 3,000 to 5,000 members in the last couple of years, reckoned the ADL.

he explained. "But if I wanted to, I could put a mask on and stand out front on my private property, and nobody could say a thing."

But Davidson said he stoutly opposes the kind of masked violence that has been so often attributed to Klansmen through the years.

"It doesn't do any good to go out and molest with anybody," he said. "That's just defeating the purpose of the Klan."

He emphasized that his organization has no connection with the very "activist" Alabama Klan group headed by Robert Shelton.

"Shelton used to be with us, but he got to be a fanatical in politics," said Davidson. "He helped to get John Patterson elected governor of Alabama. Now Shelton's got his own independent group; Montgomery is his stronghold."

The Alabama division of Imperial Wizard Davidson's organization has been led in recent months by the Reverend Alvin A. Horn of Talladega, a middle-aged evangelist who caused a small tizzy in the Invisible Empire in 1957 when he married a teenage girl. But the publicity created by his marriage has long since quieted down, and according to Imperial Wizard Davidson, Horn is still considered a "good Klansman—a Ku Klux man from the word 'go.' "

In addition to dissociating his group from Shelton's Klan, Davidson said he wanted to make it clear that his Empire has had no connection with John Kasper's Seaboard White Citizens' Council, George Lincoln Rockwell's Nazi party movement, or Dr. Edward Fields' National States Rights party.

"I don't get myself connected with any fanatical movement," Davidson said. "I can't go around lambasting Jews, Negroes, and Catholics and expect to get a national following."

But while Davidson does not "condone" the groups considered by him to be "fanaticals," neither does he choose to fight them, he said.

"I believe in using any and all of the forces to preserve segregation," he said. "I'd believe in using a rattlesnake to preserve segregation, if that's necessary.

"I'm not radical and I don't believe in violence," he added. "But we'd have to do something if the Negro knocks on our door and says he's going to sit on the porch till he dates our daughter. I hope that it never comes to the point where we'll have to have vigilante law. But a man has a right of self-preservation—the right to protect his wife and his children. You wouldn't want the Congo to take over your home, would you?"

Davidson, like almost all other Dixie segregationists, asserts that "the Communists" are behind the present difficulties in American race relations.

"Even the radio and TV are communist controlled and communist inspired," he remarked glumly. "Every time you turn on the TV to a cowboy show, you find a nigger playing in the lead. Now, *everybody* knows there were no nigger *cowboys.*"

Davidson conceded that there are many grave organizational problems in the Invisible Empire.

"But the Klan will live forever, anyway," he said confidently. "We have over ten million men in the country who've been Klansmen at one time or another. The Klan will live on and on—like the Minute Men—like the torch of liberty."

2. THE RECALCITRANT DRAGONS

THE MOST nettling problem for Wild Bill Davidson, just as it was for his predecessor Imperial Wizard and likely will be for successor Wizards, was the fact that Klan groups in the several states are so schism prone—so subject to the temptation to engage in free-enterprise Klansmanship. This kind of defection from the parent group seated in Georgia obviously tends to rend the solidity of the Klan, encourages oddballs to use the Klan name, and tends sometimes to promote violence—i.e., encourages some Klansmen to do the sort of thing that gives all Klansmen a bad name.

True, officerhood in the Klan has never been looked upon as evidence of great mental prowess. But no extraordinary mental ability is really required for a KKK potentate in any one of the Deep South states to one day reach the conclusion that it makes just as much sense to keep the dues in his own Klavern as it does to mail them to some Wizard away over in Georgia.

The result of this is that free-lance Klans, groups independent of the parent organization headed by Davidson, are forever springing up in the South.

The most important "defection" from the master Edwards-Davidson group in the last few years had been that of Robert (Bobby) Shelton, sometime B. F. Goodrich Rubber Company salesman of Tuscaloosa, Alabama.

Back in 1957 Shelton had replaced the Reverend Alvin Horn as Alabama Grand Dragon (i.e., state leader) of the U. S. Klans, Knights of the KKK. Horn had been Alabama's Grand Dragon for several years but had resigned (at age forty-eight) ostensibly because of publicity over his choice of a teenage girl as his bride.

But Shelton did not for long remain a satisfied subordinate of the then Imperial Wizard of the U. S. Klans, Eldon Edwards of Atlanta. For one thing, Shelton gained a great deal of prominence in Alabama politics in 1958 when he was reported to be a strong supporter of John Patterson in his successful gubernatorial race —and was reported to be a political chum of Patterson's campaign manager, Charles M. Meriwether, who later received a high administrative appointment from President John F. Kennedy (despite a fine fizz of criticism from the Liberal establishment of the North).

According to the Montgomery *Advertiser,* Patterson (who was then state attorney general) was fully aware of the Klan chieftain's support of his campaign for governor. The *Advertiser* reprinted what it identified as a letter written on stationery of the state attorney general's office soliciting campaign help from friends of Grand Dragon Shelton.

JOHN PATTERSON
ATTORNEY GENERAL
STATE OF ALABAMA
P.O. BOX 6034
MONTGOMERY 6, ALABAMA

March 19, 1958

Dear Mr. *****[1]
A mutual friend, Mr. R. M. (Bob) Shelton, of ours in Tuscaloosa has suggested that I write you and ask for your support in the coming Governor's race.

I hope you will see fit to support my candidacy and I would like to meet you when I am next in ******.

With warm personal regards, I am

Sincerely your friend,
/s/ John Patterson
JOHN PATTERSON
Attorney General

JP:db

When the *Advertiser* "exposé" was published Patterson vigor-

---

[1] The *Advertiser* reported it had agreed to delete the name and home town of the addressee from whom the copy of the letter was obtained.

ously denied having any connection with the Klan or with Grand
Dragon Shelton.

"This is amazing," Patterson declared to the *Advertiser*. "I am
not a member of the Ku Klux Klan. I have never been a member.
I don't know anyone named Shelton."

There was nevertheless a popular assumption that Shelton had
an in with the incoming state administration. This undoubtedly
added to his prestige in the Alabama provinces of the Invisible
Empire. According to the very dependable *Southern School News,*
Shelton, as a salesman for the B. F. Goodrich Company, sold the
Patterson administration a million-dollar order of merchandise.

Not many months after Patterson had become governor Shelton
had severed his official connection with the U. S. Klans (the Edwards-Davidson group) and had established his own organization: the Alabama Knights of the Ku Klux Klan.

Shelton has made it fairly obvious in the last year or so that his
ambitions for leadership in the Invisible Empire extend beyond
the borders of Alabama. In recent months he has chosen to identify himself as "National Grand Wizard of the Knights of the Ku
Klux Klan." This would seem to indicate that he has become of
a mind to challenge the Imperial Wizardry which, since the 1920's,
has been located in Georgia.

Although only thirty-two years old and a busy family man at
that, Shelton nevertheless takes an active layman's interest in matters of psychological and physical science as well as in the subject
of segregation.

A few months ago, for instance, he was expressing concern over
the fluoridation of water in some areas as a purported method of
preventing tooth decay.

"You ought to read a report I saw recently on this subject," he
said. "It proved that the whole program is inspired by the Communists so that someday they will be able to poison millions of
people. You know that there is no antidote for fluoride. It's a
deadly poison."

Shelton was even more disturbed by his analysis of the Mental
Health Society:

"This is the most dangerous organization in America today.
. . . They have already passed a bill in Congress which allows

federal agents to come down here and declare you and me mentally ill and ship us off to a hospital in Alaska.

"When they get you there they can perform an operation on you to give you the mentality of a three-year-old. The do this by going in behind the eye and deadening part of the brain tissues. And when they get you in this condition they can teach you to be an integrationist or anything else. They have already performed this operation on 500,000 people in Russia."

And as a long-time resident of Tuscaloosa, the site of the University of Alabama, National Grand Wizard Shelton has, perhaps understandably, taken a special interest in developments in the field of higher education.

At this writing the University of Alabama is still under a federal injunction to admit Negro students if they are scholastically qualified to enroll. The injunction, issued by United States District Judge Hobart Grooms in Birmingham, has been "in effect" since 1956 when Autherine Lucy, a winsome-looking young Negro woman, was briefly matriculated. But she had hardly selected her textbooks for study before an inhospitable outburst of riots prompted her swiftly to leave the campus. Soon afterward she was expelled by University officials for accusing them of complicity in the untidy disturbances (and, to the chagrin perhaps of Miss Lucy's NAACP legal staff [unaccustomed as they were to losing matches in federal courts], United States Judge Grooms ruled that her expulsion was a valid exercise of the University's right to discipline its students).

The Klan had been accused of taking a leading role in the violent Lucy episode. Among the demonstrators were numerous workers from the Tuscaloosa rubber plant where Shelton was employed.

Shelton has indicated he believes the NAACP will soon again attempt to get one or more Negroes enrolled in the University of Alabama. Will violence again occur on the campus?

"The Negroes resort to violence when they attempt to integrate," he said recently, "because they are attempting to break the law [i.e., the state segregation law]. The Klan does not wish to break any laws, but it may have to bend a few. If anyone can stop integration at the University, the Klan can do it."

Some months earlier, when the Reverend Martin Luther King spoke of the need for a new Negro challenge to school segregation in Alabama, Shelton declared:

"[If] Martin Luther King's . . . announced plans . . . are carried out it will bring bloodshed to Alabama. . . . Let this be a warning that we are ready to take whatever steps are necessary to maintain segregation and our Christian ideals in the state of Alabama."

And he added:

"We mean business."

The truth that the statement, "We mean business," was not merely windy rhetoric was fairly dramatically illustrated when the 1961 "Freedom Riders" were vigorously pummeled fast upon their arrival in Alabama.[2]

Let it be emphasized that Shelton was not accused of participating in the boisterous, bloody disorders in Alabama. However, as a result of the bruising reception the riders for freedom got in Patterson's and Shelton's home state Federal District Judge Frank M. Johnson in Montgomery did deem it prudent to issue a temporary injunction against a dozen or so organizations and individuals ordering them to desist from "interfering with interstate travel." Among the enjoined individuals and organizations were Robert Shelton and his Alabama Knights of the Ku Klux Klan —along with Alvin Horn, who by June 1961 had been imperially reinstated as Alabama Grand Dragon of the U. S. Klans, Knights of the Ku Klux Klan (i.e., the outfit headed by Wild Bill Davidson of Macon, Georgia).[3]

[2] Only four months before the first great "freedom ride" into Alabama (on December 7, 1960, just as New Orleans was in a condition of screaming turmoil over the first token integration of its public schools) Alabama's Governor Patterson declared at a press conference in a spirited comment somewhat reminiscent of Shelton's:

"If you think they've had trouble in New Orleans, just wait until they try integration here. There'll be hell to pay. . . .

"You're going to have rioting on your hands if they try forced integration [in Alabama]. . . ."

While he asserted that he personally was opposed to mob violence, Patterson warned that whenever the time for a showdown came "I'll be one of the first ones stirring up trouble, any way I can."

When the first busloads of "Freedom Riders" arrived in Alabama there was, as the governor had predicted, a generous measure of "hell to pay."

But when this showdown came, Governor Patterson was not in fact "one

The Anti-Defamation League of B'nai B'rith which, because of the Klan's long tradition of anti-Semitism, takes a close interest in developments within the KKK movement, indicated in a 1961 report that it felt Shelton's star was ascending in the Invisible Empire.

"Shelton appears to be making rapid progress in absorbing local klaverns, including many formerly affiliated with the U. S. Klans [the Edwards-Davidson group], into the Alabama Knights," said the ADL report, "and it is considered possible that he may also capture the remaining klaverns of the U. S. Klans in the state.

"Best available information indicates that while the Klan situation in Alabama continues to be highly fluid, with frequent shifts of allegiance by various klaverns, Shelton's group is emerging as the dominant Klan. . . ."

Highly fluid, forsooth.

If anything can be said with certainty about the Klan it is that its organizational weave is never neatly certain. At no given moment can its woof be distinguished from its warp.

At this writing "Bobby" Davidson of Macon, Georgia, and "Bobby" Shelton of Tuscaloosa, Alabama, appear to be the most significant figures (the most masterful Wizards, as it were) of the Ku Klux Klan in the South.

But a gift of prophecy would be necessary for anyone to venture to predict whether they will still be in power or whether the Klan's over-all structure will or will not be altered by the time these words reach print—whether altered by a simple schism or a major cataclysm.

The United Klans (the Eldon Edwards-Wild Bill Davidson organization) have at least a few followers in almost every South-

---

of the first ones stirring up trouble"; he was too busy issuing proclamations that "a serious emergency [and] a state of lawlessness" existed in Alabama, too busy calling out the federally-aided Alabama National Guard in order to bring the rioting mob's violence under control.

[3] To the despair of the integrationists in the articulately humane North, Federal Judge Johnson's injunction order also was directed against the reputed leaders of the "freedom ride," among them CORE (the Manhattan-quartered Congress of Racial Equality) and Dr. Martin Luther King, Jr., individually and as president and spiritual leader of his southern Christian Leadership Conference.

ern state. But there are numerous other Klans in the South which apparently are independent of the parent KKK.

In Alabama, in addition to Shelton's organization, there has been activity in the last year or so by white-sheeted groups called the Gulf Coast Klan, the Dixie Klans of Alabama, and the Federated Knights of the KKK. In Florida there existed the Bedford Forrest Klans, the Southern Knights of the KKK, and the Knights of the White Camellia.

In Florida, too, as well as in Georgia and South Carolina, dwell the National Knights of the KKK. Tennessee's dominant group appears to be the Dixie Klans, Knights of the KKK. And in Texas, where denizens of the Invisible Empire apparently are very few in number, the least insignificant of the divers insignificant Klan groups is one called the Original Knights of the KKK.

Indeed it is not uncommon for the words *Ku Klux Klan* to be employed with grand flourish in the title of an "organization" which has only one member—plus, maybe, sometimes, two or three of his acquaintances.

Of this genre of Klansmanship perhaps the most interesting has been that practiced in recent years by a resident of Waco, Texas, named Horace Sherman Miller. The ADL has described Miller as a "disabled veteran of the First World War" who "once operated as part of Edwards' U. S. Klan."

In his literature, published in great abundance by an offset-printing process that features a fascinatingly relaxed format, Miller identifies himself as "G.D." (Grand Dragon?) of the "Aryan Knights of the Ku Klux Klan."

Miller's main informational vehicle for broadcasting his socio-political philosophy—if such it can be termed—is a small "newspaper" named *HERE IT IS!*, with the fairly singular subtitle: *White Folks News—There is no equality among men.*

In the accepted tradition of America's "radical right," Miller's publication prints cartoons and commentary which elaborate the thesis that "JEWS DECLARE WAR ON HUMAN RACE." In one cartoon a few months ago a toothy, dollar-mark-decorated python which was coiled around the Capitol building in Washington was labeled "Rabbis" and the Capitol itself was labeled "Synagogue." In the same issue he reprinted a proposal that all good men should come to the aid of their country and "DRIVE THE JEWISH PHILOSOPHY OF GOLD AND GREED OUT OF OUR TEMPLES OF FINANCE. THROW THE JEWISH HYPOCRISY OUT OF OUR NATION'S PRESS. . . ." And, as a postscript to a reprinted article about a Jewish banquet in New York City, Miller's publication recommended to the subscribers: *"AWAKE and Put the Traitors to the Stake."*

In view of the great journalistic ado that was made over the effect that the Catholicism of one of the two presidential candidates in 1960 might have on the segregationist Bible Belt of the South, it is somewhat surprising that anti-integration emotions are not tied to the anti-Catholic sentiments in the way that they are so angrily tied to anti-Jewish sentiments.

It is therefore almost revivifying, or dismaying, if you choose, to find that Horace Sherman Miller has managed comfortably to blend anti-Catholicism with his anti-Semitism and anti-Negroism. One of the minor pieces of literature which he markets is a message in the form of a post card: One side is blank (to give room for an address, a postage stamp, and a personal message if the sender is so inclined); the other side reads, *in toto,* as follows:

HAIL MARY! You All Equals!
To HELL with
*
POPERY and Death
Demand and Defend Liberty

Horace Sherman Miller — Box 5062 — Waco, Texas
(25 Small Cards for $1.00)

It is probably accurate to say that Miller's "organization" wields no great influence inside the Invisible Empire—or, for that matter, outside the Invisible Empire. Miller's own publication, *HERE IT IS! White Folks News,* some months ago quoted (without comment) a Waco *News-Citizen* item which reported that the membership of the Aryan Knights of the Ku Klux Klan consisted of Miller and one other fellow and "maybe the immediate family."[4]

---

[4] It might fairly be inferred that the Waco *News-Citizen,* at least, does not consider Horace Sherman Miller to be a formidable force against integra-

Another noteworthy free-lance "Klan leader"—whose background and literary style differ considerably from Horace Sherman Miller's—is J. B. Stoner, an Atlanta attorney who identifies himself as "Archleader and Imperial Wizard of the Christian Knights of the Ku Klux Klan."

According to one of his membership blanks, an applicant for initiation into his realm must pledge that he is "a true and loyal, patriotic White Gentile Christian American [and] a believer in Our Lord Jesus Christ, the White Race and its Preservation and the principles of pure Americanism. . . ." The initiation fee for adult men was reduced some months ago from $15.00 to $10.00 (but has remained $5.00 for women and applicants under twenty-one).

Although he is still in his thirties, Stoner has had a long and active career in Klansmanship and anti-Jewish agitation.

According to an Anti-Defamation League press release, his career in this field of endeavor began in 1942, at age eighteen, when he became a "Kleagle" (organizer) of a Ku Klux Klan group in Chattanooga. John Roy Carlson (the pseudonym of the undercover writer Arthur Derounian) reported in his book, *The Plotters,* that in the early 1940's Stoner sent to him from Chattanooga a card inviting applicants "to join a secret organization that stands primarily for WHITE SUPREMACY." A few months later, Carlson wrote, Stoner advised him that he was no longer a Klan organizer but was "now engaged in distributing anti-Jewish literature."

"Interviewed by a reporter in 1946," said the ADL press release, "Stoner admitted he thought Hitler was too moderate, and

---

tion, Judaism, Catholicism, old Modern Republicanism, or new Frontier Democratism. Yet the vested interests (the bullet-proof vested interests, as it were) apparently have chosen to take him seriously.

More than a year ago, having learned of Miller's Aryan Knights through perusal of American Jewish Committee and Anti-Defamation League literature, I wrote to Miller a letter, the text of which read in full:

In connection with a book which I'm writing on Southern politics and the current struggle between racial integrationists and those dedicated to the preservation of segregation in the South, would you please send me any information on the program of your organization?

Promptly Miller showered me with his literature disclosing that the said he was planning a new party, the essence of which would be 'to make being a Jew a crime, punishable by death.' The Stoner Anti-Jewish party emerged, and in 1948 Stoner actually ran for Congress, receiving 541 out of 30,000 votes cast."

In the early 1950's, after migrating to Atlanta, Stoner teamed up with young Edward Reed Fields, and the old Stoner Anti-Jewish party was soon transformed into the Christian Anti-Jewish party. In more recent years Fields has become chief potentate of the South's most vociferous anti-Jewish organization at present, the National States Rights party, and Stoner has on occasion served as the NSRP's legal advisor.

Stoner publishes a small *Klan Bulletin* in Atlanta every so often, and much of it is devoted to the thesis that "race mixing is Jewish!"

As might be expected, the marriage of Sammy Davis, Jr., and May Britt brought no congratulations and best wishes from Archleader and Imperial Wizard Stoner. His society-page report, as it were, ran as follows:

JEWS HONOR SAMMY DAVIS, JR.

Sammy Davis, Jr., is the negro entertainer and movie actor who married a blond white woman named May Britt. He has always dated white women because he thinks that negro women are not good enough for him. They have both turned against our Lord Jesus Christ and become converts to Judaism. They were married by a Jew rabbi in Hollywood where Mrs. Peter Lawford, Presi-

---

Jewish philosophy is one of "gold and greed" and that right-thinking citizens should say "to HELL with POPERY and Death" and racial integration.

But it also happened that Miller forwarded my letter to one Guy Bryan Harrison, director of the Texas History Collection of Baylor University in Waco. Harrison, in a letter to me which with graceful somberness agilely seesawed between constabulary alarm and academic stuffiness, reported that "the Miller papers" are "under seal—accessible only to the FBI, Mr. Miller and our staff." On occasion, said Harrison, "certified serious scholars" are admitted to "certain areas of the papers for study," but that must be done "under supervision."

It must, in the interest of candor, be confessed that the author did not go to Waco, Texas, and study the "Miller papers" under the supervision of Guy Bryan Harrison and/or the FBI—however academically valuable such a project might well have been.

dent Kennedy's sister, kissed the groom. Of course Jews never fully accept converts but they use them for Jewish purposes.

Now, the Jewish National Fund, with headquarters in Israel, has given a plaque to Davis and his wife for their "humanitarian efforts" and cited them for their "contributions to the ideals of brotherhood."

. . . The Jews are happy to have mixed degenerate marriages, like the miscegenation of Davis and Britt, because they can use them as examples to innocent young White boys and girls. The Jews have a fanatical hatred for our White race and intend to destroy it with an intermixing of negro blood. . . . Race mixing is Jewish!

Many people across the country felt that the St. Louis heiress, Ellen Steinberg, was making a generous contribution to American education when she offered some five hundred thousand of her personal dollars to the New Orleans public education system early last year after the Louisiana Legislature announced plans to cut off state school funds as an anti-integration measure. It may be said, however, that Stoner did not share this feeling.

Of Miss Steinberg's monetarily lavish gesture Stoner wrote in his *Klan Bulletin:*

JEWS FINANCE RACE MIXING

A Jewess, Miss Ellen Steinberg, has offered half of a million dollars to the New Orleans school board to help it integrate the races in New Orleans Schools. She is "deeply distressed" because the honorable legislature of Louisiana has withheld funds from two integrated schools. Miss Steinberg, now a social worker in New York, was born in St. Louis where her father, Marc C. Steinberg, a multimillionaire, was an investment broker.

Miss Steinberg is not the first Jew to generously contribute money to mix the negroes with Whites. There have been many others. Without Jew money and the Jew money power there would be no integration! . . .

A couple of years back Stoner was promoting his Klan organization in Louisville, Kentucky—where his fellow toiler in the vineyards of "anti-Jewism," Edward Reed Fields, practiced for a time as a chiropractor.

From Chattanooga to Atlanta to Louisville and back to Atlanta the Archleader has traveled. In a recent winter this author was planning a Southern trip the itinerary of which would include the Georgia capital, and it was hoped that an interview with Arch-leader Stoner might be arranged at his convenience; the author therefore dispatched a dollar for a six-month subscription to the *Klan Bulletin* along with a letter inquiring of the archleader about the possibility of a personal interview in Atlanta.

"I will be glad to see you when you visit the South," he wrote in a friendly reply. "However, during February and March I expect to be in Florida. . . ."

He explained that he planned to spend most of the winter season at—Miami Beach!

3. THE BLOODSHEDDERS

THE CONTINUAL splintering of the Klan into independent groups obviously reduces its effectiveness as a unified force for segregation in the South. But even more destructive to the Klan movement than the schisms themselves are the occasional atrocities which some of the bed-linen mutineers are wont to perform when they are freed of all centralized control (e.g., the control of some such Imperial Wizard as Robert Lee Davidson or the late Eldon Edwards).

As a case in point it is enlightening to recall an incident that occurred one balmy 1957 September night in a rural-suburban section of Jefferson County, Alabama, just outside the city of Birmingham.

That night six "officers" of a group calling itself the Ku Klux Klan of the Confederacy assembled at the home of a forty-three-year-old Birmingham area factory worker named Jesse W. Mabry to discuss matters of moment in the struggle to preserve the Southern Way of Life.

Presiding was Joe P. Pritchett, thirty-one, the "Exalted Cyclops" of the assemblage. Also in attendance were a husky carpenter, Grover A. McCullough, forty-five; a couple of grocery clerks, John H. Griffin, thirty-eight, and William J. Miller, twenty-eight; and a newcomer to the group's high echelon, one Bart A. Floyd, thirty-one.

The host and secretary-treasurer for the Klavern, Jesse Mabry, had already achieved a measure of national recognition as a dedicated segregationist; just the year before he had been convicted of disorderly conduct for attacking singer Nat "King" Cole on the stage of the Birmingham city auditorium. And Miller the grocery clerk (according to subsequent testimony by him) had only a few months earlier been appointed a Klan captain by Asa "Ace" Carter, who at the time was chief organizer of an outfit which he called the "Original Ku Klux Klan of the Confederacy."[1]

The purposes of the meeting at Mabry's house were twofold, at least twofold. One was to consider how the group might contribute to the fight to maintain white supremacy in Alabama; the other purpose was to plan "a mission to prove the worthiness" of the newcomer, Bart Floyd.

The fact is Exalted Cyclops Joe Pritchett was considering appointing Floyd to a captaincy in the group. But how could his qualifications for such an office best be tested?

After some discussion the group decided it would be a good project to go out and pick up a Negro and "scare hell out of him." It was agreed that Floyd, the captain-candidate, could prove his mettle by doing most of the "scaring," and that, incidentally, the venture would tend to discourage Negroes from seeking integration in Alabama.

The problem remained: which Negro should be selected to receive the "scare"?

Following further discussion at Mabry's house and at a nearby tavern, it was decided that *just any Negro would do.*

So, piling into two automobiles, the six Klansmen drove to

---

[1] Carter (who was not present at the meeting of Pritchett, Griffin, Mabry, *et al.,* and apparently had no knowledge of it) was probably the most widely known segregationist in Alabama in the mid-fifties. Having gained a following of sorts as a radio commentator who denounced "be-bop" and "rock-and-roll" music as part of a communist-integrationist plot to overthrow the white South, he organized the very "activist" North Alabama White Citizens' Councils following the 1954 Supreme Court decision. When this organization (which was disavowed by the large CC Association headquartered in Mississippi) drastically declined in membership, Carter devoted his energies to the organization of the "Original KKK of the Confederacy." While carrying on his white-supremacy crusades, he campaigned—without success —for the city commission of Birmingham and for lieutenant governor of Alabama. After divers difficulties, however, Carter faded out of the Alabama "race-relations" picture about 1957; since then he apparently has chosen to leave the struggle for segregation to white Alabamians other than himself.

a drugstore to pick up a supply of razor blades and turpentine, then motored about, looking for a likely Negro.

About 9:30 P.M. the two cars pulled up alongside a Negro man and woman who were strolling along the Tarrant City–Huffman highway just out of Birmingham. The man, a thirty-four-year-old house painter's helper named Judge Aaron, recalled later:

"Three white men jumped from the car and swarmed on me like wasps. . . . 'What's the matter?' I asked them. 'What have I done?' "

But the white men simply answered, "Come here, you black _____," threw him on the back floor of Bart Floyd's car, and blindfolded him.

As the two cars drove away from Aaron's puzzled strolling companion the Klansmen asked their blindfolded captive if he was a member of the NAACP or if he knew "Shuttlesworth."

The questioners obviously were referring to the National Association for the Advancement of Colored People and to the Reverend Fred L. Shuttlesworth of Birmingham, the most active Negro campaigner for school desegregation in Jefferson County at that time.

Aaron the Negro tried to explain that he did not know what they were talking about—that he knew neither who nor what Shuttlesworth and the NAACP were. One of the men interrupted his explanation with the comment: "Be quiet or I'll wear this wrench out over your head."

A few minutes of driving and the six white men arrived with their Negro at their Klan lair, a small concrete-block building near a community called Chalkville.

Aaron was ejected from the car and forced to crawl fifty feet or so to the little building's entrance.

"Go on into the slaughter pen," one of the Klansmen ordered him.

Inside, the six white men donned hoods of the variety traditionally associated with the Invisible Empire. As Exalted Cyclops of the group, Joe Pritchett decked himself out in a full robe with red trim.

On past nights the dirt-floored lair had been a place where white men had taken the "blood-brother oath." It was customary for an applicant to kneel, hold one hand on the Bible, and take the oath from a superior Klan officer; the applicant then would be required to cut his wrist with a sharp instrument and write his initials in blood on a piece of paper, after which the paper would be ceremonially burned and the applicant thereafter would be a "blood brother" in the Invisible Empire.

On this night the ceremony was slightly different.

Aaron the Negro was forced to get out of his clothes and kneel before the six Klansmen. After beating him and kicking him for a time—and asking him more "race-problem" questions which the uneducated Negro did not understand—the Klansmen knocked him unconscious.

Thereupon Exalted Cyclops Joe Pritchett turned to Captain-candidate Bart Floyd and commanded:

"Do your duty."

And then Bart Floyd did a most extraordinary thing.

With one of the razor blades he castrated the Negro.

Floyd's worthiness for a Klan captaincy having been proved, Aaron was dressed and stuffed into the trunk of one of the cars, driven a few miles, and thrown out on a roadside north of Birmingham. Law officers found him later in the night. He was in extreme pain (Floyd had poured turpentine on the wound to augment the agony), but the officers took him to a veterans' hospital nearby and, after several blood transfusions, Aaron the Negro survived—making possible the telling of this arresting (and perhaps psychiatrically very meaningful) little tale.

The horror of the story of Judge Aaron, Negro, is difficult to comment upon, for so many of its elements contain such an Erskine Caldwellian grotesquerie. Appropriate comment is difficult for the same reason that chroniclers of Nazi atrocities usually are unable to avoid simply evoking nervous laughter when they set about analyzing that handsome young Nordic woman who took esthetic delight in having *lampshades* fashioned from the skins of those of her concentration-camp prisoners who possessed especially attractive tatoos. Attempts to measure in words the inhumanity of such acts often result merely in something that sounds like one of those "sick jokes" which were popular throughout the land some few months ago.

It is significant to note, however, that the legal authorities of Jefferson County did not approve of the mutilation of the Negro or feel that the six Klansmen were acceptably representative of the citizenry of the sovereign state of Alabama.

On the basis of information gained from Aaron, deputies quickly rounded up all six of the white men and tried them in Birmingham on charges ranging from mayhem to assault with intent to commit murder.

Griffin and Miller were given five-year sentences but, because they had chosen to become witnesses for the prosecution, were placed on probation. Pritchett, Mabry, McCullough, and Floyd each were sentenced to twenty years in the Alabama state penitentiary.

In pronouncing sentence upon Exalted Cyclops Pritchett Circuit Judge Alta King declared:

"There has never been a case in all my years of law practice and ten years on the bench that has shocked me as this one has. . . ."

4. THE FUTURE OF THE KKK

PLAINLY the nether-wordly nature of some Klansmen's more spectacular acts of violence tends to sour the majority of white Southerners on the Klan as a whole—no matter how fiercely they might favor white supremacy.

In consequence, the Klan receives very little official support from state governmental bodies in the South as it did back in its great days when Hugo Black and other citizens of high repute belonged to it.

Governmental bodies in some of the states of the old Confederacy have, indeed, gone to some considerable lengths to disprove that the Ku Klux Klan has a worth-while role in the fight to preserve the Southern Way of Life.

In Florida, for example, the unashamedly segregationist State Legislative Investigation Committee devoted several days in 1959 to a public probe of the U. S. Klans, Knights of the Ku Klux Klan.[1]

[1] The practical difficulty of staging a successful investigation of the Invisible Empire in the Deep South is indicated by an exchange between Florida State Senator Marion B. Knight and Committee Chairman Charley E. Johns on the very first day of the KKK hearing:

SENATOR KNIGHT: A question occurs to me. Prior to 1936, more than twenty years ago, I was a member of the Ku Klux Klan. Am I disqualified to sit in this hearing?
THE CHAIRMAN: I wouldn't think so.
SENATOR KNIGHT: It's more than twenty years ago, but I wouldn't want somebody to come out with a newspaper story saying that here I was, investigating the Ku Klux, and I was a former member of it.
THE CHAIRMAN: No, I don't think that would make any difference.

"There is no question but what some of the men and officers of this organization are dedicated to the use of violence and the threat thereof to carry out their aims principally in the field of segregation," the Committee concluded. "Many of these men [Floridians active in the KKK] have serious criminal records and there is no doubt that some of them are directly responsible for acts of violence directed against members of the negro race. . . ."

The Committee decided that no new legislation was desirable. However:

"The Committee strenuously condemns the use of violence by the Klan, or of any other group. . . . We already have adequate statutes making such conduct criminal offenses, and it is merely a matter of local officials enforcing the law as it presently stands. This the Committee feels should be done."

The desire on the part of most Southern political leaders to make it clear they are not Klansmen has occasionally led them to succumb to the temptation of overstatement. As a case in point, former South Carolina Governor George Bell Timmerman once said he felt that the resurgence of the Klan following the 1954 Supreme Court schools' decision was the work of the Communist party.

Comments about the Ku Klux Klan are then, we see, sometimes characterized by absurdity. Nor is this totally unfitting. For in some areas of the Invisible Empire absurdity does exist in abundance—as do comedy, moist-eyed hatred, astonishing brutality, and a kind of gargoyle ignorance which seems to belong properly within the covers of a novel perhaps but not within the world of living men.

And yet, it would not be at all intelligent to belittle the importance of the Klan. It should be dismissed neither as a cornpone joke nor as an out-of-the-past manifestation of "redneck barbarity."

An Anti-Defamation League spokesman, recently discussing the

. . . I don't think that would affect you, Senator Knight.
SENATOR KNIGHT: All right, sir. . . .

This, of course, solved that little procedural problem, and the investigaton proceeded apace.

scores of bombings, floggings, cross burnings, and other threats which have been attributed to Klansmen since the May 17, 1954, decision, remarked:

"The vast majority of white Southerners, of course, reject such violence. But there are too many who are 'Klan-minded' or who condone violence—who avert their eyes—although they would not themselves join the Klans or participate in lawless acts. It can be expected that this group will continue to look the other way or remain silent as the Klans and other extremists continue their dirty work. . . .

"Continuing Klan violence is inevitable . . . because by its own principles and its very nature the Klan must use force, for if it is not coercive and violent, it is nothing and becomes merely a 'hooded White Citizens' Council.' . . .

"[T]he present Klans have not gained any appreciable measure of public acceptance or respectability in the South . . . and they are not likely to achieve the mass followings they boasted in the 1920's and 1930's. They are still the targets of denunciation from responsible quarters and from reputable newspapers.

"But it may well be"—and this is the ADL spokesman's most meaningful speculation—"that in the 1960's public acceptance and respectability [are] not an essential ingredient for Klan growth, Klan activity, or Klan violence."

The truth is—the brutal, ineluctable truth is—that the Ku Klux Klan has been in business in this country for almost one hundred years. And despite all its slipshod schisms and Caldwellian barbarities the Klan, as a whole, continues to grow in number and in strength.

And, as a matter of historical fact, no other organization in America has been as effective as the Ku Klux Klan at intimidating Negroes and integrationists and maintaining Southern white supremacy. That, too, must be recognized.

IV. THE RACISTS

Anti-Semitism Amid the Magnolias

1. OF JEWS, NEGROES, DYNAMITE, AND WISTERIA

THE ASSAULT mounted by the white South to repel the forces of integration has been accompanied by an outburst of anti-Jewish propaganda perhaps unmatched in the history of the region.

Through the years until the past decade—with the possible exception of that period in the twenties when the Ku Klux Klan was enjoying its big revival—the South has been noted for its comparative freedom from hostility to Jews. This was so for a variety of reasons: the relatively small number of Jews in the South; the fact that Jewish names and ways were not especially alien to a people whose own religion drew so heavily on the Old Testament; and, most important, there already existed for the white Southerner a perfectly satisfactory social scapegoat, the Negro.

Only since the Supreme Court's school-integration decision of 1954 have the masses of the white South been introduced in any really significant way to the rather more Northern notion that the source of America's troubles is "the Jewish conspiracy."

The bitter frustration engendered in the white South by The Decision has given many of the nation's veteran Jew baiters—mostly non-Southerners—their best new outlet for hatred since the grand old America-First days just before World War II.

Dynamitings of Jewish houses of worship have occurred in half a dozen Southern cities since 1954, the most violent of them the $200,000 bombing of the Temple of the Reform congregation in Atlanta in 1958.[1] In several of the incidents there was evidence

[1] Four men with records as anti-Jewish agitators were indicted in the

151

that the explosions were set off by persons motivated by old-fashioned Dixie bigotry as well as anti-Semitic sentiments; for example, four of the blasts—including the one at Atlanta—were almost immediately followed by anonymous telephone calls to prominent persons in the cities from men who identified themselves as members of the "Confederate Underground."

Disturbing though the several acts of violence have been, they are probably far less significant in the long run than the fact that thousands of white Southerners today regularly receive in their homes publications that tell them that the civil-rights movement is nothing more than an evil Hebraic scheme to "mongrelize" the black and white Gentiles of the South so that America may be turned into a communist dictatorship under Jewish control.

"PROOF POSITIVE—COMMUNISM IS JEWISH FROM START TO FINISH," declares a banner headline of *Common Sense,* a Union, New Jersey, semimonthly which is believed to have the largest Southern circulation of any of the Jew-baiting periodicals. "The Jewish people are taught, and believe that before their Messiah comes they are to have complete control of the world. With only 16 million in a population of two and one half billion, the Jews *must* control governments and mass membership in labor organizations. Communism and Socialism are two of the twelve hundred fronts organized by them in the U. S. alone. Judaism is a cult based entirely on the hatred of Christianity . . ."

"JEWS CONTROL NAACP—*Spingarn, Kaplan, Greenberg, Guide Race-Mixing Movements.*" So reads the streamer of a recent issue of *The Thunderbolt,* a monthly newspaper published by the National States Rights party in Birmingham. "The NAACP is not, and never has been, a Negro movement . . . The Jew is using the Negro to destroy THE WHITE RACE, the only people left blocking complete Jew domination of the world. . . ."

It is impossible, of course, to estimate how much anti-Jewish feeling has grown in the South since the decision year, 1954. It is probably accurate to say that it has not yet gone beyond the budding stage.

Atlanta bombing. After one of them, George Michael Bright, was acquitted in January 1959, following two trials, efforts to prosecute the others were dropped.

But any tourist in the land of apartheid is bound to be struck by the abundance of anti-Jewish literature being circulated, and to be struck by the number of men of high position in the South who express fears of "The Jew." Some express them only after insisting on a guarantee that they will not be quoted for publication; many others are willing to express their anti-Semitism for the record.

True, the majority of the leading Southern segregationists, when speaking of their colleagues who happen to be anti-Jewish, take care to explain that they do not share that philosophy, that they think So-and-So is unfortunately "extreme" on the subject. And yet, having read so much anti-Jewish material, which often is so very persuasively written, they—many of them—seem tempted by it.

The Councils and the Jews

Although the Association of Citizens' Councils of America has taken precautions in recent years to keep its own publications free of anti-Jewish propaganda, some of the CCs' leaders in the earlier days following the 1954 decision were quite active in promoting the distribution of Jew-baiting literature.

Robert T. Patterson, executive secretary of the Citizens' Council Association, is given much of the credit for opening the dike for the first great Southern gush of anti-Jewish material following The Decision.

Back in August 1954, when the Council movement was just beginning to proliferate in Mississippi, Patterson sent out a letter to a list of fellow segregationist leaders recommending that they obtain literature from more than a dozen non-Southern sources long known for their hostility to Jews.

"Some of the groups are anti-Semitic," Patterson noted blandly. "However, all of the religious groups, including all Protestant, Catholic, and Jewish—have been pushing the anti-segregation issue and it is time for all of us to speak out for separation of the black and white races, regardless of our race and creed."

The groups and publications recommended by Patterson included *Common Sense,* the publication of the veteran anti-Semite,

Conde McGrinley; the Christian Nationalist Crusade of Los
Angeles, headed by Gerald L. K. Smith, sometime aide of the
late Huey Long and the most persistently successful of America's
anti-Jewish propagandists; *The American Nationalist,* slick-paper
anti-Jewish sheet published in Inglewood, California, by a disciple
of Smith, Frank Britton; the late Gerald Winrod's Defenders
organization of Wichita, Kansas, publisher of *The Defender;* the
now defunct National Association for the Advancement of White
People, a Delaware-based rabble-rousing organization headed by
Bryant Bowles; and the National Citizens Protective Association
of St. Louis, then headed by another former associate of Gerald
L. K. Smith, John W. Hamilton.[2]

Since not a few members of Citizens' Councils are Jews, it was
inevitable that some criticisms would be voiced regarding the CC
secretary's remarkable reading menu. Patterson decided it would
be prudent to issue another circular letter in October 1954, giving
further explanation of his attitude toward Jews. It was hardly a
letter of apology.

"I receive literature from all over the U. S. that contains arguments against integration. Some of this literature contains anti-
Semitic propaganda. It states that Arthur Spingarn, Jewish, has
been president of the NAACP since 1932. It states that B'nai
B'rith has actively aided the NAACP." But he added: "It states
that the noted Protestant minister, Harry Emerson Fosdick of
New York, is trying to raise 100 thousand dollars for the NAACP.
I have shown friends of mine and interested people some of this
literature. I am not anti-Semitic, but I am against any man or
group [that] aids and abets the NAACP which is trying to destroy
our way of life."

In its publications the Mississippi leadership of the Citizens'
Councils has generally represented itself as not feeling ill-disposed
toward Jews as individuals but strongly disliking some of their
national organizations. This position is expressed in an engaging
way in the most widely circulated official CC pamphlet addressed
to the subject, *A Jewish View on Segregation.*

The pamphlet consists of an eleven-page article that is described
in a foreword as an "entirely voluntary" essay written by "a Jewish Southerner who prefers to remain anonymous for the simple

---

[2] The part played by Hamilton's newspaper, *The White Sentinel,* in an
unusual Mississippi "economic-pressure" campaign is discussed on page 58.

reason that the people who will agree with what he has to say or
be tolerant of it will remain silent [and] the cranks and crackpots
who will wish to revile him for his right to form his own beliefs
and act upon them will not remain silent."

The author identifies himself as a "Jewish American, not an
American Jew," who was reared and educated in Mississippi and
Alabama.

He acknowledges that "some have said that the Citizens' Councils are anti-Semitic."

"Nothing of the sort," he replies. "Where prominent Jewish
leaders have enrolled as members and taken an active part in the
duties of the Council there is no chance of anti-Semitism creeping in." But he adds with a note of regret: "There are communities where Jewish leaders have flatly refused to join, although
in these same communities prominent Catholic and Protestant
men have joined, despite the stands taken on segregation nationally by their church groups. Who can blame them for feeling
a bit bitter against white Southerners who try to stay 'neutral' on
such an issue? . . . [If] everybody decided to be 'neutral' the
silence would be pure and simple consent. So the Jew who attempts to be neutral is much like the ostrich. And he has no right
to be surprised or amazed when the target he so readily presents
is fired upon."

The Admiral

Ever since the free-wheeling days of Jew baiting back in the
thirties the nation's professional anti-Semites have searched restlessly for a "man on horseback" capable of attracting voters in
large numbers.

Probably their closest approximation of one—their biggest
"catch" in the segregationist South—is Retired Rear Admiral John
C. Crommelin of southern Alabama.

As well as being an inexhaustible crusader for apartheid, Crommelin is an admirer of Gerald L. K. Smith and Conde McGinley, a
sometime mentor and friend of rabble-rouser Frederick John
Kasper, and a hero and political favorite of the strongly anti-
Jewish National States Rights party.

An Annapolis-trained aviator with a splendid World War II

record, Crommelin was pressured into retirement from the service in 1950 following a front-page controversy between the Navy and Air Force over unification of the armed forces. Since his retirement he has run for the United States Senate four times—in 1950, 1954, 1956, and 1960—was a candidate for the governorship of Alabama in 1958, and ran for mayor of Montgomery in 1959. In addition, following his fourth Senate defeat in 1960, he was the National States Rights party's candidate for vice president of the United States.

Crommelin and his wife and three children (one daughter attends fashionable Sweetbriar College; another daughter and a son are still of high-school age) live in a handsome gray house on blossom-lined Magnolia Curve in Montgomery. However, when he is not out on the hustings he often is to be found at his lakeside home near the little town of Wetumpka, twenty miles from the Alabama capital; it is the old Crommelin family home, and he frequently goes there to work and meditate.

The country house is a rambling white structure with a wide veranda set in a hill grove of oaks and pines and wisteria high above a large lake. The place is called Harrogate Springs and is known for its excellent fishing. Down among the pines along the lake are a cluster of camp houses that are rented to fishing parties in the summertime. It is a lovely old place, peacefully far from the highway that stretches from Montgomery to the little jerry-built town of Wetumpka.

In contrast with the tenderly feminine appearance of the interior of his home on Magnolia Curve, the interior of his Harrogate Springs house is plainly masculine.

When a visitor called on him one recent drizzly afternoon, Crommelin—dressed in Navy officer's khakis and field boots—was alone at Harrogate Springs. He had been busy typing on an old upright Royal on the kitchen table.

Scattered on the table and overflowing into a couple of chairs and onto the floor were sheaves of literature telling of the "Jew-Communist Conspiracy"—issues of *Common Sense* and of Conde McGinley's anti-Semitic broadside, *The Coming Red Dictatorship;* reprints of the Jew-baiting Montgomery *Home News;* and several copies of the National States Rights party's racist newspaper, *The Thunderbolt.*

As he brewed coffee in a battered dripolator for his visitor and himself Crommelin said, yes, it is indeed true that he is rigidly opposed to racial integration. But that does not mean he feels hostility toward Negroes, he insisted.

"When I was a child in this house, my old Negro mammy—we called her 'Aunt Kitty'—slept in a little room that used to be right there where you're sitting," he said, pointing to a corner of the kitchen. "And our cook was 'Aunt Kate.' Both of them had been slaves. They were almost like members of the family."

As Crommelin was pouring the coffee, a Negro man in faded work clothes shambled across the back yard and knocked at the side door. He had come to go with the admiral to feed his cows in a pasture a mile or so away. Crommelin genially asked him if he would mind waiting until he finished talking with his visitor. The man said he wouldn't mind.

Returning to the kitchen, Crommlin smiled and said, "See that boy out there? Why, I don't feel any more hostility toward him than I do toward a good bird dog.

"No," he added, "the Negro is just a pawn for those who are behind all this agitation for racial equality. As somebody once said to me, 'The Negro is the malarial germ, but the *Jew* is the mosquito.' "

Crommelin is tall, blue-eyed, gray-haired, a very nearly handsome man. Not quite yet sixty, he is still hard-muscled and powerful looking. His nose gives his face a rugged look; it is a boxer's nose, dented at the bridge back when he fought as a middleweight at the Naval Academy. He proudly remembers that he came within a jab or two of outboxing the National AAU middleweight champion during his senior year in 1923.

He comes from a fighting family, in fact. His great-grandfather was a captain in the Revolutionary Army. Both of his grandfathers fought for the Confederacy. And he is the oldest of five brothers, all of whom graduated from Annapolis and fought in World War II. At least one Crommelin brother was in every major naval engagement in the Pacific; Crommelin Field at the Naval Air Station at Atlantic City was named in honor of two of the brothers who died in battle.

John Crommelin himself was one of the Navy's outstanding aviation officers. For a time after he got his navy wings in 1926 he was the leader of the famed stunt flying team, "The Blue Angels." In the crucial Battle of the Coral Sea, which may well have decided the outcome of World War II, he served as air officer of one of the great fighting ships of all times, the carrier *Enterprise*. Later, during the invasion of the Gilbert Islands, he was chief of staff aboard the carrier *Liscomb Bay* when it was mortally torpedoed; Crommelin had to swim from it in the buff.

"I was taking a shower when they shot that ship out from under me."

After being attached to the fleet constantly from 1942 to 1948, he was assigned to duty in the District of Columbia, first with the National War Colleges, then with the Joint Staff. Before long it became apparent that Crommelin was an officer better designed for war than for peace, a man better equipped for the direct action of air battles than for the subtleties of Washington politics.

During the bitter squabble over armed-forces unification in 1949 and 1950 Crommelin became convinced that high Air Force officials were bent on critically weakening naval aviation.

"The junior officers of the Navy thought their seniors were selling them out in Washington," Crommelin recalls. "They sort of projected me into the position where I was their unofficial leader."

Soon the downfall came. Following allegations that he had used overenthusiastic methods to build public support for the Navy, Crommelin was reprimanded by his superiors, and, as he continued his attack on unification policies, finally was "indefinitely furloughed" from the Navy in 1950.

Leaving the Navy at such a comparatively youthful age—he was only forty-seven when they "furloughed" him—was clearly a severe blow to Crommelin.

"I loved the Navy—loved all the services," he reflected. "They're our last hope. Their middle-bracket officers I'm talking about. A police state can never exist unless it's backed up by the military."

The bitterness felt by Crommelin has apparently grown steadily along with the series of political defeats suffered by him since retiring from the Navy. In the early fifties he did comparatively little campaigning against the "Jewish conspiracy." He trained his fire instead on the threat of Negro integration and the influence of Communists in Washington. In 1955 he was busy leading the nationwide campaign to secure 10,000,000 signatures for a petition protesting the Senate censure of Joseph McCarthy. Later that year he was active in a short-lived nationalist organization called "Americans for American Action." In these activities he became more and more closely acquainted with such leading Jew-baiters as Conde McGinley.

By 1956 anti-Semitism had become the cornerstone of his philosophy of life. In the summer of that year, addressing the North Alabama Citizens' Council (then led by anti-Jewish Birmingham radio announcer Asa Carter), Crommelin declared that the campaign against segregation in the South was led by "Felix Frankfurter, a Jew, [and] Senator Herbert Lehman, a Marxist Jew. Don't you know it's their kind of people who are behind this whole mess? . . . We've got to keep this last frontier of the real Anglo-Saxon race. . . . And if I am wrong, my name is Finkelstein."

The admiral and John Kasper became fast friends in 1956. The young anti-Semitic adventurer from Greenwich Village lived for a time at Crommelin's home that year, assisting him in his second campaign against Senator Lister Hill. Kasper later credited Crommelin with alerting him to the threat of integration; Kasper already was aware of the "Jewish conspiracy," and doubtless helped to stimulate the admiral's emotions on the subject. Crommelin several times accompanied Kasper on his famous forays into Clinton, Tennessee, where the young agitator eventually was jailed for inciting the townspeople to riot in protest against school desegregation.

At Kasper's trial Crommelin appeared as a defense witness. And when Kasper was released in August 1958, after his first term at the federal prison in Tallahassee, Florida, it was reported that Crommelin was there to greet him. Also present at the coming-out gathering were John W. Hamilton, sometime editor of the *White Sentinel;* Bill Hendrix, veteran Florida Klan leader; and George Michael Bright, who later that year was tried and acquitted in connection with the Atlanta synagogue bombing.

Crommelin remains a staunch admirer of Kasper.

"You will hear more from that young man," he predicted.

The admiral obviously still feels as he felt when he told a Citizens' Council rally in Clinton a few months after the rioting in their town: "You may not see it, and your children may not see it, but someday a statue will be erected on this courthouse lawn to John Kasper."

In the years since 1956 Crommelin has become ever more vigorous and far-reaching in his public pronouncements against the "Communist-Jewish conspiracy."

At the peak of the disruptions following the court order to integrate Little Rock's Central High School in the fall of 1957 he wired President Eisenhower:

"The press states you are taking steps to employ federal troops in Little Rock. Many patriots believe much information and advice reaching you is controlled by the same agents of the Communist-Jewish conspiracy or invisible government who influenced Truman to fire General MacArthur and deny ammunition to our fighting men in Korea. I feel it is my duty to attempt to inform you immediately that in employing federal troops to attempt to enforce integration you are considered by many informed Southerners to be a tool of the Communist-Jewish conspiracy."

No answer came from President Eisenhower, but this did not especially surprise Crommelin; the admiral said he understands that Eisenhower is "supposed to be a Jew."

Crommelin also asserts that Woodrow Wilson and Franklin D. Roosevelt were Jews—and participants in the great international conspiracy. He believes Jewish conspirators have been at the bottom of most of our nation's troubles throughout history.

"The Jews killed Lincoln and Garfield, and they killed James Forrestal and Albert Patterson [Alabama Governor John Patterson's father, who was slain after breaking up a notorious crime syndicate at Phenix City, Alabama]." And he added, "They commit all their murders between Friday sundown and Saturday sundown."

He blames the Jews themselves for the several bombings of synagogues in the South. He spoke with particular bitterness when recalling that agents of the Federal Bureau of Investigation had visited his Montgomery home to question him about the Atlanta temple bombing in 1958.

"Why, I had no more to do with that bombing than you did," he scoffed.

He led his visitor to a large sitting room whose picture window frames a view of a long lawn fringed with graceful pines. From a row of file cabinets he pulled a copy of an open letter he had written to FBI Director J. Edgar Hoover protesting the visit paid him by the agents. The letter asserted that the Atlanta temple was actually dynamited by "evolutionary-Kol-Nidre-Kosher jews" [sic] as a propaganda stunt.

"By their control of the major media of communication—the press, radio, and TV—the communist-jewish conspirators are trying to use their bombing of their own meetinghouse in Atlanta as a booster shot in their present hate campaign to discredit those of us White Christian Americans who understand and expose the communist-jewish conspiracy for just what it is."

Although the National States Rights party advertised Crommelin in 1960 as its candidate for vice president of the United States,[3] the admiral said he is not a member of the NSRP but is a Democrat.

Crommelin has on occasion circulated material emanating from the Ku Klux Klan. For example, during the debate in Congress over President Kennedy's appointment of Alabama Governor John Patterson's 1958 campaign manager, Charles Meriwether, as a board member of the Export-Import Bank, Crommelin reprinted a couple of telegrams to the President and other high political officers from one J. Austin Banks, "Mediator, Confederate States Lodge #11, Alabama Knights of the Ku Klux Klan, P. O. Box 7072, Montgomery, Ala." The weirdly-worded telegrams suggested that the congressional questioning of Meriwether about his alleged courtship of Klan votes for Governor Patterson was no more than a "ridiculous opera bouffe" and that Meriwether was in fact in league with conspiring Jews. However, Crommelin emphasized that he himself is not a Klansman.

His races against such popular Alabama political figures as Lister Hill and John Sparkman have inevitably resulted in defeat for Crommelin. Even so, the substantial vote received by him in some sections of the state—notably Montgomery County—has created some considerable concern among national Jewish organizations.

In 1959 Crommelin's propaganda outlet in his home county, the suburban weekly Mongomery *Home News,* reprinted a confidential

[3] At an organizational convention of the NSRP in Louisville, Kentucky, in 1958, John Kasper pushed through a resolution in which the party urged that Crommelin run for president. When election year came, the NSRP nominated Arkansas Governor Orval Faubus for president and Crommelin as his running mate; however, Faubus quietly declined the nomination.

circular letter sent out by Arthur J. Levin, southeastern director of the Anti-Defamation League of B'nai B'rith.

Levin noted that in the race for mayor of Montgomery Crommelin had run third, polling 1,760 of the total 17,338 votes cast.

"The Jewish community is deeply disturbed that Crommelin received as high as 10 per cent of the vote," wrote Levin. "You will recall that in the race for governor of Alabama [in 1958] Crommelin received less than 1 per cent of the vote in a field of fourteen candidates."

He made a poor showing indeed in his 1958 gubernatorial race, getting only 2,245 out of a total of 618,462 votes cast in the state— and finishing eleventh in a field of fourteen candidates. He displayed a fairly formidable vote-getting ability in both his 1956 and 1960 Senate campaigns, however. He ran second in both races, polling 112,579 votes against Hill and 51,591 against Sparkman in 1960 (including 28 per cent of the votes in Montgomery County).

The figures probably serve as a fairly accurate index to the extent of anti-Jewish sentiment in Alabama, for in none of his recent political campaigns has Crommelin chosen to "soft-pedal the Communist-Jewish issue" in order to attract voters.

"The key to survival is a thorough understanding of the Communist-Jewish Conspiracy by White Christian Voters." So reads a typical piece of his campaign literature. "The ultimate objective of the Communist-Jewish Conspirators is to use their world-wide control of money to destroy Christianity and set up a World Government in the framework of the United Nations, and erase all national boundaries and eliminate all racial distinction except the so-called Jewish race, which will then become the master race with headquarters in the state of Israel and in United Nations in New York, and from these two communication centers rule a slave-like world population of copper-colored human mongrels. . . ."

Since Crommelin is still technically a member of the Navy, some moves have been made by influential persons to encourage the Navy to pressure him into toning down his Jew-baiting campaign.

In a 1959 issue of the Montgomery *Home News* Crommelin published an intercepted copy of a letter that was identified as a Navy Department answer to an "inquiry" from New York Senator Jacob Javits. Printed under the boldface headline, "CROMMELIN

CALLS JAVITS 'COWARDLY CUR'!!!" the letter to Javits from Assistant Navy Secretary Richard Jackson said:

"The Navy Department has been well aware for some time of the sweeping attack upon the Jewish people made by Crommelin. As a result, intensive studies have been made of the very question you have raised—what should and can be done to prevent and repudiate activities by Crommelin such as those mentioned in the enclosures to your letter."

Assistant Secretary Jackson pointed out that the Navy does have "general court-martial jurisdiction" over its retired officers on inactive duty.

"Any contemplated exercise of control over the public or private statements of a retired officer, however, raises immediately the question of abridgement of freedom of speech and freedom of the press," the letter said. "The guarantee of free speech, of course, includes freedom to make irresponsible remarks which are repugnant as well as those which are pleasing."

Jackson also suggested to Javits the possibility that any action by the Navy against Crommelin might "effect a self-styled and self-claimed martyrdom" that could provide him with "a national spotlight for the advancement of his anti-Semitic crusade." But the letter promised that the Navy Department would keep an eye on the admiral, and added:

"I am certain that you know without my reassuring you that Crommelin's comments do not represent the view of the Navy. I am confident that the fine people comprising our Navy, who represent virtually all racial and religious groups, abhor and regret his diatribes."

Crommelin disapproves of Jews not merely on political and religious grounds; his is a racial prejudice as well.

"Ninety per cent of the Jews are Mongoloids," he said. "That's why they're particular to Asiatic communism."

Mongoloids. Yet he insists, too, that Jews are also Negroes. He uses the term "Jewlatto" in speaking of many notables toward whom he feels hostility. Woodrow Wilson, for instance, is identified by Crommelin as a "Jewlatto."

The admiral dug from his files a pamphlet entitled *Gallery of Jewish Types,* written in the 1920's by his favorite ethnologist,

Lothrop Stoddard, and pointed out a message that he found especially enlightening: "It was . . . probably during their Egyptian sojourn that the Jews picked up their first traces of Negro blood. A Negroid strain undoubtedly exists in Jewry; to it the frizzy or woolly hair, thick lips, and prognathous jaws appearing in many Jewish individuals are probably due. . . ."

"The biggest lie of all," Crommelin said with a note of disgust, "is the claim that the modern Jew is a white man."

Much of Crommelin's "current information" on the "Jewish problem" comes from the shrill publications of Gerald L. K. Smith and Conde McGinley. He has spoken at several of Smith's Christian Nationalist Crusade rallies in the West and Southwest, commending him as a man who "is trying to do a job for God and country." The admiral indicated he is even closer to McGinley. A sometime financial supporter of McGinley's Christian Educational Association, Crommelin pleasantly recalled having the elderly anti-Semite as a guest in his house at Wetumpka.

"He has sat right in that chair where you've been sitting, and we've talked for hours and hours. He's a fine fellow. Doesn't have so much formal education," Crommelin said, then tapped his temple with a forefinger, "but he's got plenty up here."

McGinley's *Common Sense* had only recently devoted an issue to expounding the thesis that the reports of Nazi atrocities during World War II were Zionist lies. The 6,000,000 Jews who were reported slaughtered by the Nazis did not really die at all but were smuggled into the United States as illegal aliens, *Common Sense* had said.

"It's a ridiculous myth that 6,000,000 Jews were killed by Hitler," Crommelin agreed.

The admiral described Hitler as a "phony" and hinted that he suspects Der Führer might have been a front man for Jewish conspirators.

Adolf Eichmann? He, too, was a Jew, said Crommelin.

Living in a world that he feels is infested with "Jewlattoes" bent on doing him evil, Crommelin has his plans for protecting his property and his person. Pointing to his file cabinets, he smiled cunningly and said:

"I have other copies of all this in other places, just in case this house ever burns down." And later he spoke of the gate at the entrance to his country place: "Anybody I'm not expecting better not come past that gate after dark. I'm a pretty good shot."

But he expressed less concern over possible physical danger than over the danger of "brainwashing," perhaps by chemical means. He denounced "mental health" and "water fluoridation" as Communist-Jewish plots psychologically to cripple our citizenry and overthrow the United States Government. He spoke of a high-ranking military officer who, Crommelin said, had mysteriously changed his political position from Right to Left.

"He was given isotopes," Crommelin said. 'You don't believe that's possible, do you?"

Engrossed in his subject as he was, Crommelin apparently had almost forgotten his Negro man who had been sitting out in the admiral's car, waiting to go with him to the pasture. Now the sun had set, and little time was left to deal with the problem of the cows before nightfall.

"The ultimate weapon of the Jews, I think, is the mental-health movement," Crommelin said conclusively. "But if we can just hold the line till the word gets out, then I think any party that represents the American way of life can win a national election."

And what should then be the fate of America's Jews?

"They'd be sent to Israel or Madagascar." But he added with a shrug, "That's something not for me, but for the American people to decide."

And America's Negroes?

"I think a back-to-Africa movement would be the best thing. If we can't have that, nothing else would be acceptable but well-enforced segregation which I consider a poor substitute."

The admiral said some of his friends have on occasion accused him of being "against everything." But this is simply because they have not given as careful study to national and international problems as he has, he said.

"We're living in an age of confusion," he said, then added with a vigorous laugh, "but you're looking at one guy that's not confused."

Walking outside with his visitor, Crommelin, in an almost apologetic tone, asked his Negro man, "Reckon it's too late for us to go see about those cows?"

"Nawsuh," the man replied in the voice of one accustomed to waiting, "it ain't too late."

So the admiral bade his visitor farewell, climbed under the steering wheel beside his Negro, and handling the machine with the deftness and assurance that long ago made him one of the Navy's ablest aviation officers drove swiftly past the wisteria and off into the darkening afternoon.

2. THE SOUND OF THE THUNDERBOLT

THE MOST active Southern-based organization with a Jew-baiting as well as Negro-baiting program is the National States Rights party, the group that nominated Rear Admiral John Crommelin for vice president in 1960.

A party directory published recently by the NSRP listed units in thirty-one states, among them all the states of the South. Its total membership is considered small—perhaps only a few hundred persons—but it compensates for its lack of size by the volume of noise it makes. From the party's fountainhead in Birmingham flows a stream of anti-Jewish propaganda even more turbulent than the roiling polemics of Gerald L. K. Smith and Conde McGinley.

Formed at Knoxville in 1957 from fragments of a short-lived oganization called the United White party, the NSRP promotes a racism reminiscent of some of the uniform-wearing groups of the late 1930's. The hero of the party's literature is a sort of pseudo-Nietzschean imaginary fellow called "Whiteman."

"We of the National States Rights party believe in the Christian heritage of our people, the White race and the Nation which the Whiteman created out of the wilderness of this continent." So says the preamble to the party's constitution and bylaws. "We believe in the principles laid down by our forefathers in the United States Constitution and the Bill of Rights contained therein. . . . We will not allow the blood of our people to be polluted with that of black, yellow, or mongrel peoples. . . . All that is patriotic, good, clean, and decent springs forth from the foundations of our White folk. . . . We dedicate ourselves to the task of saving America and the White

Race and the preservation of the pure blood of our forefathers, so that all future generations which come after us will be born as White children with a creative intelligence that will strengthen our civilized influence over the world for the good of all mankind."

Most of the key leaders of the party are rather young men; nevertheless, they are long-experienced campaigners in behalf of anti-Semitism. The most significant of them, Dr. Edward Reed Fields, Jr., of Birmingham, information director and editor of the party newspaper, is not yet thirty but has been energetically campaigning against "Jewism" since he was fourteen. Jesse B. Stoner, thirty-nine-year-old Atlanta attorney who has served as the party's legal adviser, has been an organizer of anti-Jewish parties and Ku Klux Klan groups since the mid-1940's. Matt Koehl, Jr., of Milwaukee, Chicago, and New York, listed variously as the NSRP's "national organizer" and "security officer," was described in the House Un-American Activities Committee's 1953 report on *Neo-Fascist and Hate Groups* as a leader of the young "elite guard" of the Hitler-emulating National Renaissance party headed by James H. Madole of Beacon, New York.[1]

The most generous amount of national publicity which the National States Rights party has so far received came a few weeks after the $200,000 Atlanta synagogue dynamiting of October 12, 1958. Five men who were arrested as suspects in the case were identified in newspaper reports at the time as followers of the NSRP. All were eventually freed of charges after the trial of one of them, George Michael Bright, culminated in an acquittal. Koehl and Fields, who claimed Bright was not a member of the NSRP, testified as defense witnesses; among the other witnesses who appeared in Bright's behalf were Arthur Cole of LaFollette, Tennes-

[1] A typical message from National Renaissance Party Director Madole, printed beneath a militant portrait of the late Führer, declares: "International Jewish-Communism has always been a threat to Aryan Civilization and that Great German Statesman ADOLF HITLER was the FIRST to combat this deadly enemy before the world. What Adolf Hitler gave to the German Nation cannot be denied. What National Socialism bestowed upon the German people stands before the world as a monument to all of the Western World. . . . The Western World will never forget . . . how foolish some of them were to oppose Adolf Hitler's New Order. Now we see that only NATIONALISM CAN NEUTRALIZE AND DEFEAT JEWISH-INTERNATIONAL-COMMUNISM!!"

see, listed as chairman of the NSRP, and the late Eldon Edwards of Atlanta, then Imperial Wizard of the nation's largest Ku Klux Klan organization.

After Bright's acquittal the party's monthly newspaper, *The Thunderbolt,* commented that "the Atlanta case was a triumph of concerted effort by NSRP, together with allied patriotic groups."

The Thunderbolt, whose masthead emblem is identical with that of the late Atlanta storm-troop-type organization called The Columbians, is published in Birmingham under the editorship of young Fields, who was a practicing chiropractor before deciding a few years ago to channel his energies full time into the campaign against the "Communist-Jewish Conspiracy."

Much of *The Thunderbolt's* content is familiar stuff to readers of *Common Sense* and *The Cross and the Flag.* Indeed it consists largely of offset reprints of articles and pictures clipped from those and other anti-Jewish publications. Right in the mainstream of anti-Jewry, for example, are recent headline *Thunderbolt* articles "exposing" the fact that the head of the NAACP is Jewish ("JEWS CONTROL NAACP"), and the fact that several of President Kennedy's cabinet and subcabinet appointees are Jewish ("REDS MOVE INTO WHITE HOUSE").

But many of *The Thunderbolt's* exposés seem to be uniquely the NSRP's own.

Still smarting from the memory that the key prosecution witness in the Atlanta temple bombing case was a man identified as an FBI undercover agent, *The Thunderbolt* declared not long ago that "the phony fight between the FBI and the Communists is a fraud and a deception designed to conceal the fact that the FBI is a part of the Communist-Jewish Conspiracy."

FBI Director J. Edgar Hoover, who is idolized by most of the "nationalist, anti-communist" organizations of the county, is described by *The Thunderbolt* as a pro-mongrelization "tyrant" who is "not concerned with investigating Negro or Jewish subversion and treason in America" because he is kept in office by the "INVISIBLE POWER."

The Thunderbolt even disapproves of Georgia's Senator Herman Talmadge. Of all the Dixieland congressmen who have thundered against the 1954 integration decision, none has received higher segregationist acclaim as a defender of the Southern Way of Life than Talmadge. Even so, *The Thunderbolt* portrays him as an integrationist tool of the Jews.

Reporting that Talmadge had joined the "race-mixing" National Conference of Christians and Jews, *The Thunderbolt* exclaimed: "He even allows them to use his name on their official literature. Herman Talmadge, the integrator, uses his father's White Supremacy reputation to get White votes while working with Governor Vandiver, Ralph McGill, the Atlanta newspapers, and the Jews to drag the White people of Georgia and the South down into the cesspool of racial intermixture."

Since it is in the grand tradition of the "radical right" to picture United States presidents as tools of Communism, it comes as no surprise that the NSRP recommended—hardly before he and his wife had unpacked their bags at the White House—that President Kennedy be impeached.

Unlike the John Birch Society, however, the NSRP does not suggest that Chief Justice Warren be impeached. Instead, the party proposes that all nine Supreme Court justices be *put to death*.

"The number-one plan of communist subversion is to destroy the Whiteman through Mongrelization with the Blackman," a recent *Thunderbolt* explained. Federal Law provides for the DEATH penalty for all who 'give aid and comfort to America's enemies.' It is our position that the present members of the Supreme Court are guilty of Treason and should be thusly tried and given the ULTIMATE PENALTY."

A thread of violence runs through almost every issue of *The Thunderbolt*. Following the Jacksonville "lunch-counter riot" in 1960, the paper published photographs showing police and civilian "Whitemen" beating "Blackmen" with fists and ax handles. Many of the issues feature one or more highly emotional accounts of Negro rapes or murders of white females in the integrated North. Last year almost a complete issue was dedicated to glorifying the long-ago killers of Leo Frank, Jewish victim of Atlanta's most famous lynching.

The Thunderbolt's favorite campaign through much of 1961 was to convince its readers that the trial of Adolf Eichmann in Israel was a "GIANT PROPAGANDA HOAX." Like McGinley's *Common Sense*, *The Thunderbolt* insists that the reports of Nazi atrocities against Jews are phony, and that the Eichmann trial has been a

Communist-Jewish stunt to develop the "myth" that several million Jews were exterminated by the Nazis. Unlike Admiral Crommelin, however, *The Thunderbolt* did not advance the theory that Eichmann was actually a Jew in Nazi's clothing; instead, Eichmann was described as a "Christian patriotic German soldier."

"The Jews were out to get Eichmann because, during the war against communist Russia, he was in charge of arresting Communists and other treasonous enemies of the German government," said *The Thunderbolt*. "Since *most* Jews are Communists & have always been enemies of White Christian nations, an overwhelming number of Communist traitors arrested did turn out to be Jews. Some were tried for treason and rightly executed. The wild Jewish claim that 6,000,000 Jews died in Germany during World War II has been disproved by many authorities.[2] There were not 6,000,000 Jews in Europe at that time, and at the end of the war the world Jew population had increased. The bloody Jews [wanted] vengeance on Eichmann because he did his duty as a Christian patriotic German soldier in a war against world Communism, and against world Jewry. Note that the Jews planned to kidnap Eichmann's wife and innocent children. Those inhuman monsters must be made to pay for their Hideous crimes."

When the trial of Eichmann started, the NSRP began advertising

[2] The claim that the history of Nazi atrocities is a hoax has so frequently appeared in anti-Jewish publications such as *The Thunderbolt* that Jewish organizations have taken pains to reassert that 6,000,000 Jews did, in fact, die in Hitler's concentration camps. In a recent article by Arnold Forster, Anti-Defamation League offical and author of several books on anti-Semitism, the "hoax" charge is described as the "ultimate cruelty" to the Nazis' victims.

Forster notes that "the overwhelming number of Jews killed under the Nazis were not German Jews." He asserts that "all authoritative studies and documentation" indicate that approximately six million Jews were murdered during the Hitler regime—2,800,000 of Poland's Jews, 1,500,000 of occupied Russia's, 425,000 of Romania's, 260,000 of Czechoslovakia's; the remainder were Hungarian, Lithuanian, Dutch, French, Latvian, and German.

"The ultimate cruelty to the 6,000,000 Jews killed under Hitler—the denial of the fact that they ever existed, suffered, and died—is now being practiced by the haters, professional and amateur, here and abroad," Forster writes. "It is a constant theme in their literature and speeches; through repetition it is beginning to find its way into the responsible press and, presumably, the minds of respectable people. . . ."

an "Adolf Eichmann Trial Facts Committee" and called for "emergency contributions" of ten to one hundred dollars. In a special statement published in behalf of the "committee," Party Information Director Edward Fields spoke of a "final solution" to the Jewish problem:

"If spies, traitors, and Communists were executed in Germany during the war, and they turned out for the most part to all be Jews—SO WHAT? Are we going to crawl in the dirt in the name of Jewry, and beg the Jews to forgive the White Race because a Whiteman once meted out Justice to the Jews? I say NO, A THOUSAND TIMES NO! We are going to fight these greedy, scheming Jews, who seek to destroy our Race, Nation, and Faith and everything we hold dear. Whatever the final solution to the Jewish problem turns out to be, it will be the Jew who will bring it upon himself. The wrath of all the peoples of the world is upon his head. . . ."

Beyond its occasional praise of Nazi Germans, the National States Rights party's basic racial philosophy is remarkably reminiscent of the mystical Nordic racism of the 1930's. This is indicated in the NSRP constitution's explanation of the party symbol, a red thunderbolt in a white circle, and the party flag, the circled thunderbolt superimposed on diagonal blue stripes in a field of red:

"The Thunderbolt is an ancient symbol of the White Race. It is the thunder from the heavens which first awed our forefathers as they looked into the storm clouds and listened to the thunderous roar. The White Race has always used different forms of the flash of light to symbolize strength and power. The Thunderbolt has always been a warning to the Whiteman's enemies. . . . The flag of the National States Rights party is the patriotic red, white, and blue. The red stands for the pure Nordic blood of our people which we seek to preserve for our posterity. The blue represents the vast future of our people stretching into time and eternity: as long as God's blue sky is above us, the White Race shall live. The cross in the background is the Cross of St. Andrew which was part of the battle flag of the Confederacy. . . . The white circle stands for the purity of our white womanhood and our beloved little children who are the basic reason for our united stand; we struggle for them. We are ordained by God to save the White Race so that civilization will exist as long as the world stands."

The Chairwoman

In a trim brick bungalow on a quiet, leafy street of Little Rock the middle-aged lady in the perky little blue hat stood at her dining-room table, folding copies of *The Thunderbolt* into envelopes for mailing to her fellow supporters of the National States Rights party in Arkansas.

"I believe you're from the FBI," she said, skewering her visitor with a sharp hazel glance. But then she shrugged and smiled. "Oh, well, I don't care if you are. I always talk from the heart and not from the teeth."

The truth was, Mrs. Ann Bishop, national vice-chairman of the NSRP, was in a sunny mood.

At home with Tinkle, her Persian cat, she was having a delightful time making arrangements for an NSRP rally that was to be held in North Little Rock in just two days. The rally was to be addressed by the party's brightest star, Edward Fields, the young editor of *The Thunderbolt*. Fields and the party's secretary-treasurer, Ned Dupes of Knoxville, would be weekend guests of Mrs. Bishop and her husband. She had just made an appointment with her hairdresser to help prepare her for the occasion.

Mrs. Bishop, an erect, lean-featured woman of perhaps sixty, became active in politics for the first time in 1960. However inexperienced, she proved to be the best campaigner in the NSRP. Driving several thousand miles over the highways and byways of Arkansas, she managed to get 29,552 signatures on a petition to place the NSRP on the state ballot.

Arkansas Governor Orval Faubus had been nominated as the NSRP's presidential candidate at the party's 1960 convention in Miamisburg, Ohio, but he eventually rejected the nomination and supported the Kennedy-Johnson ticket. This was of considerable disappointment to Mrs. Bishop; she said she had gone to the Ohio convention under the impression that Faubus wanted to run as an NSRP candidate.

"The governor told me, 'Mrs. Bishop, you go on up there and put my hat in the ring. I don't know what'll happen, but I'll go along.' He also told our people in Florida they could put his name on the ballot down there. But then he got scared. He talked with

Kennedy and Collins [Leroy Collins, then governor of Florida],
and changed his mind. 'Mrs. Bishop,' he told me, 'I've been
threatened. I've done the best I could.' "

Despite Faubus' withdrawal, the National States Rights party
polled 28,952 votes in Arkansas—by far the best showing among
all the states where the party was able to get on the ballot.

Mrs. Bishop is not discouraged. The NSRP, she said, will try
again in 1964.

"That is," she added with a dash of bitterness, "we will if there
is another election. If Kennedy has his way, the Communists will
take over—unless there's an uprising of the people.

"The Jews control Kennedy, and I think he knows it. He studied
under Harold Laski, you know."

Behind her spectacles the twinkle in Mrs. Bishop's hazel eyes is
replaced by a hard, determined glare when she speaks of Negroes
and Jews, and her lips tighten.

All Jews, she said, are Communists and "psychiatrists." They
are in control of the governments of both Russia and the United
States. This, she said, has been true ever since World War I days,
"when 276 Jews left East Side New York and went through Kaiser
Bill to make Russia what it is today."

She interrupted her *Thunderbolt*-folding operation to fetch a
little leaflet from a buffet drawer. "Here. I want you to take a look
at this."

The leaflet, entitled *Government of the Soviet Union: Invisible*
[and] *Visible* and written by one S. D. Fedorov, features crude
Jewish caricatures and free-wheeling syntax.

When Jewish Sionism took control over the world propaganda,
then Jewish millionaires of Kuhn Loeb Co. financed 48 million
dollars the Communistic Revolution in Russia, and sent 276
Jewish leaders from America who with the Jewish leaders of other
Countries took over the Russia and rule until now. They took off
all material goods of country and all private property of the population and turned it over to the Jewish government, all Gentile
population made own slaves for Chosen Jewish people. In Soviet
Union Jews believe that all Gentile population are own cattles of
the Jews. Jews have such number of Gentile cattles which neces-
sory to produce material goods for the Chosen Jewish people and

for the military reasons, but who do not need for the Jews, Jewish secret police liquidates them. . . .

Beneath the verbal fog there seems to reside the thesis that the Soviet Union has not actually been run by such "front men" as Joseph Stalin and Nikita Khrushchev but by a "Jewish Secret Board" bent on destroying "Gentile Civilization."

The leaflet's main illustration is a cartoon showing a dragon with Semitic features about to attack a fair maiden who is bound to a tree labeled "Civilization." In the background dawdles a knight in Christian armor. "Get a move on, St. George!" the caption reads. "The Jewish Talmud says, 'torture and kill the Gentile people and raise holiness for Israel.'"

A lucky investment in an oil well was, in a way, responsible for leading Mrs. Bishop to her present politico-racial philosophy.

She grew up in Dallas, Texas, and in Arkadelphia, Arkansas. Although she recalls that her parents "were very much against the Jews," she gave the matter little thought while a young woman. But following the death of her first husband, while she was clerking at a store in Little Rock in the early 1930's, something happened that helped to introduce her to the world beyond Texas and Arkansas.

"A fellow came along one day and said he needed five hundred dollars to sink an oil well down at El Dorado," she recalled. "I'd saved up seven or eight hundred dollars. I asked God what to do, then I gave him the money.

"I wasn't sure I'd ever see him or the money again. But in sixty days I had a check for twelve hundred dollars. Before long I had three little old oil wells producing, and for years I got two thousand dollars a month out of them."

With some of the money she paid for a college education for her son, who lives now in Louisiana. She spent the rest, she remembers with pleasure, "a-traveling and a-going."

While visiting the World's Fair in 1939 she happened to enter the New York Public Library. And it was there that she had her first encounter with books that spoke of the "Jewish menace."

"I read a book called *Sex and Character* that said the Jew was communism—and explained it all."

Later she read *The Protocols of the Learned Elders of Zion* (an anti-Gentile document that Jewish organizations have repeatedly branded as a forgery perpetrated by Jew-haters), and she became a subscriber to Conde McGinley's *Common Sense.*

"*Common Sense* educated me on the Jews more than anything else I read."

She interrupted her reminiscing to inspect one of the envelopes she had just stuffed with a *Thunderbolt* and an invitation to the forthcoming NSRP rally. The envelope was addressed to the Ku Klux Klan at a post-office box in Little Rock.

"What in the world is the Ku Klux Klan doing on this list?" she exclaimed. "Now, I don't believe in *that.*"

But with a shrug she went ahead and tossed it on the stack of letters to be mailed.

Mrs. Bishop is, of course, a staunch segregationist. She feels that the current agitation for civil rights has tended to encourage violence among Negroes. And many of her women friends, she said, are "worried about Negro rapists."

But she reserves her very angriest comments for the subject of white men who are libidinously violating the rules of segregation.

"If I was president for one month," she declared, "I tell you what I'd do: I'd take all these white men that are keeping Negro women and making mulatto children—and there's a lot of 'em doing that right here in Little Rock; all you've got to do is go to the Negro section and look around—I'd take those men and I'd *tar* 'em, and I'd *feather* 'em, and I'd *burn 'em at the stake.*"

A call came from one of her women friends. She later identified the caller as "a little Catholic woman who just despises Kennedy." Mrs. Bishop spoke to her of a speech she planned to make at the forthcoming NSRP rally.

"Well, I'm just gonna tell 'em what's what, and I'm gonna use *that three-letter word.* I don't care if they throw eggs at me. They can put a tomato right in my face. But I'm gonna tell 'em what I think. I speak from the heart and not from the teeth."

Although she sometimes talks of the possibility that violence might be done to her because of her outspokenness, Mrs. Bishop said she had so far received only one telephone call that might be interpreted as threatening. A man who identified himself as a Jew called her, she said, after she had written a letter to a Little Rock newspaper denouncing the "Jewish conspiracy."

" 'You should get down on your knees and pray,' " he told me. I told him he was a fine one to talk. 'Why, you crucified our Lord.' 'Well,' he said, 'he was one of ours.' And then do you know what he said to me? 'What you need,' he said, 'is a psychiatrist.' I said, 'My Lord, don't tell me you believe in mental health, too.' "

Actually, said Mrs. Bishop, she does not hate Jews. She regularly trades at several stores owned by Jews in Little Rock, and she recalled that she worked for a number of years as a clerk in a Jewish-owned store in Memphis. She has never personally had any unpleasant experiences with Jews, she said.

But she remembers what she has read.

"Do you know that for every Jew that was killed in the war there were a thousand of our boys killed? Now, that's not right. They ought to be made to suffer, too."

She thought about the matter.

"They ought to cut the throats of some of these Jews," she said, and, smiling brightly, swept a forefinger across her throat.

Mrs. Bishop sealed an envelope over the last one of the *Thunderbolt*s she had folded, then discovered there were still a few empty envelopes, among them one addressed to the Sons of Liberty.

"Well, I'm just not gonna fold another one of these things," she said. "I'm tired out. They'll just not get one."

And she cast the surplus envelopes away.

As she saw her visitor to the door, that suspicious expression returned to her face.

"You might be a Jew for all I know," she said. "What'd you say your name is? Cook, huh? Well, you never can tell. The other day at a luncheon I was talking about the Jews, saying this and that about 'the kikes,' and there at the table was a man named Jones. Well, this Jones spoke up and said he was a regular contributor to B'nai B'rith. Jones. Hmph.

"Oh, well, I'm not afraid to say what I think. They could do a lot of things. They could bomb my house, I guess. But if they killed me, it wouldn't matter. This movement would go right on."

As she spoke, Tinkle the cat made a move to squeeze past the screen door and into the front yard. Mrs. Bishop picked him up gently.

Tinkle, at least, would be there to defend her, the visitor suggested.

"That's right." She laughed. "You know, Tinkle used to growl at the postman every day. But he's getting older—he's six or seven now—and he doesn't growl so much any more."

And Mrs. Bishop, who has not similarly let the years subdue her, smiled with gay defiance as she said good-by.

The Chiropractor

"When we take power," said Dr. Edward Reed Fields, Jr., editor of *The Thunderbolt* and guiding spirit of the National States Rights party, "we will remove all Negroes, Jews, and Orientals from the United States. Then we will open the doors to real immigration from northern Europe to improve our racial stock."

He sat relaxed in an overstuffed chair in Mrs. Bishop's flowery little living room, a remarkably handsome young man with a graceful voice. A blue-eyed, sandy-haired, rosy-cheeked fellow, he is in his late twenties but looks hardly eighteen.

The suit he wore was dark and nicely cut. But some of his haberdashery was fairly singular: his wide necktie was Confederate gray and decorated with the National States Rights party flag; and an encircled thunderbolt—the symbol of the NSRP, woven in red and white—was stitched to his left lapel.

"We are going to follow Abraham Lincoln's plan and repatriate the Negro to Africa. We would subsidize those of our Negroes who would voluntarily go back to Africa. Those who didn't go voluntarily wouldn't be rewarded.

"A good plan for our Orientals would be to set up a separate state for them in, say, Hawaii."

And the Jews? Are they to be dispatched to Israel?

"Oh, no," said Fields. "Anti-Jewish groups for many, many years have stated that Palestine should belong to the Christians and Arabs. A good place to settle the Jews might be Madagascar."

Fields did not indicate whether he felt that the citizens of Madagascar would welcome the several millions of Jews from America.

But he did remark that his party has been trying to "work out something with Tubman" (President W. V. S. Tubman of Liberia, presumably) in preparation for the removal of America's Negroes to Africa.

And what of the Jews, Negroes, and Orientals of America who might not wish to make a trip abroad?

"Later on," Fields said casually, "the country would have to be purified."

Whatever else might be said of the young chieftain of the National States Rights party, there is no gainsaying the fact that he has been very consistent in his politics and racial philosophy through the years. They have been almost exactly the same ever since 1946.

It was in 1946 that Fields happened to attend a meeting of the Columbians in Atlanta, where he and his middle-class parents had lived since his earliest childhood days in Chicago. The Columbians was a Bundist-style organization that flourished briefly in the Georgia capital until its leader, a slender, voluble young man named Emory Burke, was sent to prison on a charge of usurping police authority in connection with the beating of a Negro.

Burke has remained a hero to Fields. In a recent issue of *The Thunderbolt* Fields recalled the excitement he felt on first seeing the Columbians decked out in their uniforms with the thunderbolt shoulder patches.

Fields was just fourteen years old at the time.

"I was a student at Marist College [a Catholic prep school in Atlanta] and leader in a student movement for the late Eugene Talmadge," he remembered. "A friend told me that a White Supremacy group was holding a meeting in West Atlanta. We played a game of golf in the West End that afternoon, and dropped by 'The Columbian Hall' that evening.

"We were enthused at what we saw. A huge Thunderbolt banner hung behind the speakers' rostrum. A record player blared out Nordic marching music.

"Then Burke entered in uniform, followed by the other officers. He began by telling the audience of our racial heritages, the reasons for the founding of America, and of the evil elements seeking to destroy White Freedoms and Liberty.

"About that time a group of men wearing Jewish War Veterans' caps entered the hall. They began booing the speaker and tearing up Columbian literature. A scuffle broke out and the police entered. The meeting was ended by a police order that the hall be cleared. I walked up to a police captain and told him the meeting should not be stopped, that it was the Jewish War Veterans who should be arrested for inciting a riot. He replied, 'We have our orders.'

"I picked up a torn piece of literature off the floor, and copied down the Columbian address. After class the next day I went by their office and learned that persecution was expected and only through sacrifice could America be saved."

Burke was an Atlanta architect who had been reared in Montgomery, Alabama. In the 1930's he had worked in New York on the staff of *The Storm,* a racist paper published by Ernest F. Elmhurst, author of the anti-Jewish volume, *The World Hoax.* That period of Burke's life, wrote Fields, was at a time when "Roosevelt and the Jews were fast moving to end the depression by starting a war and set up World Communism by knocking out the only White, Christian Anti-communist power in Europe—Germany."

Many of the trappings of the Columbians have been put to use by the NSRP, most notably the red thunderbolt as the party emblem.

"The Columbians are gone, but the spirit still lives," Fields declared. "The symbol of Emory Burke was The Thunderbolt. He designed this emblem to stand for the Whiteman's way of life. The sign of The Thunderbolt still marches on. In the end, Truth and Justice will Triumph."

While Burke was serving time in the prison at Reidsville, Georgia, Fields worked on a "Free Emory Burke Committee." One of his fellow committeemen was the late General George Van Horn Moseley of Atlanta, an influential leader in American anti-Jewish circles since the 1930's. Moseley died in 1960.

"I always admired General Moseley, particularly for the stand he made during the Roosevelt era. I'd often go over to his apartment in Atlanta. I valued what he said.[3] I was sorry when he passed away."

[3]A sample Moseley opinion, written just a few years before his death, is the following: "Although there are over thirteen million Jews of all

From his acquaintance with General Moseley, Burke, and the Columbians, young Fields soon became familiar with the names of many of the leading Jew-baiters in the country.

In 1949 and 1950 he was corresponding with *The Broom,* an anti-Jewish weekly published on the West Coast by C. Leon de Aryan, one of the group of alleged Nazi sympathizers during the early part of World War II. One of Fields' letters to *The Broom* protested the arrest in Atlanta of Edward James Smythe, another super-nationalist.

"Three weeks ago Edward James Smythe was arrested and thrown into 'Fulton Tower' here in Atlanta," Fields wrote to *The Broom* in 1949. "I noticed a small article in an Atlanta paper telling of his arrest. So I and a few of my friends who are followers of Emory Burk[e], went to see Smythe. We found him in a small dungeon-like cell all alone. . . . He is being denied all his rights provided by the constitution and is being held a political prisoner here in Atlanta by the Anti-Defamation League. . . ."

Fields urged all *Broom* readers who were interested in the case to write to him. Then in a letter a couple of months later in *The Broom* Fields was soliciting members for a "Defense Committee" to "protect Americans from the terror of the Kike."

"The persecution of such patriotic Americans [as] Emory Burke, and Edward James Smythe cry [*sic*] to heaven for justice," Fields wrote. "Unless there is an organized opposition to such persecutions, the Jews will run roughshod over us. They will imprison everyone who stands in their way, as they now do in Russia. . . ."

Fields was nineteen at this time.

According to the Anti-Defamation League of B'nai B'rith, which keeps careful tab on such matters, Fields was distributing anti-Jewish handbills in Atlanta in October 1950, when the first school integration suit was filed there. The handbills were headlined, "Jewish Communists Behind Atlanta's School Segregation Suit," and bore the imprint of the Atlanta Anti-Communist Society.

---

classes in our Republic they have not, as yet, entered the life blood of our race so seriously that a purge is impossible. Let us work and pray for that day when an aroused Congress [will] frame a charter which the President of that day will be forced to sign, issue, and execute. Such a charter should give the Jews a limited time in which to close their affairs and leave our shores, at home and abroad. Nothing less will save the United States of America. . . ."

This organization, reported the Anti-Defamation League, was Fields' own creation.

About 1952 Fields teamed up with Jesse B. Stoner of Chattanooga and Atlanta in a paper organization which they called the Christian Anti-Jewish party. A typical piece of promotional literature from Fields and Stoner's Christian Anti-Jewish party in the early 1950's declared that "we Christians are GOD's Chosen People, not the Jews. The Jews are the children of the devil."

The Stoner-Fields message explained: "Anti-Jewism is a leading Christian virtue and an essential American virtue. Anti-Jewism says that America rightfully belongs to us Americans, not to the Jews; Jew-devils have NO place in a Christian Country."

In contrast with Fields' more recent plan to cleanse Palestine as well as America of Jews and send them to Madagascar, his and Stoner's Christian Anti-Jewish party proposed: "Since the Jews now have a Country of their own, let them go to it. Our party demands that the American Government expel the Jews to Palestine and Confiscate their ill-gotten wealth for the benefit of the American people. . . ."

Fields and Stoner both attended law school in Atlanta in 1951 and 1952. Stoner was admitted to the Georgia bar. But Fields, a physical-culture enthusiast and sometime weight lifter, spurned a career in the law in favor of becoming a chiropractor. He attended the Palmer School of Chiropractics in Davenport, Iowa, from 1953 to 1956, but in his spare time continued to pursue his main interest, the campaign against Jews.

In Iowa in late 1953, according to the ADL, Fields and another Atlanta youth attending the chiropractic school were investigated by Davenport police after they were reported to have posted stickers on stores in the area; the stickers read "This Place Owned by Jews" and "Anti-Jew Week February 21–28."

A year later Fields and Stoner and four of their Christian Anti-Jewish party sympathizers were reported picketing the White House with anti-Jewish placards.

During the national election in 1956 Fields was for a time a leader of the Iowa America-Constitutional party, one of the dozens of rightist splinter groups that backed former Internal Revenue Commissioner T. Coleman Andrews for the presidency. The party polled 3,202 of the total 1,234,564 votes cast in Iowa that year.

Marrying and moving to Louisville, Kentucky, Fields began practicing as a chiropractor. But as the months passed, more and more of his time was devoted to segregationist and anti-Jewish activity. Through 1957 he worked closely with one Millard Grubbs in expanding a White Citizens' Council organization in Louisville. Then he busied himself with organizing the United White party. In 1958, at a meeting of about twenty people in Knoxville, the United White party (whose symbol was a "W" in a white circle) was transformed into the present National States Rights party.

Fields said he believes that racial integration can be prevented only if segregationists take direct political action.

"I think the Citizens' Council organization is very worth while, but it's not a political movement—and neither is the Klan. The only way we [the Whitemen] can win an ultimate victory is through the political action of a third party."

The NSRP is affiliated with neither the Councils nor the Klan, said Fields.

"We think the Klan has done a lot of good, and we're not against it. But we're not a part of it; we don't have a single Klan member."

Fields said he had on occasion met with other groups to discuss cooperation in supporting such segregationist candidates as Crommelin and Faubus.

"But we support them without losing our own individuality," he said. "I wish the best of luck to other groups with our goals, but I'm opposed to alliances. When you make alliances, you weaken your movement."

Neither Crommelin nor his friend, John Kasper, is a member of the NSRP, said Fields. But he spoke highly of them—especially of the admiral.

"He's a wonderful leader; he just doesn't believe in allying with any group. He feels he can be more effective on his own."

Like many other organizations of the "radical right," Fields' party advocates that the Communist party in the United States be outlawed and its members arrested forthwith. The NSRP also proposes that public schools be replaced with private schools as a means of blocking integration, that the Supreme Court be made elective rather than appointive, and that the United States withdraw from the United Nations (Fields would have the United States help organize a "UN of white people").

But unlike some of the ultraconservative social proposals being tossed about in right field these days, Fields said he favors slum clearance, unemployment assistance, old-age pensions, and other measures of "aid to the poor and downtrodden."

"We don't believe in going back to the cave era," he said.

He remarked that his followers in the NSRP are mostly "working-class people; we have no rich people."

As the leader of a "working-class" movement, Fields maintains that the kind of "moss-backed Republicanism" symbolized by Arizona Senator Barry Goldwater (a favorite in some quarters of the "radical right") has no chance of winning political power in the future. Fields noted, moreover, that Go!dwater is of Jewish descent.

"That's reason enough not to vote for him."

Fields and his attractive young wife and baby son had driven to Little Rock from Birmingham with Ned Dupes of Knoxville, a retired salesman who is secretary-treasurer of the NSRP. Dupes, an elderly Tennesseean wearing a light-brown suit, maroon shirt, and elaborately flowered tie, remarked that he serves the party without pay.

Dupes' political opinions are not so intellectualized as Fields'; in explaining his dislike of Franklin D. Roosevelt, for example, Dupes said he had known right away, back in the 1930's, that FDR was not a man to be trusted, because he "had eyes close together like a rat's."

In what seemed to be a move to distract Dupes from his Tennessee cracker-barrel-style discussion of this and that, Fields asked him to help unpack their supply of books and their party flag.

As they stood holding the flag, which matched the young chiropractor's necktie, Fields explained its various symbolic values. Although the NSRP uses the same thunderbolt insigne that was used by the old Columbians, Fields said: "To my knowlege, no former Columbian is a member of my organization."

Fields also stoutly denied that the NSRP was connected in any way with the 1958 Atlanta temple bombing. The temple was actually dynamited by an agent of the Anti-Defamation League of B'nai B'rith, he declared.

"They did it to stir up public opinion and bring about federal action," he said. "But the case came so close to bringing out the fact that Jews were behind it that the bombings in the South have stopped."

Furling the big flag again, Fields dug into a box of books which he had brought along for sale at the Little Rock rally he planned to address.

"Right now I'm not as concerned with our ultimate goals as with indoctrinating people. We want our people to know we're right—one hundred per cent right. I don't want anyone at any level of leadership in the party to have any doubts. I don't want anyone to join who doesn't believe."

And he struck his chair arm with his fist for emphasis.

Among the "approved books" displayed by Fields were Ernest Elmhurst's *The World Hoax; The Anti-Defamation League and Its Use in the World Communist Offensive,* by Major Robert H. Williams; *The Protocols: World Conquest through World Government,* by Victor E. Marsden; *Our Nordic Race,* edited by Richard Kelly Hoskins; and *The Jewish War of Survival,* by Arnold Leese.

"We have an NSRP bookstore at Wilkes-Barre, Pennsylvania," Fields mentioned. "We're trying to get college students to buy there."

Fields' child, a blond, remarkably handsome little boy, toddled out from the kitchen where he had been playing under the care of his mother and Mrs. Bishop. He held out a colorful rubber ball to his father.

Fields interrupted his discourse long enough to accept the ball from his son and to say gently, "Hi." Then he rolled the ball across the living-room floor, and the boy happily ran and brought it back to him.

"Several fuzzy-headed professors in our colleges are saying that future generations in the United States will have brown faces and dark eyes—in other words, that we'll look something like Egyptians."

Fields rolled the ball again, and his son scampered after it.

"There's already a lot of interdating going on between the

races. *Crisis,* the NAACP magazine, is bragging that there's more intermarriage now than ever before." And he added: "You know, of course, that black genes are dominant over white. So the Negroes could outbreed us until only a dark people would populate our world.

"But we of the National States Rights party don't choose to visualize the possibility that there will be no blond children in the future. I want to go to my grave knowing that a thousand years from now a blond child will be born."

Fields said he is aware that his party is considered by many people to be a copy of the Nazi party in Germany. But this is not true, he said—and he spoke with even more emphasis in denying that the NSRP is affiliated in any way with the neo-Nazi group headed by George Lincoln Rockwell.

"We don't want to be associated with Rockwell in any shape or form. We feel he's hurting us. As far as I'm concerned, he doesn't exist."

Unlike Rockwell's organization, said Fields, the NSRP is "a native American movement."

"The Nazi party in Germany was a socialist party," he said. "The NSRP is opposed to socialism in every form. Ours is a *conservative* movement. We believe in free enterprise, free elections, and free political parties; I'd like to see *fifteen* parties in America."

If a National States Rights party candidate were to be elected president, said Fields, opposing parties (except the Communist party) would not be outlawed as they were in Hitler's Germany.

He paused to accept the ball again from his little boy.

"No, in a four-year term we would have time to repatriate all the Negroes and Jews," he said. "After a four-year term we would be willing to step down. Our task would be completed."

And, half-smiling as he meditated on that prospect, he gently rolled the ball across the floor for the delight of his beautiful son.

V. THE LAWYERS

With All Deliberate Protest

1. THE SPIRIT OF '96

ONE DAY in the early 1890's a man named Plessy boarded an East Louisiana Railway passenger train in New Orleans, bound for the town of Covington just on the other side of Lake Pontchartrain. It was a "Jim Crow" train, with some cars reserved for white ticket holders, some for Negroes. Citizen Plessy entered one of the coaches reserved for whites; he was, in fact, an octoroon—seven-eighths Caucasian and one-eighth Negro—so "white," it was later testified, that "the mixture of colored blood was not discernible in him."

After Plessy had settled himself, the conductor—who apparently suspected that the passenger's family tree had a dark branch or two—ordered him to vacate the seat and go to a car reserved for Negroes. When Plessy refused to budge, the conductor summoned a policeman and Plessy was "forcibly ejected from said coach and hurried off to and imprisoned in the parish jail of New Orleans." Judge Ferguson of New Orleans found him guilty of violating a Louisiana law that provided a jail term of up to twenty days for "passengers insisting on going into a coach or compartment other than the one set aside for the race to which he or she belongs."

Plessy appealed the conviction all the way to the United States Supreme Court, claiming—among other things—that it was in violation of the Fourteenth Amendment of the federal Constitution.[1] The Supreme Court's decision in the case of *Plessy* v. *Fergu-*

[1] It is the first clause of the Fourteenth Amendment that declares: "All persons born or naturalized in the United States, and subject to the jurisdic-

189

son in 1896 was to be the most important legal factor in American race relations for more than half a century.

The court—with only Justice Harlan dissenting—gave its approval to the fateful phrase, "equal but separate." In the opinion, delivered by Justice Brown, the court ruled that it was constitutional for the Louisiana State Legislature to have enacted a statute providing that "all railway companies carrying passengers in their coaches in this State shall provide equal but separate accommodations for the white and colored races by providing two or more passenger coaches for each passenger train, or by dividing the passenger coaches with a partition so as to secure separate accommodations. . . ."

The 1896 court's opinion gave an interpretation of the Fourteenth Amendment which, in effect, endorsed the multitude of Jim Crow laws which were passed by southern legislatures following the Reconstruction period. While the amendment guaranteed Negroes equal rights, the court ruled, it did not prohibit segregation.

"The object of the amendment was undoubtedly to enforce the absolute equality of the two races before the law," Justice Brown wrote, "but in the nature of things it could not have been intended to abolish distinctions based upon color, or to enforce social, as distinguished from political, equality, or a commingling of the two races upon terms unsatisfactory to either.

"Laws permitting, and even requiring, their separation in places where they are liable to be brought into contact do not necessarily imply the inferiority of either race to the other, and have been generally, if not universally, recognized as within the competency of the state legislatures in the exercise of their police power. The most common instance of this," he added, in a comment which was to have great significance for systems of public education in the South, "is connected with the establishment of separate schools for white and colored children, which has been held to be a valid

---

tion thereof, are citizens of the United States and of the State wherein they reside. No State shall make or enforce any law which shall abridge the privileges or immunities of citizens of the United States, nor shall any State deprive any person of life, liberty, or property without due process of law, nor deny to any person within its jurisdiction the equal protection of the laws."

exercise of the legislative power even by courts of states where the political rights of the colored race have been longest and most earnestly enforced."

Taking up the question of whether the Louisiana law under which Plessy was convicted was "reasonable," Justice Brown said: "[The legislature] is at liberty to act with reference to the established usages, customs, and traditions of the people, and with a view to the promotion of their comfort, and the preservation of the public peace and good order. Gauged by this standard, we cannot say that a law which authorizes or even requires the separation of the two races in public conveyances is more obnoxious to the Fourteenth Amendment than the acts of Congress requiring separate schools for colored children in the District of Columbia, the constitutionality of which does not seem to have been questioned, or the corresponding acts of state legislatures."

The 1896 court's concluding bit of philosophy was the oft-stated idea that improvements in race relations cannot successfully be legislated, but must come about through changes in individuals' (presumably white individuals') attitudes.

"If the two races are to meet upon terms of social equality, it must be the result of natural affinities, a mutual appreciation of each other's merits, and a voluntary consent of individuals. . . . Legislation is powerless to eradicate racial instincts or to abolish distinctions based upon physical differences, and the attempt to do so can only result in accentuating the difficulties of the present situation. . . ."

And so the conviction of Citizen Plessy was affirmed, and the Southern Way of Life was made secure until the middle of the twentieth century. Although subsequent decisions eroded it slightly, the "separate but equal" doctrine established by the *Plessy* v. *Ferguson* decision stood as the keystone of the South's system of racial segregation until May 17, 1954.

Onto the Horns of an American Dilemma

It was on that date—"the day of the second Emancipation Proclamation" to opponents of apartheid; "Black Monday" to the South's segregationists—that another United States Supreme Court abolished the "separate but equal" doctrine of *Plessy* v. *Ferguson,* thereby lifting the gates for a torrent of litigation that promised to destroy the entire Southern structure of Jim Crow laws.

It is customary to speak of May 17, 1954, as the day of *The* decision. Actually, the court handed down *two* decisions that day against public-school segregation: one, the case of *Brown* v. *Topeka,* ruled that it violated the Fourteenth Amendment; the other, *Bolling* v. *Sharpe,* ruled that it violated the Fifth Amendment.[2] The opinions in both cases were written by Chief Justice Warren, with all eight other justices concurring.

To understand the present-day segregationists' legalistic arguments against integration of schools and other public facilities, it is helpful briefly to review the most famous of the May 17, 1954, decisions, *Brown* v. *Topeka,*[3] in comparison with the *Plessy* v. *Ferguson* ruling.

Chief Justice Warren conceded in his opinion that the Negro and white schools involved in the *Brown* v. *Topeka* cases "have been equalized, or are being equalized, with respect to buildings, curricula, qualifications, and salaries of teachers, and other 'tangible' factors." But such "tangible factors" were not the point of this decision, he said.

"We must look, instead, to the effect of segregation itself on public education. In approaching this problem we cannot turn

[2] In the case of *Spottswood Thomas Bolling et al.* v. *C. Melvin Sharpe et al.,* Bolling and other Negro students had petitioned for admission to previously all-white schools in the District of Columbia. The court held that by being required to attend a segregated school they were being denied their rights under the "due-process" clause of the Fifth Amendment ("No person shall be . . . deprived of life, liberty, or property, without due process of law. . . ."

[3] *Brown* v. *Topeka* is the commonly used identification of the opinion, even though it actually applied to four cases which had been instituted in behalf of several Negro students in each of four states: Kansas (*Brown* v. *Board of Education of Topeka*), South Carolina (*Briggs* v. *Elliott*), Virginia (*Davis* v. *County School Board of Prince Edward County*), and Delaware (*Gebhart* v. *Belton*).

While deciding the merits of the cases on May 17, 1954, it was not until May 31, 1955, that the Supreme Court remanded them to the federal district courts in the various states with an order that Negro petitioners be admitted to the public schools "on a racially nondiscriminatory basis with all deliberate speed. . . ."

the clock back to 1868 when the [Fourteenth] Amendment was adopted, or even to 1896 when *Plessy* v. *Ferguson* was written. We must consider public education in the light of its full development and its present place in American life throughout the nation."

The Warren court held that the opportunity for an education, "where the state has undertaken to provide it, is a right which must be made available to all on equal terms." But the opinion went a step further—in a significant departure from *Plessy* v. *Ferguson:*

"Does segregation of children in public schools solely on the basis of race, even though the physical facilities and other 'tangible' factors may be equal, deprive the children of the minority group of equal educational opportunities? We believe that it does. . . . To separate [pupils of a minority group] from others of similar age and qualifications solely because of their race generates a feeling of inferiority as to their status in the community that may affect their hearts and minds in a way unlikely ever to be undone."

A couple of references were made to previous school cases in which the Supreme Court "resorted to intangible considerations." However, Warren indicated that the court now was relying heavily on modern "psychological knowledge."

"The effect of [school segregation] was well stated by a finding in the Kansas case [*Brown* v. *Topeka*] by a court which nevertheless felt compelled to rule against the Negro plaintiffs: 'Segregation of white and colored children in public schools has a detrimental effect upon the colored children. The impact is greater when it has the sanction of the law; for the policy of separating the races is usually interpreted as denoting the inferiority of the Negro group. A sense of inferiority affects the motivation of a child to learn. Segregation with the sanction of law, therefore, has a tendency to retard the educational and mental development of Negro children and to deprive them of some of the benefits they would receive in a racially integrated school system.'

"Whatever may have been the extent of psychological knowledge at the time of *Plessy* v. *Ferguson,* this finding is amply supported by modern authority. Any language in *Plessy* v. *Ferguson* contrary to this finding is rejected."

In a footnote the Warren court listed this "modern authority" as: "K. B. Clark, *Effect of Prejudice on Personality Development* (Midcentury White House Conference on Children and Youth, 1950); Witmer and Kotinsky, *Personality in the Making* (1952), Chapter VI; Deutscher and Chein, 'The Psychological Effects of Enforced Segregation: A Survey of Social Science Opinion,' 26 *J. Psychol.* 259 (1948); Chein, 'What Are the Psychological Effects of Segregation under Conditions of Equal Facilities?' 3 *Int. J. Opinion and Attitude Res.* 229 (1949); Brameld, *Educational Costs in Discrimination and National Welfare* (McIver, ed. 1949), 44–48; Frazier, *The Negro in the United States* (1949), 674–681. And see generally Myrdal, *An American Dilemma* (1944)."

The opinion's heavy reliance on the factor of "psychological knowledge" since 1954 has been the source of an endless stream of Southern lawyers' protests that the court's decision was not based on sound legal precedents but on faulty "social science." In addition, the footnote has been the source of the segregationists' claim that The Decision was the nefarious work of "left wingers" and "communist fronters."

A Serving of Louisiana Gumbo

Of all the many Dixieland attorneys who have lashed out at the May 17, 1954, decision as a Red-inspired outrage, one of the ablest, most influential, and most flamboyant, has been a little pistol of a man named Perez.

A key leader of white New Orleans' resistance to school integration, a chief architect of the awesome structure of anti-integration laws enacted by the Louisiana Legislature, Leander Henry Perez, Sr., has been the most powerful force for segregation in his state.

His has never been the "soft-sell" approach preferred by the rather more velvety segregationist leaders such as Bill Simmons of the Citizens' Council Association over in Mississippi. Perez favors blunt talk.

"Don't wait for your daughters to be raped by these Congolese," he shouted to a crowd of 5,000 at a recent CC rally in New Orleans. "Don't wait until the burr heads are forced into your schools. Do something about it now."

But it would be inaccurate indeed to interpret Leander Perez's unrestrained racist talk as simply thoughtless Dixie emotionalism. He is, in fact, a man of considerable learning and sophistication— one of the South's outstanding constitutional lawyers, and, to boot, a shrewd politician who preserves a cool decisiveness beneath the flames of his oratory.

In one of the richly furnished dining rooms of New Orleans' Roosevelt Hotel one day not long ago, in the company of a visitor and a clerkly looking fellow who serves as his office aide, Perez was spooning into a midafternoon serving of Louisiana gumbo ("The cup I want is right at the bottom of the pot," he had told the waitress) and predicting that the 1954 decision could well mean catastrophe for the nation.

"The objective of the Communists is to use the Supreme Court to destroy our public-school system by forced integration, and ultimately to destroy white civilization in this country. Unless the Southern states can set up a more powerful bloc of votes in coming presidential elections, our constitutional government is doomed. Unless something is done, Khrushchev's prediction that Eisenhower's grandchildren will live under a communist government will follow as the night the day. Oh, the destruction of our white civilization won't come in this generation, but it can happen in four or five generations. I ask you: what would lead to the more certain destruction of our country than a mongrelized race? How much resistance do you think would be offered to the Communists by a mongrelized race?"

Perez is a rapid-fire talker. He seems almost to explode with energy. When not eating his gumbo, he puffs constantly on a cigar through a blunt black holder. He is a napkin flapper. He is a brusher of imaginary crumbs and tobacco ashes from the tablecloth. And whenever there is the slightest hiatus in the conversation, he gives the table top a smart slap.

He is seventy years old, but looks considerably younger. Recently a reporter described the color of Perez's flowing mane of hair as "pewter"; it was an apt description. The shock value of his pewter-colored coiffure is intensified by the thick darkness of his eyebrows. Behind his rimless glasses his blue-gray eyes are normally lidded closely by a scowl as he talks, but now and then, even when he is right in the middle of a violent denunciation, he will wing his fierce eyebrows high, letting his face fall into an irrelevant, almost clownishly astonished expression which seems to transmit the sudden thought: "By the way, where are we?"

Perez's enormous influence in Louisiana politics stems primarily from the fact that he is the political boss of Plaquemines and St. Bernard, the two parishes (i.e., counties) that lie just south of and reach part of the way into New Orleans. Son of a Plaquemines Parish farmer, he finished at Tulane University Law School in New Orleans and was appointed a judge in his home parish at the age of twenty-seven. Everybody in Louisiana still addresses him as "Judge." Four years later, in 1924, he was elected district attorney of both Plaquemines and St. Bernard parishes; he served in that office until December 1960, when he turned it over to one of his sons, Leander, Jr., and forthwith allowed his son to appoint him as his assistant district attorney. ("The judge" has, however, chosen to remain president of the Plaquemines Parish Council, its governing body).

The swampy land below New Orleans has some of the richest oil deposits in the country, and through the years Perez has become a very wealthy man. He lives on his cattle ranch in Plaquemines Parish. For several years he spent his home life in a house on fashionable Newcomb Boulevard in New Orleans—just down the street from the target of some of his most blistering oratory, J. Skelly Wright, the federal judge who in 1960 ordered the first desegregation in New Orleans' public schools.

As spokesman for Plaquemines and St. Bernard parishes Perez has been a significant figure in Louisiana politics since the twenties. He was an ally of Huey Long until his assassination. However, he was to some extent forced into a secondary position in Louisiana politics by the fact that he and Huey's brother, the late Governor Earl Long, never could get along happily in politics. In 1956, for instance, when an appointment to a Plaquemines ward post would have given Governor Earl a voice in the parish's government, Perez simply abolished the ward.

Since the decision of 1954 he has become recognized as Louisiana's major spokesman against the evils of integration. Add to this the fact of Earl Long's colorful decline and death, and the fact that Perez was savvy enough to pick Jimmie Davis as his candidate for governor in the last race, and the sum of it has been a great increase in Perez's political prestige and power in the last few years.

Perez's fiery maledictions against The Decision, which have been echoed repeatedly throughout the segregationist South since 1954, center mainly on the Warren court's dependence on intangible considerations and modern psychological "authorities" rather than—or at least more than—on the tangible factors in the *Brown* v. *Topeka* case and the "authority" of past Supreme Court decisions.

"After the court cited several of its previous decisions upholding the 'separate but equal' doctrine in the field of public education, and finding that the Negro and white schools involved had been equalized with respect to buildings, curriculums, qualifications, and salaries of teachers, and other 'tangible' factors, the court held that their decision could not turn on merely a comparison of these tangible factors. The court then said it must look into the effect of segregation itself on public education, and that in approaching this problem the nine justices could not turn the clock back to 1868 when the [Fourteenth] Amendment was adopted, or even to 1896 when *Plessy* v. *Ferguson* was written.

"In so many words," Perez has declared in testimony to a congressional committee, "the United States Supreme Court said that they could not go along with the Fourteenth Amendment or construe the provisions of [it] as applicable to these school desegregation cases because the history of its adoption showed that it had no application to public schools. . . . The court, in so many words, actually repudiated the Fourteenth Amendment."

Continuing this line of thought, Perez said:

"After the court repudiated the Fourteenth Amendment, and finding no basis for its holding in the history of the adoption of the Fourteenth Amendment applicable to public education, the court then floundered around to justify its decision on policy regarding the importance of education to our democratic society. . . ."

Since it had no constitutional grounds for its decision, commented Perez, "the court went into the realm of psychological and sociological speculation" to reach the conclusion that segregated school facilities—whether "equalized" or not—have a bad effect on Negro children. The court changed the word "equal" in the Fourteenth Amendment and adopted the word "same" for public schools and other facilities.

"That was that. No law, no Fourteenth Amendment. Only psychology and sociology."

And who, he asks, were the "authorities" listed by the court in its controversial footnote to the decision?

"First, there was K. B. Clark, employed as social-science consultant for the legal staff of the NAACP, the real plaintiff in the 'Black Monday' cases; and then Kotinsky and Chein; and then Theodore Brameld, a ten-time commy-front member; and E. Franklin Frazier, an eighteen-time commy-front member.[4] . . . Isn't it more than passing strange that the court did not cite one white American Christian as its authority on psychology and sociology as the basis for its Black Monday 'announcement' for compulsory integration?"

Perez expresses even greater scorn for the book listed by Chief Justice Warren as the court's "general" sociopsychological authority for the *Brown* v. *Topeka* decision, Gunnar Myrdal's *An American Dilemma*. This 1,483-page work, financed by the philanthropic Carnegie Corporation, was written by Myrdal, noted Swedish sociologist, with the aid of a large staff of American scholars, many of them veteran Negro civil-rights campaigners. Published in 1944 (by Harper and Brothers, publishers), the book still stands as the most exhaustive study of American race relations ever printed. But however highly recommended it is in some quarters, *An American Dilemma* is not Perez's cup of tea.

"In the first place, Myrdal is not by any means the sole author of the book," he has said. "It is a project of the Carnegie Corporation, of Alger Hiss fame.[5] Between 75 and 100 anti-Southern writers, many of them Negroes, such as Ralph Bunche and Walter

[4] Perez takes these statistics from a May 1955 speech made in the Senate by James O. Eastland of Mississippi, chairman of the Senate Judiciary Committee and a noted critic of The Decision.

[5] Although he persistently identifies the Carnegie organization as the "corporation of Alger Hiss Fame," Perez—when questioned—readily concedes he knows that Hiss, who later served for a time as its head, was not connected with it at the time of the Myrdal project.

White, head of the NAACP, spent about six years working up this propaganda against the South and wrote four books and thirty-five manuscripts which were used by Myrdal and his immediate assistants in putting together his *An American Dilemma.*"

Besides, Perez has said, Myrdal "was a socialist and had no knowledge of the Negro question in the United States." Perez explained, with apparent amazement, "His [Myrdal's] solution was racial integration *because he held there is no such thing as race.*"

Perez has said that he himself prefers the ethnological observations presented in such works as Professor Ruggles Gates' *Human Ancestry,* published in 1948:

"[Gates] showed that the members of the human race were composed of three distinct species of man, namely: *Homo Caucasius* (the white man); *Homo Mongoloideus* (the yellow man); and *Homo Africanus* (the Negro). Whether one accepts the scientific doctrine of the evolution of life on earth from lower to higher forms, it takes no expert to see at a glance the physical differences between the Negro and the white man. Intellectually and spiritually there is no comparison between the two. Strictly speaking, the proper place to make the comparison is in the jungles of Africa. The American Negro, by virtue of his short accidental sojourn in this country, has taken on a veneer of our way of life, but he is still rooted in the mores of his ancestors in the savage jungle life."

Feeling as he does that the Supreme Court's *Brown* v. *Topeka* opinion was based on alien and leftist "social science" rather than on precedents in home-grown American law, Perez has concluded that it was an opinion designed to ruin the country.

"That decision, based upon direct repudiation of the Constitution and its framers, was nothing more nor less than a fellow traveler blank check to the pro-communist dominated NAACP to go into any and all of the federal courts of the land and secure bogus communistic decrees for forced racial integration, regimentation, and the ultimate amalgamation of the American people, to our certain destruction and, in the end, the surrender to the world-wide communist conspiracy."

A political acquaintance of "the judge" joined the luncheon table for a dessert of apple slices. But, guying Perez broadly, he said he sure enough was not going to pick up the check.

"Judge, I'ma let you pay for this lunch," he declared, with an exaggeratedly sly expression. "Now, if you was still a district attorney, I'd pay for it, figuring I might could get something outta you. But now't you're nothing but an assistant district attorney, you pro'ly got nothing for me to get. So I'ma let you pay the check."

Perez, accepting the check, spanked the table with one of his strong hands and laughed generously. It has been the source of much amusement in Louisiana that he allowed his son to appoint him as assistant district attorney of Plaquemines Parish.

"The judge" is a great kidder, and does not mind when his friends give him a bit of ribbing. He can display an appealing warmth, but he can convert it in an instant to bitter frost. As he walked from the Roosevelt he nodded in the direction of a frail fellow in a suit that could benefit from a pressing, and identified him as a former news reporter.

"Every time he did an article about me," said Perez, "he always managed to leave the impression he would be willing to accept a little payoff if I ever wanted him to do a little 'public-relations work' for me."

But then a while back his editor had caught him goofing off on the job and had canned him, Perez recalled with satisfaction.

"Hmph," he snorted. "If I'd wanted dog meat, I'd have gone to the pound."

Dozens of pedestrians waved and called out "Hiday, Judge," to Perez as he bustled up Barrone Street in the direction of his office. When Perez walks in company, he is the locomotive and his companions are the freight that follows. He had to clutch his high-crowned cattleman's hat as he steamed along, for a ferocious wind was gusting down the narrow street.

"That wind off the Gulf, George?" he snapped to his aide.

"Naw, Judge," his aide answered, "this one's right out of the east."

Perez, holding onto his hat, frowned disapprovingly, as if he suspected that the gale might possibly be buffeting his parishes without having obtained his permission.

From Perez's penthouse suite of offices on the eighteenth floor of the glistening new Commerce Building portions of his political fief to the south of New Orleans can be seen on a clear day. His is a handsome office, all in a beige that dramatizes the effect of his pewtery swell of hair—beige furniture of leanly modern design, a thick beige rug, and floor-to-ceiling beige drapes ribbed out over two long glass walls.

And it is a busy office: secretaries and aides—a key one of whom is his youngest son—scurry in and out, with charts for him to examine, documents for him to sign. The telephone buzzes every two or three minutes; answering it, Perez swivels and tilts his chair, almost disappearing behind his king-size desk, and voices a few staccato remarks and a political laugh or two into the mouth-piece before hanging up.

He wastes no time, for he is a man of many works—a lawyer with a rich and busy practice, a director of political and govern-mental affairs in two parishes, a statewide political string puller, adviser to the governor, Citizens' Council chieftain, drafter of legislation, cattleman, oil-lands expert, *assistant* district attorney, and *de-facto* director of the hurriedly organized school in St. Bernard Parish attended by children of white parents who chose to boycott New Orleans' "integrated" schools.

When not tackling these chores at his desk Perez is likely to be flying off to a neighboring Southern city to deliver a speech criticizing Negroes for being "willing tools of the communist con-spiracy to destroy public education and our institutions," or to Washington to appear before a congressional committee and testify against the latest proposals for new civil-rights legislation.

He was preparing for a trip just the next day to Baton Rouge to meet with state officials to devise new legal strategies to fend off the latest barrage of federal integration orders. Perez has spent a good portion of his seventy years wheeling over the straight stretch of highway between New Orleans and the state capital; at a recent testimonial banquet in Perez's honor "the judge" was presented with a special certificate from Governor Davis entitling him to exceed the speed limit while driving to and from Baton Rouge.

In the interstices of his late-afternoon work schedule Perez took time to pepper both Jewish and Catholic leaders with charges of creeping integrationism.

"The official Catholic position favoring school integration," said Perez, "is due to being drawn into the National Conference of Christians and Jews—and to accepting grants from the Ford, Carnegie, Rockefeller, and other such foundations. Just look up how much is being given to Catholic colleges by them, and you'll see what I mean."

Perez, like most other residents of his parishes, has been a member of the Catholic Church since infancy. But he said he had not made any financial contributions to the Church in the local archdiocese since 1956, when New Orleans Archbishop Joseph Francis Rummel issued a pastoral letter declaring that segregation is "morally wrong and sinful."[6]

The judge's persistent public criticisms of the Church hierarchy's proposal to integrate the parochial schools of ten south Louisiana parishes in 1962 prompted Archbishop Rummel eventually, in April, to excommunicate Perez—along with two other leading segregationists in the New Orleans area. It was the first time in Rummel's thirty-five years as a bishop of the church that he had issued an excommunication order.

The excommunication was pronounced on the ground that Perez had "flagrantly disregarded" Rummel's "fatherly counsel" by ignoring his warning to stop attacking his desegregation decision.

Although Church officials denied it, Perez claimed the excommunication order was designed to increase Church revenues and "frighten or terrorize" parents into not withdrawing their children from parochial schools as they are integrated.

"The real truth of this so-called excommunication," Perez declared, "is the fact that our Catholic friends throughout the archdiocese have learned firsthand from many priests that their Sunday collections have dropped to less than 40 per cent of normal collections, and these friendly priests further advise that if this low rate of Sunday collections continues or is further reduced, the archbishop's integration order may well have to be recalled. . . ."

Saying he planned to remain a Catholic as always, Perez added that "excommunication can't send you to hell, but integration could send your children to hell on earth."

As for Zionist Jews:

"Communism and Zionism are almost synonymous. They're un-

[6] See Chapter VI (2) for an account of the remarkable controversy over Catholic school integration in New Orleans.

American co-conspirators in the drive for integration as a means of destroying both our white Christian civilizaton and our power to resist communism."

Perez has been a front-page favorite of the anti-Jewish National States Rights party. At a New Orleans Citizens' Council rally addressed by him a few months ago hundreds of copies of *The Thunderbolt* were distributed by NSRP enthusiasts; they featured a page-one portrait of Perez under the banner headline: "PEREZ TURNS SPOTLIGHT ON THE ENEMY" (i.e., the Zionist Jews).

However, Perez dismisses the NSRP with a wave of the hand.

"I don't think any third party has any hope of success."

Hope for the segregationist South, he believes, lies rather in the election of presidential electors who are not committed in advance either to the Democratic or Republican party. He realizes that Southern senators and representatives who choose not to support the Democratic presidential candidate *could* be punished with a loss of their seniority privileges in Congress.

"If they *were* kicked out of their seniority," said Perez, "they then could form a coalition that would lead the party to become conservative rather than liberal."

Since the federal courts ordered desegregation of the first two elementary schools in New Orleans in 1960, one of Perez's pet projects has been the arrangement of schooling in his St. Bernard Parish for the children of white parents who have boycotted the schools—the children of, among others, the TV-famed "screaming mothers."

Perez employs some of his harshest language when speaking of school integration. He pictures it as the first great stride toward communistic destruction of the South and of the nation.

"How do the commy fronters, through the NAACP, propose to accomplish this integration? Here is the pattern. Beginning at the age of six, little white and Negro children—boys and girls—would be forced into continuous physical contact with each other in public schools and public-school activities. They would study together, recite together, sing together, play together, sit together, talk together, and dance together. They would eat lunch together. In this manner they would go through grade school, through high school, through college, and university. The social theory behind this procedure is that this close and intimate association during the entire formative period of their lives would, in itself, produce integration or, in other words, amalgamation of the races.

"Fantastic as it may appear, the social aim is a negroid South."

It is a fairly reliable rule of thumb that the degree of any Southern politician's racism is in direct proportion to the number of Negro voters in his bailiwick. In St. Bernard Parish only 777 of the 14,692 registered voters are Negroes; in Plaquemines Parish, only 47 of 7,212 are Negroes. Whether or not such statistics encourage Perez, he is undoubtedly the most unrestrained spokesman for white supremacy of all the South's men of large political influence. He never softens his comments with such traditional Dixieland prefaces as "We love our colored people, but . . ." or "I'm not anti-Negro, mind you, but. . . ."

Speaking of the money spent by Louisiana for the education and social welfare of Negroes, Perez said:

"At a cost of more than two hundred million dollars annually, we're supporting the bastards. And what is their contribution? They contribute more illegitimates."

On occasion Perez quotes from the *Encyclopedia Brittanica*—the 1902 edition—in support of his belief that the Negro is an inferior being: "The cranial sutures [close] much earlier in the Negro than in other races. To this premature ossification of the skull, preventing all further development of the brain, many pathologists have attributed the inherent mental inferiority of the blacks. . . . Nearly all observers admit that the Negro child is on the whole quite as intelligent as those of other human varieties, but that on arriving at puberty all further progress seems to be arrested. . . . 'It is more correct to say of the Negro that he is non-moral than immoral.' . . . No full-blooded Negro has ever been distinguished as a man of science, a poet, or an artist, and the fundamental equality claimed for him by ignorant or willful philanthropists is belied by the whole history of the race throughout the historic period."

Beyond his expressions of concern about communism and Zionism and the decline of constitutional government, Perez repeatedly elaborates on the fear that school desegregation will before long result in a spate of Congo-style rapes of white women, then a deluge of mixed marriages.

"He [the Negro] is not too far removed from the jungle in his morals, and make him believe that he is the equal of the whites, he wants that white woman," he recently declared. "We know that the objective, that the aim ultimately is not better education for the Negro, but is social equality and marriage and the bearing of mongrel children."

Perez stabbed a new cigar into his holder and clamped it between his teeth. He fired the cigar and puffed vigorously.

"Can all the double talk of the 'liberals' erase the communist-sponsored black cloud over our nation? One has to be weak-minded and thoughtless not to see the danger to our civilization," he said. "But damned few people are giving serious thought to this situation."

Then he winged his fierce eyebrows high, giving his face that disconcerting, supremely irrelevant expression of astonishment that seemed to say: "By the way, where are we?"

VI. THE CRUSADERS

Defending the White Faith

1. THE CLERGYMEN

The Bible Students

THE Reverend Dr. Thornton Stringfellow preached in Culpeper County, Virginia:

The subject in dispute is whether involuntary and hereditary slavery was ever lawful in the sight of God, the Bible being judge. I have shown by the Bible that God decreed this relation between the posterity of Canaan and the posterity of Shem and Japheth. . . . God executed this decree by aiding the posterity of Shem [to] enslave the posterity of Canaan in the days of Joshua. I have shown that when God ratified the covenant of promise with Abraham, he recognized Abraham as the owner of slaves [and] recorded his approbation of the relation by commanding Abraham to circumcise them. . . . God, as their national lawgiver, ordained by express statute that [Abraham's descendants] should buy slaves of the nations around them (the seven devoted nations excepted), and that these slaves and their increase should be a perpetual inheritance to their children. . . . When Jesus ordered His gospel to be published throughout the world, the relation of master and slave existed by law in every province and family of the Roman Empire, as it had done in the Jewish commonwealth for fifteen hundred years. . . . Jesus ordained that the legislative authority, which created this legislation in that empire, should be obeyed and honored as an ordinance of God. . . . [When] His professed followers [attempted] to disturb this relation in the apostolic churches, Jesus ordered that fellowship should be disclaimed with all such disciples, as seditious persons—whose conduct was not only dangerous to the state, but destructive to the true character of the gospel dispensation. . . .

The Reverend Dr. E. E. Colvin preached in Orangeburg, South Carolina:

The Old Testament scriptures recognize the existence of things as they are. We find that also in the New Testament. Jesus did not attempt to change or reform society in His day by the use of force. There was slavery in His day [but] never did Jesus attempt to use force or advocate force. . . .

Paul sent Onesimus, the slave, back to his former owner, Philemon. Paul did not write to Philemon and say, "You have no right to own this man." Not at all. Paul respected the law and the right to private property back in that day.

In the New Testament we find instructions given to slaves and to masters telling them what to do. "Servants, be obedient to them that are your masters according to the flesh . . . and, ye masters, do the same things unto them, forbearing threatening; knowing that your Master also is in heaven. . . ." (Ephesians 6:5, 9.)

We find no attempt whatever to overthrow slavery suddenly and by force. "Let every man abide in the same calling where he was called. Art thou called being a servant? Care not for it. . . . For he that is called in the Lord, being a servant, is the Lord's freeman: likewise also he that is called, being free, is Christ's servant. Ye are bought with a price. . . . Brother, let every man, wherein he is called, therein abide with God." (Corinthians 7:20–24.) The light of the Scriptures shows what we know by experience, that social changes take time. . . .

These two biblical justifications of slavery might well have come straight from that ante-bellum period of the South when ministers of the Gospel were energetically defending the "peculiar institution" against the attacks of the despised Abolitionists.

One did: The Reverend Dr. Stringfellow's message was delivered in the 1850's, not long before the outbreak of the Civil War.

The other did not: The Reverend Dr. Colvin's sermon was delivered in the 1950's, not long after the Supreme Court's school integration decision.

Just as the King James Bible was searched more than a century ago for arguments in favor of slavery, so it is gleaned today for passages that can be interpreted as justifications for racial segregation.

This is one of the most important and effective activities of the organized segregationists—for the South, despite all the years of witty assaults by the Darrows and Menckens and divers other evolutionists, skeptics, and scoffers, is still the "Bible Belt" of the nation.

The Reverend Dr. Stringfellow of Culpeper was credited with writing the most influential biblical rationalization of ante-bellum slavery, his *Scriptural and Statistical Views in Favor of Slavery.*

Of the many tracts published since May 17, 1954, in elaboration of the thesis that God and Jesus favor *segregation,* probably the most influential—certainly the most widely distributed—has been a little sermon composed by a Jackson, Mississippi, clergyman named G. T. Gillespie.

The late Reverend Dr. Gillespie's *A Christian View on Segregation* has been distributed by the hundreds of thousands from the officers of the Citizens' Council Association. First published less than a year after The Decision, it continues to be one of the most popular items on the CC Association's list of "educational literature."

Dr. Gillespie was born and reared in Mississippi and trained in theology at Union Seminary in Virginia, and Columbia University. He served in Presbyterian pulpits in Oklahoma and Mississippi before becoming president of Belhaven College, a small denominational school at Jackson, in 1921. It was in November of the year of his retirement as Belhaven's president, 1954, that he delivered his *Christian View on Segregation* before the Mississippi Synod of the Presbyterian Church.

It is helpful to examine Gillespie's sermon in some detail, for it is something of a compendium of the religio-racial beliefs of great masses of white Southern Christians. It is a presentation of the biblical "evidence" of what so many religious white Southerners "feel in their bones"—that surely God would not insist that they integrate with Negroes.

"While the Bible contains no clear mandate for or against segregation as between the white and Negro races," Gillespie con-

ceded, "it does furnish considerable data from which valid infer-
ences may be drawn in support of the general principle of segregation as an important feature of the Divine purpose and Providence
throughout the ages."

The first act of apartheid performed by God—as discerned by
Gillespie—was the placing of a mark upon Cain which distinguished his descendants from those of his brother Seth. (Genesis
4:11–26.)

The "promiscuous intermarriage" of Seth's descendants ("sons
of God") with Cain's descendants ("daughters of Men") "resulted
in the complete breakdown of family life and such widespread immorality and wickedness as to provoke the Lord to destroy the
earth with the flood." (Genesis 6:1–7.) From this tragic story
Gillespie drew the inference that "the intermarriage of dissimilar
groups, whether the differences be moral, cultural, or physical, is
not conducive to the preservation of wholesome family life or to
morality, and therefore is contrary to the purpose and will of God."

It is from the ninth chapter of Genesis that the segregationists
have always developed their main argument that God intended to
divide mankind into three races and keep them separated. Especially interesting to them are verses eighteen through twenty-seven
in the chapter, the familiar passage which describes Noah's overin-
dulgence in alcoholic spirits. The King James version of the passage
reads:

And the sons of Noah, that went forth of the ark, were Shem,
and Ham, and Japeth: and Ham is the father of Canaan.

These are the three sons of Noah: and of them was the whole
earth overspread.

And Noah began to be an husbandman, and he planted a vine-
yard:

And he drank of the wine, and was drunken; and he was uncovered within his tent.

And Ham, the father of Canaan, saw the nakedness of his
father, and told his two brothers without.

And Shem and Japheth took a garment, and laid it upon both
their shoulders, and went backward, and covered the nakedness of
their father; and their faces were backward, and they saw not their
father's nakedness.

And Noah awoke from his wine, and knew what his younger
son had done unto him:
And he said, Cursed be Canaan; a servant of servants shall he
be unto his brethren.
And he said, Blessed be the Lord God of Shem; and Canaan
shall be his servant.
God shall enlarge Japheth, and he shall dwell in the tents of
Shem; and Canaan shall be his servant.

Using Genesis 9 as a starting point, the Reverend Dr. Gillespie
fashioned the following ethnological history:

"After the flood the three sons of Noah—Shem, Ham, and Japheth—became the progenitors of three distinct racial groups,
which were to repeople and overspread the earth. The descendants
of Shem migrated eastward and occupied most of Asia; the descendants of Japheth migrated westward and ultimately occupied
the continent of Europe, while the children of Ham moved generally
southward toward the tropics and occupied the continent of Africa,
and possibly southern Asia and the islands of the Pacific.

"This brief record, while affirming the unity of the race[s], also
implies that an all-wise Providence has 'determined the times before
appointed, and the bounds of their habitation.' Which same Providence, by determining the climatic and other physical conditions
under which many successive generations of the several racial
groups should live, is thereby equally responsible for the distinct
racial characteristics which seem to have become fixed in prehis-
toric times, and which are chiefly responsible for the segregation of
racial groups across the centuries and in our time."

Moving on to Genesis 11, Gillespie interpreted the Lord's "confusion of tongues" which wrecked the Tower of Babel project as
another phase of His segregationist campaign. "[It] was an act of
special Divine Providence to frustrate the mistaken efforts of god-
less men to assure the permanent integration of the peoples of the
earth."[1]

[1] Commenting on the frequent employment of Noah's curse and the
Tower of Babel work stoppage as biblical defenses of segregation, the
general board of social and economic relations of the Methodist Church
remarked not long ago:
"Genesis 9:18–27 is occasionally used as the basis for saying that God
placed a curse on Ham and his descendants, turning them black and assign-

Dr. Gillespie found numerous other pieces of evidence in the Old Testament which convinced him that God was a segregationist who disapproved of "mixed marriages." Referring to later chapters of Genesis, Gillespie pointed out that "the Covenant of Circumcision instituted by God provided a sign or seal which was to distinguish and set apart in a most significant way the 'Seed of Abraham,' or the Hebrew people, from all the other people of the earth throughout all generations." The Mississippi minister also found guides to the solution of today's race problems in Moses' regulation against the crossbreeding of diverse strains of cattle and the mixing of wool and linen in a garment (Leviticus 19:19), and the opposition expressed by Moses and Ezra to the intermarriage of Jews with heathens (Deuteronomy 7:3 and Ezra 9–10).

The New Testament did not yield Dr. Gillespie quite as much segregationist evidence as did the Old. He had to concede that Jesus made it "abundantly clear that the redeeming love of Christ knows no limitations of class or condition or nationality or race." He could only make the negative argument that Jesus did not specifically denounce the "racial distinctions" existing at the time He lived, "nor did He set plans on foot to abolish them and to bring about amalgamation of the Jews and the Samaritans, or of any other races."

It might be expected that Gillespie would have encountered some difficulty in identifying the apostle Paul as a segregationist, for Paul had written to the Colossians that once they became faithful servants of Jesus Christ "there is neither Greek nor Jew, circumcision or uncircumcision, barbarian, Scythian, bond nor free: but

---

ing them a place of inferiority and servility in society. It should be noted that the purpose of the passage is to explain why the Israelites came to a position of dominance over the Canaanites—not over the peoples of Africa. This is accomplished by appealing to the curse of Noah, a curse being thought by ancients to have permanent effect. It will be noted in a careful reading of the passage that: (1) God placed a curse on no one; (2) Noah did the cursing after being awakened from a drunken stupor; (3) Canaan was the one actually cursed, not Ham; (4) there is no indication of God's having approved Noah's act or of his having implemented it in any way; and (5) no reference is made to anybody's having been given a different color.

"Genesis 11:1–9 records the incident of God's confounding the builders of the Tower of Babel by confusing their language and scattering them

Christ is all, and in all." (Colossians 3:11.) But Gillespie had no trouble with it; he identified this "unity of all believers in Christ, regardless of their racial differences," as a *spiritual* relationship rather than a *social* or *physical* relationship.

"That Paul had in mind the absolute uniformity of believers in external relations and the wiping out of all distinctions of race, nationality, social status, sex or cultural heritage, is disproven by the fact that Paul never ceased to identify himself as a member of the Jewish race, and he made very practical use of his right to Roman citizenship. He recognized the master-slave relationship prevalent in Greek and Roman society, and enjoined obedience to the reciprocal duties arising therefrom. . . ."

Aside from biblical matters, Gillespie—like fellow white Mississippians who are not men of the cloth—felt that the attack on the Southern Way of Life that commenced with the May 17, 1954, decision was a communist-inspired movement to foster mixed marriages and thereby destroy the white race.

"[A] very considerable part of the violent agitation against segregation stems from sources outside the Negro race, and outside of America, and coincides with the worldwide movement for racial amalgamation which has its fountainhead in Moscow," he declared. "Here, therefore, is the crux of this whole problem of racial relations, whether we face it in America or in the world at large. It is essentially a choice between the Anglo-Saxon ideal of racial integrity maintained by a consistent application of the principle of segregation and the Communist goal of amalgamation, implemented by the wiping out of all distinctions and the fostering of the most intimate contact between the races in all the relations of life. . . .

"A recent issue of the Pittsburgh *Courier*, a representative Negro newspaper, in voicing intense resentment against Dr. Norman Vin-

---

over the face of the earth. The passage can hardly be used to support the idea that God ordained separate 'races.' It should be noted: (1) that the scattering of men was a judgment of God on man's arrogance, not a part of his original intention for the human family; (2) that the story of Pentecost in Acts 2 clearly indicates that it is God's intention in the messianic age to reverse the disruption of Babel (representatives of 'every nation under heaven' heard and understood the apostles, and all men were incited to join the Church of Christ). The Tower of Babel story is evidence of what God does not want, rather than of what He intends!"

cent Peale of *Look* magazine for advising a negro girl against marrying a white boy, said: 'It is not possible to have people of different race, nationalities, and religions living together, working together, and playing together and bar them from marrying. . . . Intermarriage is as necessarily Christian as interfaith and interracial education. We will have to have desegregation in that area of life, and it has already begun to move heavily.'

"Under our system of compulsory education," said Gillespie, "abandonment of the principle of segregation and the enforcement of the policy of integration in the schools, especially in the South and in other communities in which the negro population approximates or exceeds the white population, could have but one or two possible results: either a state of constant friction and tension would develop between the two groups, which would greatly complicate the problem of discipline and administration, and ultimately destroy the morale and impair the efficiency of the public-school system, or, on the other hand, it would lead to the cultivation of such attitudes and social intimacies as would normally and inevitably result in intermarriage."

At the November 1954 Mississippi synod which was so addressed by Dr. Gillespie a vote was taken on a memorial from the Presbyterian Church's general assembly. The memorial called for the opening of Presbyterian churches and schools to Negroes. The Mississippi synod rejected it by a vote of 62 to 40.

A Diversity of Conviction

In contrast with the great sunderings experienced by several American religious groups during the ante-bellum controversy over slavery, the *national* and *regional* spokesmen for the largest denominations today have been almost unanimous in expressing disapproval of racial segregation.

Statements endorsing the 1954 Supreme Court decision have been issued by major governing bodies of the National Council of Churches of Christ, the Roman Catholic, Methodist, Episcopal, Presbyterian, and Congregational churches, the American Baptist Convention, and several others—even the Southern Baptist Convention.

Fairly representative of the statements approving The Decision is the resolution adopted by the Texas synod of the Presbyterian Church, United States (South), in September 1954:

The synod affirms that enforced segregation of the races is discrimination which is out of harmony with Christian theology and ethics, and that the church, in its relationships to cultural patterns, should lead rather than follow;

That trustees, directors, and officers of institutions and agencies of the synod be urged to adopt policies for operating [them] on an unsegregated basis;

That the presbyteries be requested to urge sessions of local churches on the scriptural basis of faith in the Lord Jesus Christ without reference to race. . . .

But however united the denominations' higher clerical leaders have been in their stand against segregation, it is nevertheless a fact that no impressive amount of integration has yet occurred in the actual church houses and denominational schools of the South. The ringing pronouncements of the various church-governing bodies have not, in truth, had a decisive influence on the attitudes of their several flocks toward segregation in public schools or elsewhere.

The Reverend Dr. George M. Brydon, registrar and historiographer of the Episcopal Diocese of Virginia, recently commented on this apparent cleavage between the clergy and laity: "[M]any of the clergy of the Episcopal Church and of the Protestant denominations have accepted the newly stated ruling concerning integration in the public schools as though it were the enunciation of a Christian principle, and have issued statements to that effect, while vast numbers of the laymen of all churches are equally strong in their conviction that enforced segregation of all public schools is an evil which must be resisted at all costs. As a result of this diversity of conviction there is growing among the laity of all the churches [a] sense of resentment against the clergy which is capable of bearing bitter fruit."

Brydon, who strongly favors maintaining segregation, makes—with graceful restraint—a point which is often missed by champions of integration who dwell north of the Mason-Dixon line:

"One would be exceedingly ill-advised to take the stand that refusal to integrate the public schools in the Southern states is the result of domination of state governments by criminal or lawless elements, and that the Christian forces in these states have been cowed into silence by such forces. And one would be equally ill-advised to make the patronizing statement that 'some devout Christians believe in segregation.' Speaking for Virginia alone, I can say that from my own wide experience and correspondence I am convinced that outside of the transmontane counties of southwestern Virginia, the city of Norfolk and its suburban section, and the Washington-suburban area of counties and cities on the south side of the Potomac River, 80 or more out of every 100 lay members of the Episcopal Church in this state will stand up and be counted in favor of separate schools for the children of the two races. . . . This percentage I believe to be true also in the leading Protestant churches in the state; and I believe it to be true generally throughout the Southern states."

Christ and Antichrist in Texas

The Reverend Dr. Brydon's observations appear in a slim volume entitled *Essays on Segregation,* which has enjoyed nothing like the mass circulation of Dr. Gillespie's *A Christian View on Segregation* but which has had perhaps even greater influence on some of the more cerebral theologians of the South—certainly among those of the Episcopal persuasion.

In addition to Brydon's composition, the little book contains defenses of racial segregation written by the Reverend Edward B. Guerry, rector of the parishes of St. James and St. John in Charleston, South Carolina; the Reverend Albert S. Thomas, retired bishop of South Carolina; the Reverend Henry T. Egger, rector of St. Peter's Episcopal Church in Charlotte, North Carolina; the Reverend James P. Dees, rector of Trinity Church in Statesville, North Carolina; and the Reverend T. Robert Ingram, rector of St. Thomas' Church and school in Houston, Texas.

Ingram, the editor and publisher of *Essays on Segregation,* directs the activities of a church and school of severely modernistic design in one of the vast, new, affluently barbecue-pitted residential subdivisions of Houston. From his parish house, a modified ranch-style structure whose architect obviously relished the use of glass and cement, Ingram also runs a small publishing operation called St. Thomas Press. The books on the St. Thomas Press list are directed against "radical" modernism in the Episcopal Church, government participation in education, the movements to abolish the death penalty, and racial desegregation.

The interest of the rector of St. Thomas' in preserving segregation does not stem from a Southern heritage. Denver, Colorado, was the town of his birth and youth. Nor was the religious impulse very strong in him during the first thirty-odd years of his life.

"I was reared in a Baptist family," he said to a recent visitor, "but I quickly became agnostic and 'Liberal.' I didn't go to a church for many years."

After schooling in journalism, he worked for the *Oil and Gas Journal* in Tulsa, Oklahoma, then during World War II served as a line officer in the Navy amphibious forces. Returning to newspapering after the war, he worked for the Honolulu *Star-Bulletin,* then the Boston *Globe.*

The inclination to Christianity had been gaining strength within him since the war, and while living in Boston he decided, in his late thirties, to enter the Cambridge Episcopal Seminary. After being ordained as a minister, he served at churches in Weirton, West Virginia, and Abilene, Texas, before taking up his duties at St. Thomas' in Houston in 1953.

Now forty-eight, with a ruddily attractive wife and an extraordinarily pretty blond stepdaughter of kindergarten age, the former amphib officer and newspaper beat reporter is a man of settled life and, he says, settled convictions.

He is a lean, dark-haired, dark-eyed man of studied composure, who makes black-or-white, either-or declarations which seem never to be sullied by doubt.

"The movement toward integration is a denial of Christ," he said, gently but firmly. "It is part of an effort to create *one* society in which there are no distinctions or differences. This is part and parcel of the spirit of the Antichrist."

In his churchly dim, book-walled study his desk is dramatically situated. Beyond the room's single window behind him a large crucifix rises from a low wall; as Ingram sits and talks, the cross remains constantly in view, just above his right shoulder.

"The nature of the Christian faith is that it resists any attempts to achieve its goals in *this* world. To attempt to do so is to try to get along without God. It is a rebellion against God to try to achieve on earth the fruits of *heaven*."

The "race problem," like wars between nations, is something to be solved in heaven rather than in this life, Ingram believes. Indeed —so goes his thinking—imperfect institutions and conditions on earth are desirable and necessary; for they provide pains and discouragements for earthlings to *overcome* in order to reach heaven.

"Faith . . . demands that we turn to no other support, we reach out for no other power, we contend for no other salvation, we seek no heaven other than that held out to the eyes of faith through the Resurrection," he has written. "We cannot escape the awful personal demands upon us of the Gospel of Jesus Christ by trying to eliminate the very powers His grace enables us to overcome. We cannot be a victor over this world if we destroy the powers of this world which we must battle; for without a battle there is no victory."

It is "obvious" to Ingram that in heaven there will be "unity," with none of the discontents or "aberrations" that are characteristic of life on earth.

"All will be integrated [in heaven], with neither male nor female, black nor white."

However, the hope of achieving such "unity" on earth—such "heaven on earth," if you please—is a Judaic hope and a "socialist hope," but not a Christian hope, said Ingram. It is his conclusion that the erroneous, "liberal Christian" notion that the Gospel should be made "relevant to this world" goes back to the "Unitarian heresy in New England."

Ingram feels it is unchristian to try to alter (i.e., destroy) "the basic nature of things" on earth, for these things provide Jesus Christ with "enemies" to overcome—to overcome, that is, for the benefit of the faithful.

"[Christ] could not both destroy them and overcome them. The destroyer, therefore, works against Christ, especially if he would destroy the enemies of Christ."

Such patterns of reasoning are at times a bit difficult for the uninitiated to follow. Much easier to grasp is the fact that Ingram considers racial segregation a part of "the basic nature of things."

He feels it is in accordance with God's "rules of harmony" for there to be "blacks" and "whites"—and it would be disharmonious for them to integrate.

In a turn of thought which, for Ingram, is rather atypically terrestrial, he expressed the old Dixieland horror of having a Negro for a son-in-law and, in consequence, a grandchild who does not inherit his hue from the maternal side of the family. "Have you," asked the rector of St. Thomas', "tried to imagine fondling a little black baby that's not your own?"

But Ingram's objection to racial intermingling is presented not simply as an expression of distaste at the thought of it. He claims it is his desire to prevent the "Negro community" from being *destroyed* (a favorite word of the rector's).

"The people who are most enraged at something they call genocide, that is, the murder of a whole race or nation or culture of people, make no bones about their own passion to destroy any vestige of what the South has long known and loved as the Negro community, though without open advocacy of violence."

The "long-known and loved" Negroes of Houston, said Ingram, have a "well-developed community" just as there is a well-developed community of whites in the city.

"We've lived side by side for a long time and we get along pretty well. Now we are told it is contrary to the will of God to have two separate communities."

And he asked, "Can one absorb the other without destroying it?"

Ingram's answer is "No"—and his implication is that everyone will be better off if segregation is maintained in all the social institutions this side of Paradise. It is crystal clear to Ingram that the current campaign for desegregation in Houston and elsewhere is part of a broad program drafted by the devil to bring about world government, "unity," "socialism," and "destruction."

"Unity, socialism, and the world, then, are the real issues involved in what is called 'integration,' " Ingram writes in the introduction to the *Essays on Segregation*. "The very word bespeaks that much. For the South, where the kingdom of God is taken seriously and where a very workable social order has flowered under the Providence of God for a people, both Black and White, who give God both the glory and the sovereignty, the issue is whether the Southern culture, independent, distinctive, and unwilling to acknowledge a national divinity that must be enthroned to achieve heaven on earth, shall be 'eliminated.' The South is clearly 'obstructionist' to the vision of an 'earth-located spirit state.' The real question is not whether Christians should love one another, or whether they sit next to each other in school, but whether our pilgrimage is limited to the march of the masses toward a unified or 'integrated' heaven on earth, or whether heaven would cease to be heaven if it were cast in terms of this world. As long as the argument rages in the field of something called 'race relations,' the real struggle will go on in blind fury. For it is not the races only that must disappear and be brought into conformity with the requirements of a world state: so with the sexes, so with parents and children, so with nations, states, tribes, and empires. All must go and be swallowed up in the maw of the great monad, theologically familiar to students of oriental mysticism as religion, and to traditional Christianity as Satan."

Strolling outside, the rector and his visitor were surrounded by the bright banks of flowers of his wife's patio garden. The weather had been muggy and tense all that day, but now there was the sweet beginning of a gentle rain, and his little stepdaughter skipped through it joyfully. The raindrops stirred the white camellias and seemed to sharpen the fragrance of the jasmine and the olivewood.

Reflecting on the evils that would result if integration and "unity" ever came to pass in this world, Ingram nevertheless indicated with a knowing little smile that he was not unduly alarmed. All such earthly problems will be solved when the prophecy that God will *destroy* the earth is fulfilled—and he feels that the day of the great holocaust is not far off. It is true that Houston has a civil-defense program, but the rector of St. Thomas' is convinced that nuclear bomb shelters will not give anyone protection *that day*.

Mozart in North Carolina

The spirit of apartheid that prevails in many areas of the Southern ministry is expressed not merely in occasional sermons and essays. Some pastors have become very active leaders in the organization of Citizens' Councils and similar white supremacy groups. Clergymen seem particularly active in defending the segregationist faith on the seaboard: for examples, the Citizens' Councils of Virginia have been headed by the Reverend Henry J. Davis, and the Reverend James P. Dees has been president of the Tar Heel version of the CCs, the North Carolina Defenders of States Rights, Inc. Both Davis and Dees have been members of the editorial board of *The Citizens' Council,* the official CC Association newspaper published by Bill Simmons in Mississippi, and Dees has long served as a member of the board of directors of the segregationist Federation for Constitutional Government.

The North Carolina organization headed by Dees recently issued the following statement of principles as an "outline for an educational program that is in need of being set before the people of the South to counteract the propaganda of the ultraliberals":

Racial segregation is in accord with the natural law which is a product of God's creation. It provides the opportunity for members of different races to mature more wholesomely in their own schools, churches, and other institutions. . . . Federal and State constitutions and legislative acts do not deny the right to segregate racially, nor do they require racial integration. Judges do not have the power to make the law. . . . Where racial integration is effected, instances of crime soar, and academic standards and school discipline deteriorate, and economic values are destroyed. . . . Reliable anthropologists tell us that racial integration is among the major factors contributing to the decay and fall of the Egyptian, Greek, and Roman civilizations, among others, and has resulted in some quarters in a decadent and disease-ridden people.

"Of one thing we are certain," Dees emphasized. "The races of the earth are not equal. They are not equal mentally, morally, nor are they the same in any number of ways physically. And when you mix a lower with a higher, then you drag down the higher."

The Reverend James Parker Dees is rector of Trinity Episcopal Church and priest-in-charge of Holy Cross Church in the small city of Statesville in western North Carolina. He was born in Greenville in the tidewater flatlands of North Carolina in 1915, and can lay claim to such illustrious forebears as William Bradford, the first governor of the Plymouth Colony in the 1620's, and Samuel Johnston, the first man elected "President of the United States" under the Articles of Confederation.

Like his fellow Episcopal clergyman in Texas, T. Robert Ingram, Dees came late to the ministry. After graduating from the University of North Carolina as a political-science and economics major in 1938, he worked a few years for the Atlantic Coast Line Railroad in his home town of Greenville. Then during World War II he served with the 88th Infantry Division in North Africa and Italy. He was ordained as a minister in 1949, at the age of thirty-four, after three years of study at the Virginia Theological Seminary in Alexandria.

He and his family live in a roomy old frame house on a pleasantly shaded street within easy walking distance of downtown Statesville.

As he spoke to a visitor about the inferiority of the Negro race, Dees—his white shirt collarless, his black trousers supported by suspenders also of clerical black—sat in an ancient rocking chair. A huge grandfather's clock of rich, dark wood gleamed softly in a corner of the vast living room, hypnotically ticking away the morning's minutes.

"Down here in the South we have a biracial culture that has just grown up naturally. After the war [the War Between the States] Negroes attended white churches for a time, but after a while they got out and built their own churches. Mixing the races doesn't make them equal; it results in the disintegration of the cultures of each one.

"It doesn't help anybody to tell him he's inferior, and I don't like to do it; I don't want to alienate the affection of Negroes. But even a Negro preacher over in Charlotte told me the other day that Negroes have had nothing to contribute to the scene except what they got from the whites.

"I know those are pretty hard words," he added. And he voiced a regretful laugh, as if to say it grieves him to bear such unpleasant tidings about fellow creatures of God.

Dees has an impressive earnestness. He is a stocky, rough-hewn fellow who is given to bursts of chesty laughter. His eyes are pale blue, and about them is a constant expression of puzzlement at the fact that the truths which he grasps so easily seem somehow to elude many other people.

By championing segregation, Dees feels that he is helping to protect the racial interests of Negroes as well as whites.

"What is at stake here is the maintenance of the Negro race. The loudest voices are proclaiming indirectly that there is virtue in the destruction of the Negro race. This I fail to see, and I declare, I believe that it is contrary to divine will."

If integration were to come to Statesville, Dees foresees, crime would increase and present property values would decrease.

"And why should white people be compelled to take such a loss?" he asked, in an engagingly earthly, materialistic turn of thought. "White people have a right to their own property and have a right to preserve the value of it."

He foresees, too, that Negroes would not be content merely with *school* integration. The NAACP, he has written, "is concerned with forcing total race mixing, with the Negro's sitting down with and among members of the White race, placing their children with our children, attending the same hotels, eating in the same restaurants, sitting with you in the theaters, living in your neighborhood; through the bloc vote to run your government, sit with you and your children in busses, trains, airplanes, and so on and so on. . . . I [am] dreadfully concerned about efforts to induce racial integration, which will lead to racial amalgamation, which will lead to a Negroid or mulatto culture in the South and finally throughout our country."

In a pamphlet entitled *The Destroyers* Dees quotes a comment made by General Sumter Lowry in a 1958 talk to the United Daughters of the Confederacy at Tampa, Florida: "If you throw little white and colored children of both sexes together in an intimate social relationship from the time they are five or six years of age . . . it can end at only one place . . . with or without the benefit of marriage."

So nightmarish is this vision to Dees that he feels it is bound to be a Red plot.

"Our chief adversaries in the racial crisis are not the overzealous and misguided leaders of the Negro organization, but rather the agents of international communism." Nor is the enemy outside our gates, he is convinced. "I am of the opinion that the forces of international communism are centered, not across the sea in Moscow, but in these United States, in New York City. I have read much to the effect that the Bolshevik Revolution was financed by Wall Street money."

Speaking of Nikita Khrushchev's tour of the United States, Dees said he had read "evidence" that indicated the "major object" of the Soviet premier's visit "was *not* to put the American people to sleep with his peace talk and his coexistence rubbish, but to get money to bolster his sagging economy."

Such views as these are strikingly similar to those expressed by the veteran Jew-baiter, Gerald L. K. Smith of Los Angeles, in his monthly magazine, *The Cross and the Flag*.

In fact, Dees and Smith express great admiration for each other. The November 1960 issue of Smith's magazine featured a portrait of Dees on its cover and predicted that "his name will go down in history as one who dared to be courageously right when the whole church bureaucracy of America was threatened with modernism, communism, and treason." Smith enthusiastically offered to mail his readers Dees' pamphlet, *The Destroyers*—at twenty-five cents a copy.

"I think Gerald L. K. Smith is the greatest patriot in this country today," said Dees. "He is a profound Christian. I know him personally, and I have a deep respect for him."

Dees left the living room for a minute, then brought forth a copy of Smith's "handbook for Patriots dealing with issues on which America will rise or fall," a 1958 pamphlet entitled *Matters of Life and Death*.

In his "handbook" Smith pictures and describes various Americans who "personify the RIGHT" (i.e., are working for the "survival of our precious America") and others who "personify the WRONG" (i.e., are working in behalf of the "communist-Jewish conspiracy" to mongrelize and enslave America).

Among the pairs of RIGHT guys and WRONG guys in the Gerald L. K. Smith lineup are these:

RIGHT: Mississippi Senator James Eastland—WRONG: Chief Justice Earl Warren.

RIGHT: Arkansas Governor Orval Faubus—WRONG: former United States Attorney General Herbert Brownell.

RIGHT: the late Senator Joseph McCarthy—WRONG: Mrs. Eleanor Roosevelt.

RIGHT: Virginia Senator Harry Byrd—WRONG: the late General George Marshall.

RIGHT: General Douglas MacArthur—WRONG: Golda Meir.

RIGHT: Lawrence Welk—WRONG: Louis Armstrong.

The suggestions that Smith has had "fascistic" inclinations are "malarkey, a lot of baloney," said Dees. "Anybody who fights communism is going to be smeared from 'A' to izzard—and they've done a good job of discrediting Mr. Smith."

Dees conceded that he "detects a bitterness in Mr. Smith toward his enemies."

"I feel like there are good Jews and bad Jews; to Mr. Smith they're all bad." Dees laughed, but then added: "I've seen a lot of evidence that seems to substantiate his contentions."

Some of those contentions, said Dees, have been "substantiated" by Robert Welch of the John Birch Society, who also is much admired by the Statesville rector. Dees remarked incidentally that he had "got word" well in advance that the "Liberals" were planning to mount the recent public attack on Welch.

"But Welch is going to come out of this better off than ever," he predicted.

As do most segregationists sooner or later, Dees employs the old bird-watchers' and cattle-breeders' argument in defense of the Southern Way of Life.

"Among the things that support me in the view that integration is contrary to the moral law revealed in nature is enlightened common sense as you look around you. Do black birds intermingle with the blue birds? Does the redwing fly with the crows? Would it make sense for my senior warden to mix Black Angus cattle with his pure-bred Herefords? Common sense, knotty-headed common sense, cries out against it, 'No!' It is abhorrent to the natural created order."

The rector of Statesville would prefer that both races "not force issues" but "let the spirit of God work through them," thereby permitting the "normal" development of the two racial cultures.

"These crackpot integrationists are trying to take nature and bend it to their own will," he protested.

Dees finds in all cultures "an element of spirit—either the Spirit of God or the Spirit of Man." The "Negro culture," he feels, is dominated by the Spirit of Man—by "the elements of jungle culture."

"That's the spirit behind the beatnik movement and rock and roll. They are primitive and predominantly sex motivated. I think it's fairly well recognized," he added, "that jazz came to this country through the brothels of New Orleans."

As Dees was speaking of musical matters, his wife—a slim, neat lady who is descended from a fine old North Carolina family—entered the room to remind her husband that he was scheduled to address a school gathering that morning and therefore must get a move on.

Dees agreed, but he first wished to play a record on the hi-fi for his visitor.

After a bit of fumbling he finally got the needle in place, and there was music.

It was Mozart's "Concerto in C Major for Flute, Harp, and Orchestra," and its sounds were pure and beautiful indeed.

"Can you conceive of this in a Negro culture?" he asked. And after a pause he added with quiet emphasis: "That's all the answer you need."

Then another thought occurred to him.

"Can you conceive of this on *Ed Sullivan's integrated TV show?*"

And the rector's chesty laughter rose grandly with the delicate melody of Mozart's harps and flutes.

2. SIN AND SOCIOLOGY IN NEW ORLEANS

THE "diversity of conviction" about the rights and wrongs of racial segregation has troubled the souls of God-fearing people all through the South. But nowhere has The Problem caused as much spiritual agony as it has among the Roman Catholics of New Orleans.

For the past seven years the Church's hierarchy in New Orleans has repeatedly issued statements denouncing segregation as "morally wrong," "unjust," and/or "sinful," and has again and again expressed an intent to integrate Catholic schools forthwith and with all morally deliberate speed. At this writing, the latest order from the New Orleans Archdiocese is that Catholic schools will operate on an integrated basis during the 1962–63 academic year. When summer vacation time arrived in June 1962, however, the parochial schools of the New Orleans area were as segregated as ever.

This delay in Catholic desegregation in New Orleans has resulted from a remarkable debate of the "theological issues" of the race question—the most fascinating such debate, perhaps, in the history of the South.

Of course the famous "screaming mothers" of New Orleans in late 1960 were gratifyingly colorful subjects for human-interest newspaper articles. But, actually, they were minor characters indeed in the story of segregation v. integration in New Orleans.

In reality, much more prominent roles in "the New Orleans story" have been played by one man and one institution. The institution: the Roman Catholic Church. The man: a brilliant, somewhat gloomy-visaged, harassingly persistent banker-lawyer named Emile Wagner.

The dialogue between Wagner, a lifelong Catholic, and the church hierarchy of New Orleans has been not merely an exercise in theology, not merely an argument over whether the angels on the pinhead are integrated or segregated. It has had crucial "practical" significance for both the parochial and public schools of all Louisiana—and of all the South.

The story of the "Second Battle of New Orleans" has often been misunderstood simply because a few elementary statistics have not been adequately reported by the press. One important fact is that about one-fourth of Louisiana's pupils attend parochial schools—most of them in the 140-odd white Catholic and 40-odd Negro Catholic schools of New Orleans and the ten surrounding parishes of southern Louisiana (the area of the Catholic archdiocese of New Orleans). Another fact: of the 49,000 pupils in the segregated *parochial* schools of the city of New Orleans about 8,000 are Negro. And still another: of the 91,000 *public*-school pupils in the city, 54,000 are Negro.[1]

If the Catholics of New Orleans had accepted their hierachy's conclusion that segregation is "unjust," "morally wrong," and "sinful," then 8,000 Negro parochial-school pupils in the city of New Orleans alone would probably have been desegregated several years ago. And almost inevitably then a full one-fourth of Louisiana's grade-school pupils would have become "integrated"— practically so, or, at the least, in principle.

Had this occurred, it is inconceivable that segregation could have been maintained—maintained for long, anyway—in the public schools of Louisiana. The South's stiff resistance to the Supreme Court's 1954 decision would have had its back broken. For Louisiana is Deep South. When white Louisiana surrenders, the skirmishes (in Mississippi, say, and in Alabama and Georgia

[1] As of June 1962, 12 of New Orleans' 54,000 Negro public-school pupils were attending classes with whites. In other words, public-school integration of Negroes in New Orleans was by then approximately 00.02 per cent complete.

These 12 were the only ones of the 271,000 Negro public-school pupils in Louisiana who, so far, had been desegregated. Thus at the close of the 1961-62 academic year public-school integration in Louisiana as a whole was approximately 00.004 per cent complete.

and South Carolina) will continue, but the war over segregation will have ended.

In the realm of reality, however, there are not many signs that white Louisiana will abandon the Southern Way of Life any time soon. Nor does Emile Wagner of New Orleans appear to be in the mood to surrender.

About the time of the Supreme Court school-desegregation decision Archbishop Joseph Francis Rummel of New Orleans, an elderly man with failing eyesight, announced that he was considering a plan for the integration of Catholic schools in the southern Louisiana parishes under his spiritual jurisdiction. But so many segregationists in his flock—among them Emile Wagner— reacted so strongly against the idea that the archbishop chose soon afterward to assure the faithful that parochial schools would not be integrated "in advance of" the integration of New Orleans' public schools.

This was scant assurance to segregationists, for public-school integration—at least in token form—seemed inevitable. A school desegregation suit, *Bush* v. *Orleans School Board,* had been drifting through the courts for many months. A decision on it was bound to come sooner or later, and after the May 17, 1954, Supreme Court ruling, it seemed obvious that the decision promised to be in favor of the Negro petitioners for public-school integration.

By August 1955 Archbishop Rummel—and his diocesan advisers—apparently decided anew that he should let his flock know that he intended soon to desegregate the Catholic grade schools. He did this with a curiously indirect statement that announced that they would not be integrated in the fall of 1955, but which hinted strongly that they might be integrated in the fall of 1956.

"Although the ruling of the Supreme Court is thoroughly in accord with the principles and teachings of the Catholic Church, immediate integration would not be prudent or practical," the archbishop stated. "We are confronted with the tradition of segregation over a period of one hundred and fifty years. . . . [But] obviously it would not be just to defer integration indefinitely. . . . During the intervening year pastoral letters and other instructive communications will serve to prepare the way for the most propitious plan to be followed."

The archbishop's statement was accompanied by a comparatively quiet campaign on the part of New Orleans' more "liberal" clergy to "prepare the way" for integration by equating segregationist sentiment with "un-Catholic behavior." At the same time quite a few "conservative" clergymen in the archdiocese opposed integration, and the great majority of white Catholic parents opposed it.

Wagner was sorely nettled by the Catholic campaign to pave the way for peaceful integration. Also, after a personal chat with the archbishop, he became convinced that parochial-school integration was planned for 1956—and he recognized that this probably would hasten public-school integration.

So it was in December 1955 that Wagner wrote the first significant letter in his extraordinary dialogue with Archbishop Rummel.

"[I]t seems that it is quite the mode," he wrote the archbishop, "for some 'liberal and progressive' clergymen and laymen to stamp any Catholic who is intellectually convinced that segregation per se has no moral significance, as un-Catholic, not having the 'Catholic viewpoint,' and lacking in 'Catholic mindedness'. . . .

"The bald fact is that although it is glibly stated by integrationists that to favor segregation is un-Catholic, none of these integrationists has ever taken the trouble to prove the assertion. . . .

"[T]he morality of segregation was not even questioned prior to some ten or fifteen years ago coincidental with the coming into prominence of the NAACP.

"In my estimation of the matter," wrote Wagner, "something more than the mere unsubstantiated declaration of any one man or group of men, of course with the exception of His Holiness the Pope, when speaking 'ex cathedra,' is required to convince intelligent Catholics that they are guilty of sin when they espouse the cause of segregation.

"In fact, since the denunciation of segregation implies the promulgation of a matter of morals, it would appear beyond the power of any bishop or group of bishops to make such a pronouncement. . . ."

And Wagner cited a section of canon law that declares that "bishops, singly or in groups, cannot authoritatively decide dog-matic controversies, even in their own territory, since this involves the SUPREME power of the Church's MAGISTERIUM. . . ."

He compared the plight of New Orleans' segregationist Catholics to the plight of Catholics in sixteenth-century England when almost all of the bishops repudiated the Pope and acknowledged Henry VIII as the supreme head of the Church.

"[I]f segregation per se is morally wrong, then the Catholic is entitled to be informed as to the rational basis for this conclusion—as he was so informed when the immorality of birth control was denounced. . . . It is my belief that the thinking Catholic resents even more the foisting upon him of an unproved principle, whatever it be, than he does the integration of the Negro with the white, as much as he finds the latter distasteful. . . ."

Beyond the range of the Church's canons Wagner's letter emphasized "the disparity existing between the races in the areas of health, morality, education, and culture," and declared that many sincere Catholics who were campaigning for integration were "unwittingly sponsoring and furthering communistic aims and objectives."

Wagner's letter undoubtedly was read with interest down at the archbishopric. It was obviously not to be looked upon as just another bit of correspondence from the laity.

In truth, Wagner was a man of considerable standing in the Catholic community of New Orleans. A man just approaching middle age, a widower with five chlidren, a noted lawyer and "civic leader," and former president of the Loyola University Alumni Association.

Even more pertinent to the parochial-school race question Wagner had been a member of the Orleans Parish school board since 1952 and was its key leader in the fight to preserve segregation in the public schools.

Perhaps Archbishop Rummel was especially stimulated by Wagner's letter. Perhaps not. Whatever the motive, less than two months after receiving Wagner's note the archbishop, in February 1956, issued a "pastoral letter" to the clergy and laity of his domain. The letter was headlined: *The Morality of Racial Segregation.*

"Racial segregation as such is morally wrong and sinful because it is a denial of the unity and solidarity of the human race as conceived by God in the creation of man in Adam and Eve," the archbishop declared. "Throughout the pages of the Old Testament and the New there is constant recurrence of [the] truth that all mankind has in Adam and Eve one common father and mother and one common destiny, namely to serve God in this world and find eternal happiness with Him in the world to come. . . ."

As for his eligibility to make such pronouncements, the archbishop cited several Church precedents to prove that "bishops, too, share the teaching authority of the Pope."

"Racial segregation is morally wrong and sinful," he continued, "because it is a denial of the unity and universality of the Redemption. . . . 'For in one Spirit were we all baptized into one body, whether Jews or Gentiles, whether bond or free; and in one spirit we have all been made to drink.' . . .

"Racial segregation is morally wrong and sinful because it is basically a violation of the dictates of justice and the mandate of love, which in obedience to God's will must regulate the relations between all men. To deny to members of a certain race, just because they are members of that race, certain rights and opportunities, civic or economic, educational or religious, recreational or social, imposes upon them definite hardships and humiliations, frustrations and impediments to progress which condemn them to perpetual degradation which is only a step removed from slavery. Such indignities are grievous violations of Christian justice and charity, which cannot be justified in this modern age of enlightenment and loudly proclaimed democracy. . . ."

True, the archbishop remarked, the Church had considered it "wise and necessary" to maintain separate church and school facilities for Negroes all through the years since the Civil War. But, he asserted, "this arrangement was never intended to be permanent. . . ."

"We come now to the reasons for segregation at least in the school," he said, shifting into a sociological gear. "These reasons are for the most part unwarranted generalizations in which it is aimed to give the impression that all members of the Negro race and especially all Negro children are tainted with virtually all the alleged defects. The amazing fact is that 'as a race' they are not still more generally lacking in mental ability, culture, moral self-control, immunity from social diseases, criminal propensities, etc., when you consider the neglect and barriers to which they have been exposed in education, general culture, economic opportunities, respectable housing facilities, contact with stable social institutions, and the more dignified ways of life. . . ."

The archbishop had spoken.

But with a recalcitrance perhaps unequaled in the history of the Catholic Church in America, a stunningly large number of devout Catholics in New Orleans declined to accept his dictum that "racial segregation is morally wrong and sinful." And Emile Wagner was the chief ideologist of the dissenters.

Within a month of Rummel's pastoral letter, in mid-March 1956, several dozen of his flock joined to organize an Association of Catholic Laymen. Eventually a membership in the thousands was claimed. According to its official charter, membership in the Association was "limited to persons of the Caucasian race who profess the faith of the Holy Roman Catholic Church." The announced purposes of the Association were, among other things, the "investigation and study, in all its aspects, of the problem of compulsory integration of the black and white races" and to "seek out, make known, and denounce communist infiltration, if any there be in the integration movement."

Emile Wagner was elected president of the Association.

The Association, in a letter signed by Wagner, immediately notified Archbishop Rummel of its existence.

"My immediate reaction," the archbishop promptly responded, "is that such an organization seems unnecessary, ill-advised, and capable of causing much scandal, confusion, and dissension among our Catholic people. Per se your organization stands without parallel among the religious denominations of our city and state and will hardly escape the imputation that it is intended to embarrass and handicap the proper authority designated according to the sacred Scriptures, canon law, and tradition for the decision of questions of moment within diocesan administrations. . . ."

However, the archbishop said he was willing to talk it over. He agreed to meet with leaders of the Association on April 5.

But a week and a half later, on March 28, 1956, the archbishop indicated that his mood had become less easygoing. He had just had read to him an advertisement of the Association of Catholic

Laymen in the New Orleans *Times-Picayune* and, plainly, he was grieved by it.

"Appalled by the advertisement which appeared on page 5 of the *Times-Picayune* under this date, March 28, 1956, in which you solicit members of the Roman Catholic Church of the Caucasian race to join your organization called 'Association of Catholic Laymen,' " he wrote in a letter to Wagner, "I consider it eminently important that we have a personal conversation over the issue."

Wagner and several other leaders of the lay Association met twice with the archbishop and his right-hand clergymen during the next few days, but Rummel did not manage to convince them that they were treading a sinful path. On April 12, after the two meetings, the Association of Catholic Laymen (in a letter signed by its executive secretary, Jackson G. Ricau) advised Archbishop Rummel that the organization planned to "continue its policies" and "not restrict itself in the securing of additional active members."

Straightway the archbishop dispatched a telegram to each of the thirty board directors of the Association, declaring:

PLEASE BE INFORMED THAT THE RESOLUTION OF THE "ASSOCIA-TION OF CATHOLIC LAYMEN" TO CONTINUE THE FORMATION OF AN ACTIVE MEMBERSHIP GROUP IS UNACCEPTABLE. DETAILED REPLY WILL FOLLOW WITHIN THE COMING WEEK, MEANWHILE ALL AC-TIVITY RELATIVE TO SUCH MEMBERSHIP SHALL REMAIN SUS-PENDED. JOSEPH FRANCIS RUMMEL ARCHBISHOP OF NEW ORLEANS

In his letter that followed the archbishop vigorously chastised the laymen of the Asssociation for not displaying more "considera-tion or regard for ecclesiastical authority," and he firmly ruled:

"[W]e deem it our duty to define and decree that the Associa-tion of Catholic Laymen shall be entirely discontinued and that there shall be no further solicitation, public or private, for mem-bership. . . ."

Making it plain that he was not just kidding around, the arch-bishop added:

"Failure to accept the definition and decree . . . not later than Tuesday, May 1, 1956, will make you . . . liable to the penalty of excommunication. . . ."

To underscore this warning, Rummel attached to his letter several sections of canon law which explain that any person who is excommunicated is denied the Church sacraments and ecclesiastical burial, and is not permitted to share in the indulgences and public prayers of the Church.

Since the thought of being excommunicated from the Church is a fairly uncomfortable one for any serious Catholic, the directors of the Association of Catholic Laymen decided to obey the archbishop's command—at least temporarily.

On May 1 Wagner wrote a letter to the archbishop reporting that he and his fellow directors of the Association had adopted a resolution "accepting your definition and decree that the Association of Catholic Laymen shall be entirely discontinued. . . ."

"[A]lthough we must obey your command and acknowledge your episcopal authority," wrote Wagner, "we respectfully question the propriety of your decision to require the discontinuance of the Association of Catholic Laymen. We shall, therefore, avail ourselves of our rights as Catholics to appeal this matter to higher authority, and this letter will serve as notice of our intention to prosecute an appeal to the Holy See. . . ."

The appeal to the Pope was not prepared until the following year. But later in that same month of May 1956 Wagner wrote and published a letter to Rummel analyzing the segregation-is-morally-wrong pastoral letter which the archbishop had written three months earlier.

"It does not appear that you have proven that 'racial segregation as such is a denial of the unity and solidarity of the human race as conceived by God in the creation of Adam and Eve and hence morally wrong and sinful,'" Wagner wrote. "If segregation on the basis of color alone is wrong for this reason, then the division of people into nations solely because of nationality, into states and municipalities because of residence, and into families because of consanguinity is also wrong for the same reason. . . . Judged by [this criterion] it would be morally wrong and sinful to exclude women from ordination to the priesthood solely because of sex! . . .

"If it is wrong to segregate racially, as we see it, it is wrong to segregate nationally, and to hold that it is wrong to segregate nationally is to adopt the 'One World' ideology, than which there is nothing so dear to the communist heart. . . ."

In a rather more familiar Southern tradition, Wagner cited various statistics to support his contention that Caucasians are superior to Negroes in mentality, health, and morality.

He reported that about 20 per cent of the Negroes born in Louisiana are illegitimate, while only about 1 per cent of the whites are born out of wedlock.

"There are more than twenty-two times as many new cases yearly of venereal disease among Negroes as whites," Wagner noted. "Twenty-eight per cent of Negro pupils are below average in mentality and 43.17 per cent border mental retardation or are definitely mentally retarded, whereas 16.79 per cent of the white children are below average and only 9.59 per cent border mental retardation or are definitely mentally retarded. . . .

"Parents are endowed and charged by God with the direct right and obligation of developing to their fullest capacities the virtues and talents of their offspring, to the end that their children will serve God and save their immortal souls. This," asserted Wagner, "is a right and duty with which no one else, no matter how highly placed, can rightfully interfere. . . .

"White parents do not indict Negro children because they are illegitimate, nor do they maintain as a proven fact that venereal disease is easily contracted, although there is considerable evidence to this effect as to some types, but they do maintain without fear of contradiction that children who are illegitimate or who have venereal disease have a home life and background which make them improper and possibly dangerous associates for their own offspring. . . ."

Wagner indicated he did not believe that the archbishop knew his sociology from his theology.

"It appears to us that the proper distinction between the physical and social order on the one hand and the spiritual and supernatural order on the other has not been made, and that while we must recognize complete identity of the rights of the races in the spiritual and supernatural order, we are not obliged to, nor do we recognize, the identity of rights in the physical and social order."

Moreover:

"We deny absolutely and unequivocally that racial segregation is a 'violation of the dictates of justice and the mandate of love.' It has never been charged that it is morally wrong and sinful for the United States to pass immigration laws whereby northern and western Europe are given a large quota of admission to this country and Orientals are practically excluded. . . . If it is wrong not to allow Negroes to attend white schools, is it not a far greater wrong to deprive all peoples from sharing the rich natural resources which we, in the United States, claim as our own? . . ."

Perhaps Wagner's most telling point was made in countering the archbishop's remark that the denial of civil rights to Negroes subjects them to "indignities" which cannot be justified "in this modern age of enlightenment."

"If they [the 'indignities' cited by the archbishop] are inherently wrong, they have always been inherently wrong no matter the age or what people think about them," Wagner wrote.

And he contested Rummel's ecclesiastical authority to issue such a "definition" on the subject of segregation.

"[W]e do not think that the teaching authority of a bishop includes the power of definition. In a word, a bishop can teach what the Pope has defined, for then he is in 'communion' with the Pope, but he cannot, on his own, pronounce a matter as inherently good or bad, for then he is not in communion with the Pope, but only speaking for himself alone. . . . To put it baldly, you have seen fit to declare that racial segregation is unnatural, when the Pope himself has not seen fit so to do. And if the bishops of other dioceses, as we believe they do, disagree with your logic, the Catholic layman is placed in the impossible position of sinning in New Orleans if he practices segregation, and being virtuous in the same practice in Mobile, Alexandria, Lafayette, or in many other dioceses throughout the world. And if, possibly, you could be wrong, as all humans oftentimes are, you could be leading your flock into error and causing them to sin.

"And what of your own position, Your Excellency?" Wagner asked. "If segregation . . . is morally wrong and sinful, how can you continue your parochial schools on a segregated basis? This is not merely a toleration of, but an actual participation in, an inherent wrong. . . . Are you not indeed participating in that which you have denounced?

"We beg you, do not order the integration of the schools. . . ."

Again it is impossible to reckon how much or how little Wagner's letter influenced him, but ten weeks later the archbishop did, in fact, issue a new pastoral letter announcing that the parochial schools would not be integrated in 1956. Maybe later.

"[W]e deem it necessary to postpone integration in schools in which it has not yet been effected at least until September 1957," the archbishop wrote. "In the meantime we hope to overcome difficulties and make necessary preparations. . . ."

Monsignor Henry C. Bezou, who was generally accepted as a spokesman for the archbishop, remarked that when integration came it would come under a grade-a-year plan and "under moderate conditions."

But in 1957, as in 1956, the parochial schools remained segregated.

It was in July of 1957 that Wagner composed his appeal to the Pope (Pius XII) in behalf of the Association of Catholic Laymen.

"For over two years now," Wagner wrote in a letter accompanying the appeal, "conscientious and sincere Catholics in the Archdiocese of New Orleans have been confronted with the strange new doctrine, propounded by our Archbishop, His Excellency Joseph Francis Rummel, that the segregation of the white and Negro races is 'morally wrong and sinful.' Indeed this concept is both new and strange, for even the Clergy and the Church itself have participated and are participating in the perpetuation of this type of segregation by, among other things, sanctioning the establishment and maintenance of separate churches and schools.

"Despite the fact that no competent attempt has been made to offer conclusive proof to establish the validity of the principle, nor to demonstrate a Bishop's authority to define a matter of morals, Catholics have been admonished that they are bound in conscience, under pain of possible serious sin, to accept it. As a result, educated Catholics have become demoralized and uneducated ones scandalized. . . .

"Having reached this grim realization, we must of necessity turn to you, Holy Father, for there is no one else who can at once resolve the disquietude of conscience and allay the scandal and demoralization that beset Catholics of this Archdiocese and endanger their immortal souls. . . ."

The letter expressed the hope that the Pope would not feel that the race problem in New Orleans was too local in nature to require the direct attention of papal authority.

"Far from being a local problem, it is one of universal concern. It is true that there has been considerable propaganda to the effect that segregation of whites and Negroes is peculiar to the southern portion of the United States of America, but although the practice obtains openly here, it is equally true that it obtains throughout the rest of the nation, although great pains are taken to deny the fact in many areas. . . .

"Catholic consciences are not merely seeking the answer whether the separation of the Negro from the white in the Deep South of the United States is, in itself, 'morally wrong and sinful,' but whether the separation of the Negro from the white anywhere, or whether the separation of any people or race from any other people or race is, in itself, 'morally wrong and sinful.' We respectfully submit that, viewed in this light, the resolution of this question of worldwide significance becomes a most serious obligation of Your Holiness. . . ."

Pending such a pronouncement by the Pope, the appeal asked that Archbishop Rummel be "requested to take no further steps toward the integration of white and Negro Catholics."

The appeal, wrote Wagner, "discussed rather freely our Archbishop's unfortunate physical handicap of loss of sight. This was done so with reluctance, the letter said.

"His Excellency has always been a man of great religious zeal, dedicated to the flock over which he is shepherd. However, where a man is no longer able to acquire information as to important questions for himself and on his own and must rely totally on subordinates for facts on which to make great decisions affecting the consciences of hundreds of thousands, then, even though regretfully, delicacy and diplomacy must give way to frankness and forthrightness, for the fate of souls may hang in the balance. . . ."

No answer came from the Vatican—neither from Pope Pius XII, who died in 1958, nor from his successor, Pope John XXIII.

After letting 1957 and 1958 slip by in the same old segregated way, in August 1959 Rummel authorized the official Catholic weekly of the archdiocese to publish a statement saying:

"It is the sentiment and opinion of the Archbishop that integration must come . . . [C]ertainly as far as the parochial-school system is concerned, it will come at the earliest possible opportunity, and definitely that time will not be later than when the public schools are integrated. . . ."

And yet when the first few Negro pupils were ordered integrated in New Orleans' public schools in the fall of 1960—the season of the "screaming mothers"—the parochial schools did not follow suit. And again in the fall of 1961, when the number of "integrated" Negroes in New Orleans' public schools was increased to 12, the parochial schools of the archdiocese remained segregated as usual.

In contrast with previous statements from the archbishopric that parochial-school integration would "definitely" take place no later than public-school integration, Monsignor Bezou declared at the beginning of the 1961–62 school year that the Catholic schools would be desegregated when integration becomes *effective* in the public-school system.

"I personally feel where you have less than a handful of children in the schools it would be less than effective integration," said Bezou.

But a few months later, in March 1962, Archbishop Rummel issued a new directive which promised to have a pronounced effect on the complexion of schools in south Louisiana. The directive simply said:

"All Catholic children may apply for admission to the schools of the Archdiocese, both elementary and secondary, parochial and private, according to accepted educational standards."

Although it made no mention of "race" or "Negroes" or "desegregation," the directive was generally interpreted by all concerned as meaning that racial integration would begin in the Catholic schools of the New Orleans Archdiocese in the autumn of 1962.

The apparent desegregationist intent of the Catholic hierarchy seemed to be dramatized strongly three weeks later when the archbishop ordered the excommunication of three segregationist leaders who had vociferously protested against the new directive. The excommunicates were Jackson G. Ricau, executive secretary of the Citizens' Council of South Louisiana and sometime official of the Association of Catholic Laymen; Leander H. Perez, Sr., for years one of the South's major spokesmen for white supremacy; and Mrs. B. J. Gaillot, Jr., president of a New Orleans segregationist group called Save Our Nation, Inc.

It is, of course, impossible to forecast how much and how fast integration will in fact take place in the parochial schools of the archdiocese, and to what extent it will, in turn, affect the battle over integration in the public schools.

At this writing the fate of Catholic souls in New Orleans—to use the words employed by Emile Wagner in his letter to the Pope —is still hanging in the balance.

The Negroes attending the so-called "integrated" classrooms in New Orleans have indeed been few in number. But Wagner recognizes the significance of their presence in previously all-white schools.

"New Orleans is the bell cow for the rest of the state," he said recently at his downtown office. "And Louisiana may be the bell cow for what happens in the rest of the Deep South."

True, the statistics would seem to indicate that by June 1962 only "token integration" had taken place in the city's public schools.

"But 'token integration' is a myth," said Wagner. "It is naïve to think otherwise."

But only 12 Negro pupils—handsome, clear-eyed first- and second-graders—had been admitted to the "white" schools.

"The few little Negro children in their finery are not the issue. It is intellectually dishonest to maintain that they are," he said. "Our people are being sold the idea that this is only 'token integration.' But this is a false idea. For soon will come court cases saying that Negroes are not being admitted fast enough."

Wagner spoke of a "pupil-placement law" which had been passed in a nearby state as a means of postponing integration.

"I'm a lawyer, and as a lawyer I know this is a device and a deceit," said Wagner. "Sooner or later the NAACP will have it thrown out by the federal judiciary as unconstitutional. No, the issue is not 'token integration.' The true issue is whether we'll have public integrated schools or private segregated schools."

Wagner clings—or at least indicates that he clings—to the

notion that school segregation can be maintained by the establishment of tuition-free private schools supported by state "grant-in-aid" funds paid to individual students. With such state grants-in-aid, white parents could send their children to all-white private schools if they did not want them to attend classes with Negroes: so Wagner proposes, and he has composed state legislation to that effect.

Perhaps this, on Wagner's part, is just a bit of politico-legal whistling in the dark. To a layman in the law certainly it would seem that the federal judiciary could declare the grant-in-aid device unconstitutional just as easily as it might declare the pupil-placement device unconstitutional.

There is hardly any doubt, however, that Wagner is fully sincere in his feelings that the present "token integration" must perforce lead to "total integration" of New Orleans' public schools.

"And the city could not remain half integrated and half segregated," he said, speaking of the relationship between the racial policies of the public schools and the parochial schools. "If the public schools are integrated, I feel they will be wiped out."

Many men in New Orleans feel the same way. Why, among them, has Wagner chosen to take such an active part in the battle against desegregationists?

Some of his critics suggest that it is because he has political aspirations to gain an elective office higher than that of membership on the Orleans Parish school board. It is especially strongly suggested that he yearns to become mayor of New Orleans.

When speaking of his possible future role in politics he speaks in an oblique, "I-do-not-choose-to-run" manner which seems somehow disconsonant with his other, firmer expressions.

"I have no aspirations for public office," he said. "If I ran for an office, it would be at a personal and financial sacrifice. I am not by nature a politician."

But:

"I would run if I thought I could be of material help in solving this thing [i.e., preventing integration]."

Wagner expresses a strong resentment at the way he and his role in the New Orleans school controversy have been described by newspapers, magazines, and books.

"Some writers have depicted me as a nineteenth-century figure

—the old Southern aristocrat. Others have used such words as 'corpulent' and 'Prussian' in describing me."

In truth, he is neither Prussian nor corpulent.

His forebears came to New Orleans from Alsace, which explains the seeming contradiction between his rather Gallic first name and his rather Germanic last name.

He is a stocky, wide-shouldered man of middling height. His hair, which is spattered unevenly with gray, is worn in a short, carelessly collegiate brush cut. He occasionally sports a bow tie, and dresses tastefully and neatly—and yet perhaps because of his somewhat bearish build he somehow gives the impression of being *rumpled*. He is not an unhandsome man, but neither has he any prettiness; his features are rough in design, and his ears are aggressively large. Were he of lower rank in the socioeconomic order, his appearance likely would earn him some such nickname as "Biff," or, perhaps, "Spud."

He wages his war for segregation from a windowless ground-floor office of the Hibernia Homestead and Savings Association at the corner of Carondelet and Gravier streets. Emile Wagner's office, too, like his name, is slightly contradictory: it is unsunny and heavy and rather austere, and yet there are beside his desk a scattering of bright pictures of his beautiful daughters and a couple of prints of sunnily romantic street scenes in creamy French provincial frames.

In contrast with the almost intimidating orderliness of his mind his files seem to be in an unhappy state of disarray. When searching for copies of his Association of Catholic Laymen correspondence one day recently he rummaged several times through divers desk drawers and through cardboard boxes in his office closet, not infrequently failing to find what he was looking for.

Perhaps such contradictions in his appearance and personality have been responsible for the difficulty reporters have had in describing Wagner completely successfully.

But he feels that much more sinister factors are involved in the press's coverage of him and other segregationist leaders in the white South.

"In every field where opinion can be influenced, people are being propagandized," he said. "I'm bitter about the press treatment we have received. There has been a travesty of justice all the way up [to the Supreme Court]."

Whether or not he chooses to run for mayor of New Orleans, it is obvious that Wagner feels a strong personal identification with the city, and takes a sincerely intense interest in its racial traditions.

"I grew up here. My family dates back to the early 1800's in New Orleans. . . . And I know that to mix the races here now would be horrible. It not only would affect education but would affect morality generally.

"I am a person of strong convictions, and my purpose is to achieve what I believe to be right," he said. "The segregation issue has portents, and I feel an innate obligation to do what I can to solve it. It's something I cannot get away from."

VII. THE COUNTERATTACKERS

Campaigning Against the Alien Isms

ONLY comparatively recently has it finally dawned on segregationist leaders down South that broadcasting merely the fear of racial "mongrelization" is not sufficient to arouse any effective amount of public opinion beyond the Mason-Dixon line—certainly not in the dozens of states where Negroes are still such a small minority that the idea of a black threat to their white masses seems preposterous.

But as the months of the great segregation-v.-integration struggle have transpired, white supremacists have learned better and better that Northern emotions *can* be stimulated by the fear of communism.

The more thoughtful segregationist groups therefore have more and more in the last few years moved to associate themselves with organizations outside the South who are in the business of inflaming the public's terror of the "Red menace."

With nobody of the hair-raising personality of, say, Joseph McCarthy, on the present sociopolitical scene, the task of giving the body politic a case of the shivers is not an easy one.

But it is a fact that the South's propagandists for apartheid have grown a bit more suavely sophisticated than they were in the blazing, bombastic old days of 1954 when Judge Tom Brady's pyrotechnic *Black Monday* was composed. No longer do they hold righteously rigidly to the position, "If you're not for us you're against us." Rather, they are now willing to use organizations and propaganda sources that might not themselves be campaigning for segregation but which might be of *indirect* aid to the white South's cause.

The Fisherman

Carved beside the entrance to the skyscraper Louisiana capitol building at Baton Rouge are a few words enunciated by Robert R. Livingston in 1803 fast upon signing the treaty papers that sealed the purchase of Louisiana from France:

"The instruments we have just signed will cause no tears to be shed. They prepare ages of happiness for innumerable generations of human creatures."

Within the magnificent capitol structure, at the office of the Louisiana Sovereignty Commission (which was created by an instrument of the State Legislature just a couple of years ago), there sat one recent afternoon a young, auburn-haired stenographer clad in skirt and sweater of a sky-blue hue, busily updating an interesting little booklet that gives a hint of the number of "rightist" and "radical rightist" organizations that exist in these United States as potential markets for the South's salesmen of segregation.

The booklet, published by an anti-Jewish (and anti-just-about-everything-else) San Francisco organization called Liberty and Property, is entitled *FIRST NATIONAL DIRECTORY of "Rightist" Groups, Publications and Some Individuals in the United States (and Some Foreign Countries)*. With the "additions and errata" which were being noted by the comely stenographer, the *FIRST NATIONAL DIRECTORY* lists approximately one thousand organizations and publications that are anti-Negro, anti-Jewish, anti-fluoridation, anti-Catholic, anti-communist, anti-socialist—or which are promoting a back-to-Africa movement for Negroes, the passage of "right-to-work" laws, or advancing one or more other extremely "conservative" and "nationalistic" programs.

"It's enlightening," said the executive director of the Louisiana Sovereignty Commission, John Deer, "to find such a large number of organizations in the country with aims similar to ours."

Deer had in mind primarily the segregationist and "respectably anti-communist" organizations rather than the anti-Semitic and anti-flouridation groups.

"We're corresponding with many of them with the thought in

mind of encouraging some unification—of creating some basic recognition of this country's fundamental constitutional principles and encouraging a return to them."

Deer, who grew up in Greenville, Alabama, exemplifies the truth that some of the white South's very ablest and most personable young men hold positions of leadership in the fight to prevent desegregation. In contrast to the snuff-dipping ruffian or Vandyked Southern colonel customarily presented in Northern cartoons as segregationist stereotypes, Deer is a tastefully tailored, trimly barbered man in his late thirties, a former president of the student body of the Alabama Polytechnic Institute at Auburn. After graduating with honors in 1936 with a degree in chemical engineering, he operated a plastics and metal fabricating business of his own for several years in Chicago. He chose to retire young and move to Louisiana to enjoy for the remainder of his life "the best fishing in the world." When the Sovereignty Commission was established by the Louisiana Legislature in 1960, however, Deer's friend and fellow fishing enthusiast, Governor Jimmie Davis, invited him to be its chief executive.

"Fundamentally we don't look upon ourselves as a *segregation* commission," said Deer. "We're not a bunch of rabble-rousers. We think our purpose is far broader, that it far transcends the fate of our schools or even the fate of Louisiana. Our purpose is to try to establish a clear-cut boundary line between federal authority and state authority."

In addition to directing an investigatory force designed to ferret out information on "scalawags" and "carpetbaggers" who might be working for integration in Louisiana, the Sovereignty Commission staff keeps busy making speeches and distributing films and literature promoting the idea that Louisiana's segregated way of life is best for both Negroes and whites. Like the Citizens' Council Association and the Mississippi Sovereignty Commission, Deer's staff is aiming toward a wide distribution of the segregationist message in non-Southern states.

The Commission's long-range goal is an amendment to the United States Constitution that would prohibit the federal government from "encroaching on the internal affairs" of the several states. This, in effect, would permit Louisiana and other Southern states to continue segregation as in the good old days before May 17, 1954.

"I don't believe we can get such an amendment passed right at this time, speaking realistically. We could just about as quickly push this capitol over with our little finger," said Deer with a laugh. "But we're devoting our time and energy to it, exploring every avenue. We know we're not going to get it passed until we can change the political climate in the United States—and that involves far more than segregation.

"Meanwhile, we must take those little steps necessary to prevent catastrophe—and catastrophe would surely result if this social experiment of the Supreme Court were to succeed in enforcing compulsory integration in Louisiana. While striving to bring about this other thing [a changed national political climate], we must use delaying actions and devise means to parry the integrationists' thrusts."

To keep the segregationist spirit flaming as brightly as possible in Louisiana while it goes fishing for Northern support, the Sovereignty Commission staff carries on an extensive "educational" program within the state designed to equate the 1954 decision with communism and to keep traditional racial fears alive. A representative piece of educational literature issued by Deer's office reads:

The real issue is: What kind of a state do we want for our children? Do we want our children to attend racially integrated schools where they will be mixed with children of another racial, cultural, and social background? Do we want our youth thrown into close social contact with a people of different racial origin, setting the stage for interracial marriages? . . . Yes, the "Carpet Baggers" are with us again. Their modern counterparts range all the way from actual Communists, interested in creating controversy, to misguided do-gooders, frustrated crackpots, and left-wing "intellectuals." . . .

The Communists know exactly what they are doing. They are not really interested in promoting better race relations. This is a smoke screen. They are, actually, trying to stir up racial hatred that they know could weaken and destroy America. Their dirty work is being done by a sorry lot of dupes who have fallen for the false promises of socialism. . . . Your action now will determine the kind of future you want for your sons and daughters. . . .

Deer wished to emphasize, however, that he is not a "racist." In fact, he said, he has a Negro employee who lives on his lakeside property over near Shreveport, "and our whole family loves him."

"If there is any prejudice on our part," said Deer, "it is prejudice in favor of the colored people rather than against them."

The Bourbons Face North

Confronted by a federal judiciary that persistently issues integration decisions, a Congress in which Southerners are a minority, and a presidential administration which is pledged to fight racial discrimination in all areas of American life, only the most parochial segregationists still cling with any conviction to the belief that the white South can by itself preserve segregation.

The most alert of the public-relations men for segregation keep beaming to the North the message that they are fighting not merely for the Southern Way—but for the *American* Way—that their battle is not simply for the maintenance of white supremacy but for the preservation of all men's individual liberties, for states' rights, and for the protection of America's very political, religious, and economic system against the evil forces of alien isms. The white South's interests, say the segregationists, are identical with those of all Americans who have an interest in maintaining the *status quo*—i.e., in keeping what they've got.

Addressing a large banquet meeting of farm owners and businessmen in Iowa, William J. Simmons, the major spokesman for the white Citizens' Councils, asked this:

Has it occurred to you that the social revolutionaries who are working to remake the South in their own image are not just interested in racial integration? They are above all *collectivists*. They are driving for increased national power. The South has to be dealt with because it stands squarely in their way as the strongest remaining bulwark of our constitutional form of government that protects *your* property rights and *your* personal freedoms as well as ours.

How long do you think you would enjoy your own rightful interests if these revolutionaries succeed in establishing a totalitarian welfare state in Washington? . . .

The Citizens' Councils are not just a prosegregation movement. *They represent the substantial beginnings of a fundamental conservative revolt.* The thousands of men who have given unstintingly of their time and substance are moved by a deep unrest that has been growing for the past 25 years, but this unrest was not impelled to active organized form until the bald attempt to abolish the Constitution by judicial decree in 1954 precipitated a crisis.

There is a direct conflict of interest between the conservative people of this country and those totalitarian "liberals" who would use the Negro as a means of power.

It is my deliberate and considered opinion that if our friends and fellow countrymen in the other great sections of our land will organize themselves and become an effective, responsible force in their local communities and states, the growing threat of a collectivist welfare state will be speedily dissolved. . . .

The need for a link between the cause of apartheid and the cause of political and economic Bourbonism was significantly emphasized for the first time when a group of the South's most influential segregationists met at Memphis in December 1955 to organize a "Federation for Constitutional Government"—the forerunner of the present Association of Citizens' Councils of America.

Picked for the advisory committee were such inflexible antiliberals as Senator James Eastland of Mississippi and Strom Thurmond of South Carolina, and Herman Talmadge, soon to become a senator from Georgia. And present at the meeting was the core of leadership of the Mississippi Citizens' Council movement, including Judge Tom Brady and Robert "Tut" Patterson.

The conservative aims and nationwide ambitions of the organization were expressed in a keynote address by Eastland.

It is essential that a nationwide organization be set up. It will be a people's organization [to] fight the CIO, to fight the NAACP, and to fight all the conscienceless pressure groups who are attempting our destruction. . . . We are about to embark on a great crusade, a crusade to restore Americanism and return the control of our government to the people. In addition, our organization will carry on its banner the slogan of free enterprise and we will fight those organizations who attempt [to] socialize industry and the great medical profession of this country. . . .

The Rope Maker

The Bourbonic complexion of the Federation was highlighted by the choice of John U. Barr of New Orleans as chairman of its executive committee. A prosperous industrialist, an organizer of the conservative Southern States Industrial Council, a long-time officer in the National Association of Manufacturers and the United States Chamber of Commerce, Barr ever since the thirties had been in the forefront of the conservative South's fight for states' rights and against labor unionization and the "socialistic" measures of the New and Fair Deals.

In 1944 he had led a Southern fight against the fourth-term nomination of Roosevelt, trying to enlist Virginia's Senator Harry Byrd as a presidential candidate. In 1948 he was a prime mover in the Dixiecrat campaign. And in 1956, not long after he helped organize the Federation for Constitutional Government, he served as cochairman (with Dean Clarence Manion of Notre Dame) of the ill-fated campaign of former Internal Revenue Commissioner T. Coleman Andrews for president.

One day several months ago Barr talked at length of his hope of welding the South's segregationists and the North's conservatives into a single great political force.

He spoke in his office on the second floor of a machine shop in a section of New Orleans cluttered with factories and Negro shanties. Since his retirement as a rope manufacturer he had served as a sometime adviser to the machine-shop's owners, who once had been his employees.

A tall, gray-haired man of seventy-two—in his appearance there was no hint of the bellicosity he had so often expressed when denouncing racial integration and New Deal "socialism." His brown eyes, dimmed by age and the strain of poor eyesight, were free of hostility, and his face had the kind of good-humored lines that are formed by a generous amount of smiling.

Barr's racial attitudes as well as his rather nostalgically conservative view of American politics and economics were born of his boyhood experiences in Mississippi.

The son of a Presbyterian minister, he grew up in a series of

small towns. For a time his father was president of the Chicka-
saw Female College in Pontotoc.

There never was much money in the family, but young Barr
was well equipped with a spirit for free enterprise.

"When I was eleven, an uncle of mine in Porterville would ship
eggs to me at Pontotoc. I'd keep 'em cool in brine water, then go
around house to house selling them. And I picked potatoes and
beans and cotton as a kid; I remember making fifteen cents a day
picking cotton."

During his teens at Pontotoc and Houston, Mississippi, he
worked as a laborer at a brick kiln, as a hotel clerk, as a fireman
at an ax-handle factory at $1.25 a day, and as an ironing-board
salesman.

"Wherever a nickel was to be made I was there." He laughed
with the memory.

After high school there was no money for college, and Barr
went to work as a "drummer." In the tradition of the traveling
salesman who tried peddling refrigerators to Eskimos, Barr for
a time had a job selling Knox Crystal Gelatin and Quick-Work
Metal Polish in the French bayou country of South Louisiana.

"Trouble was, nobody down there had ice to freeze the gelatin
with, and there was no machinery for anybody to use the polish
on. Besides that, my company's big selling point was supposed to
be that these products were being given special advertising in a
certain Presbyterian paper. I remember one old storekeeper told
me, 'Son, if a single one of those papers comes into this town
between now and the next time you're here, I'll give you a good
order for that stuff you're selling.' Well, sir, not one of those
Presbyterian papers came to that town, not one; I'd overlooked
the fact that everybody down there was Catholic. So I finally quit
that job and started taking a business course in New Orleans."

Years later Barr remembered those jobs not as things of drudg-
ery and disappointment but as parts of golden youth.

"In those days we didn't have the luxuries we enjoy today, but
there was unbridled liberty. A great many, at times, may have felt
the pangs of want, and there was not held out before them what
is now presented to us as the 'Welfare State' and 'Social Security,'
but they did enjoy unhampered opportunity. Those were days . . .
when a dollar was truly a dollar and bought a full dollar's value."

After business school Barr worked for several years as office manager of a New Orleans printing company, then in the early twenties went into business for himself selling rope and twine. By the mid-thirties his company, Federal Fiber Mills, had hundreds of employees and a national distribution.

It was in 1943, while serving in Washington as a part-time consultant to the War Production Board, that Barr became convinced that President Roosevelt was conspiring to "socialize" American business. Barr claimed he had personal knowledge that Roosevelt instructed the chairman of a House committee to issue a report recommending that the federal government take over all war industries as soon as peace was declared with Germany and Japan.

"I realized then that while our boys were dying in the war against fascism we ourselves were headed toward a fascist government that would operate our war plants and eventually all business. When I learned that, I told my wife, 'I'm too old to carry a gun, but I'm not too old to fight to preserve what those boys have been fighting for.' I told her I'd feel destroyed if I didn't meet the challenge. She said, 'You go ahead.' "

That conclusion reached by Barr in 1943, however correct or incorrect, guided him in his political activity ever afterward.

The very next year he tried to induce the Democratic party to draft Byrd of Virginia to lead a campaign "to destroy the political dictatorship of Hillman, Browder, and Dubinsky, and to save constitutional democracy." Despite a statement from Byrd that he was not a candidate, the move for the Virginia senator—according to Barr—was strong enough to produce a compromise offer from the White House.

"FDR sent word he was willing to take Byrd as his running mate if it would stop the revolt in the South. But we made no reply. When a publicity man who was aiding me told me of the offer from FDR I said, 'Jim, you can't put a hyena and a lamb in the same cage and expect 'em both to live.' He told me that if I 'went along' I could become a 'big man.' I said, 'I'm not interested in that; I'm just interested in saving my nation.' "

Roosevelt's eventual choice of Harry S. Truman as his 1944 running mate was never pleasing to Barr, and in August 1947 he issued an open letter "To the People of the South and Their Political Leaders," a message that was very influential in harnessing the dissidence below the Mason-Dixon line into the Dixiecrat movement of 1948.

In the letter Barr urged "the real Democratic leaders in each Southern State to serve notice publicly and in advance of the 1948 Democratic National Convention that (1) they will not participate in the Convention up to a certain point, but (2) if an anti-South or Leftist platform is adopted, or a Leftist candidate is nominated, they will withdraw as a body and return to their respective States, and without bolting from the Party, run their electors on a pledge to vote in the Electoral College for a true Jeffersonian Democrat."

The "Jeffersonian Democrat" chosen by the bolters from the mother party was J. Strom Thurmond of South Carolina. Political history records that his campaign produced an abundance of oratory but not many votes; the Dixiecrats carried only four states: Alabama, Louisiana, Mississippi, and South Carolina. Rather than serving as a reassertion of the South's political prowess, it has served as a haunting reminder to workaday politicians in Dixie of the difficulty of trying to establish a third party in American politics.

Barr's cochairmanship of T. Coleman Andrews' third-party campaign for president in 1956 rewarded him with a fiasco of even greater dimensions. His candidate got only a little more than one hundred thousand votes throughout the country.

"The 1956 campaign took a lot out of me," Barr admitted.

That drubbing, together with the 1948 defeat, impressed on Barr the thought that a third political force in the United States cannot hope to succeed unless it can find a "man on a white horse"—a candidate who can whip up some enthusiasm among voters.

Barr said also that he had learned from experience that money, and lots of it, is necessary to run a national political campaign. But if segregationist-conservative leaders could ever manage to dig up an adequately attractive candidate, Barr said, there would be enough right-wing money lying around to make a strong campaign possible.

"One fellow said to me a while back, 'If you can find two individuals between the age of forty and fifty who can spark the public's imagination as did Nathan Bedford Forrest and Wade Hampton, I think I can get their campaign underwritten in the low millions.' And don't kid yourself, boy," Barr added, "money is power."

He said he had made approaches to a few national political figures who might be potential Forrests and Hamptons—among others, former Senator William Jenner of Indiana and Representative John Bell Williams of Mississippi.

"But they aren't 'buying' at this time," said Barr.

It is not easy, Barr conceded, to find a man of national stature who is willing to go to work to lure the hundreds of conservative splinter groups into one political "tent" outside the "leftist" Democratic and Republican parties.

"You have to have an individual who symbolizes things for the people," he said. "I guess the only man I know at the present time who could do it is Barry Goldwater. I think he's a real good American."

The South Side of a Conservative's Conscience

Unlike many Dixieland "conservatives" such as John Barr, Arizona Senator Goldwater advances no racial theories to prove that Negroes are inferior to Caucasians. Nor does he reach the conclusion that the Negro civil-rights protest in our country is merely a communist plot.

Indeed, Goldwater has indicated that he *personally* favors school desegregation.

"It so happens that I am in agreement with the *objectives* of the Supreme Court as stated in the Brown decision [of May 17, 1954]," he declares in his book, *The Conscience of a Conservative*. "I believe that it *is* both wise and just for negro children to attend the same schools as whites, and that to deny them this opportunity carries with it strong implications of inferiority."

But when he comes to the specifics of the matter, Goldwater takes a legalistic position that is right up the alley of the segregationists.

"[The] federal Constitution does not require the States to maintain racially mixed schools. Despite the recent holding of the

Supreme Court, I am firmly convinced—not only that integrated schools are not required—but that the Constitution does not permit any interference whatsoever by the federal government in the field of education. It may be just or wise or expedient for negro children to attend the same schools as white children, but they do not have a civil right to do so which is protected by the federal Constitution, or which is enforceable by the federal government."

Goldwater is not impressed by the claim that the Supreme Court's school-desegregation decision is now the "law of the land." Rather, he declares, it is an unhappy illustration of the present court's view that "what matters is not the ideas of the men who wrote the Constitution, but the *Court's* ideas. . . . The Congress and the States, equally with the Supreme Court, are obliged to interpret and comply with the Constitution according to their own lights. I therefore support all efforts by the States, excluding violence, of course, to preserve their rightful powers over education."

Although *personally* favoring school integration, he says, "I am not prepared [to] impose that judgment of mine on the people of Mississippi or South Carolina. . . . That is their business, not mine. . . . I believe that the problem of race relations, like all social and cultural problems, is best handled by the people directly concerned."

But Goldwater's position is not merely one of remaining aloof from the "business" of Deep Southern states. He not only encourages the states to defy the 1954 decision; he also proposes an amendment to the Constitution which, in effect, would prohibit any future federal action—by the executive, legislative, or judicial branches—related to school segregation or any other matter in the field of education. As he puts it: "I would hope that the national legislature would help clarify the problem by proposing to the States a Constitutional Amendment that would reaffirm the States' exclusive jurisdiction in the field of education."

For those citizens who find the Southern system of segregation objectionable, Goldwater gently suggests: "Let us, through persuasion and education, seek to improve institutions we deem defective. But let us, in doing so, respect the orderly process of law. Any other course enthrones tyrants and dooms freedom."

Goldwater's philosophy is, of course, the very philosophy which the South's segregationists have been striving to make flourish in the North ever since the Civil War—indeed, since slavery days.

The white South's constant message has been: "Our race problem is *our* business; just leave us alone and we will solve it." So far, of course, the solution has been to maintain segregation. And history gives little evidence that the white South, if left free of federal pressures, would reach any other "solution."

Two Sazeracs Below Valley Forge

At the discreetly luxurious International House, where a Negro waiter in a well-starched uniform served Barr and his guest excellent Sazeracs[1] followed by shrimp rémoulade and oysters en brochette, the old rope manufacturer spoke of his long, defeat-filled political career in comparison with the discomforts suffered long ago by his hero, George Washington.

"The Americans who are fighting for Constitutional principles today are in much the same position that Washington was in at Valley Forge. I guess it was even worse for Washington. There were even more traitors around then, his forces were ragged and starving and tending to be dispirited, and he was faced with what was then the greatest power on earth as his adversary—the British Empire."

Like Washington, Barr has always distrusted entangling foreign alliances. He opposed both the League of Nations and the United Nations.

"Did the League of Nations prevent Mussolini from attacking Ethiopia? And look at the Congo," he said. "The Dutchmen would still be there if it hadn't been for the UN. All the UN does is take power away from the Haves and give it to the Have-Nots. The only thing which has meaning in international politics is *power.*"

He reflected for a moment.

"And yet I distrust power. I've seen the effect it can have on

[1] One New Orleans recipe for a pitcher of three or four Sazeracs is as follows: mix 4 teaspoons sugar syrup, 4 dashes Peychaud bitters, 4 dashes anisette, 7 jiggers bourbon. Stir with ice cubes until thoroughly chilled. Pour into chilled glasses, and add a twist of lemon peel.

people. I've seen the effect it's had a few times on *me*. No," he mused, "I distrust it."

Back at his office, as he and his visitor puffed on cigars of a local brand favored by Barr, he pulled a large organizational chart from a stack of papers near his desk.

It was a chart that had been prepared by Barr in the early days of the Federation for Constitutional Government, back when he hoped to develop the organization into a strong third-party force.

In neatly ruled brackets were deployed the board of directors, the executive committee, and the national secretary with his staff: the legal department, the division of research, the public-relations department, the governmental liaison department, the speakers' division, et cetera.

"The idea, you see, was that local organizations could be built on local issues, then we could shoot the national 'Constitutional principles' stuff to them. . . . If you could find a way to help 'em [the various segregationist and conservative organizations of the country], then you could consolidate 'em."

But he folded the chart and returned it to the stack of papers. It had never amounted to more than a neatly-organized dream.

After all the years of political defeats, did Barr retain much hope that the "Liberal tide" could be turned back—that he and his fellow conservatives and states' rightists and segregationists could prevent "mongrelization," defeat the forces of "welfare statism," and restore the "unbridled liberty" that he felt existed in the days of his small-town Mississippi youth?

"No," he said, "I don't think there is any hope." But he laughed —the not discontented laugh of a man who had seen many years and did not have too many more to worry about. "That doesn't mean I won't keep on fighting, though."[2]

[2] Just a few weeks later John U. Barr died, at the age of seventy-two. "Many good men in our cause have gone to their reward," commented *The Citizens' Council*, official newspaper of the Association of CCs of America. "Few were equal to John Barr, and none were superior. We will miss him."

The Candy Man

Early the next morning Barr had telephoned to apologize for forgetting to mention one organization which he feels *does* offer some hope of arousing the nation to the dangers of integration-minded Supreme Court justices and the Reds in our midst.

"There's a fellow up in Massachusetts who has an organization that's making terrific progress down here. His name is Robert Welch and he calls his outfit the John Birch Society. This fellow Welch has regular field organizers out in the country. I understand he has eight or ten chapters right here in New Orleans."

Robert H. W. Welch, Jr., retired candy manufacturer of Belmont, Massachusetts, formed the John Birch Society in 1958. Not much was known about it by the general public until 1961, when it suddenly became a nationwide topic of controversy.

Although much of the nation's press expressed sympathy with the Society's announced purpose of opposing communism, there was considerable criticism of the fairly breathtaking charges made by Welch in some of his writings.

In a document entitled *The Politician,* Welch charged that President Eisenhower was a dedicated, conscious communist agent, answerable to his brother Milton (alleged by Welch to be Eisenhower's superior in the party), and for whose actions "there is only one word—treason." Elsewhere in the tome, first written in 1954 and since expanded, he described Presidents Truman and Roosevelt, the Dulles brothers, and various other high government officials as tools of international communism.

Welch is a pale, thinly gray-haired, rather petulant-spoken man in his early sixties. Born on a North Carolina farm, he attended the University of North Carolina, the Naval Academy, and Harvard Law School. He moved to Massachusetts in his teens and worked for many years as vice president of a candy manufacturing firm headed by his brother.

He was vice-chairman of the Massachusetts Republican Finance Committee in 1948, ran unsuccessfully for the GOP nomination for lieutenant governor in 1950, and worked for Eisenhower's election in 1952. In 1954 he was New England vice president of the National Association of Manufacturers. By 1956 he was advocating the formation of a third party. In 1960 he was a leader of the short-lived drive to get Barry Goldwater nominated as the GOP presidential candidate.

Aside from the energy he expends labeling famous Americans as communist sympathizers, one of his major efforts is to impress upon Birch Society members that the United States is not a "democracy" but a "constitutional republic."

"Democracy," says Welch, "is merely a deceptive phrase, a weapon of demagoguery, a perennial fraud."

The Society, which was named in memory of a Georgia farm boy-missionary who was slain by Chinese Communists while serving as an intelligence officer during World War II, has a cell structure not unlike that of the enemy Communist party. After looking around for a good man for the job as leader of the Society, Welch settled upon himself.

Since Welch has chosen to keep the size of his membership a secret, no estimate is possible of the Birch Society's spread since 1958. It is believed that one of its main strongholds is the South; Welch has said that Tennessee, Texas, and southern California are the best Birch Society areas.

Barr recalled that he had first met Welch in September 1956 at a National States Rights Conference in Memphis. The conference concluded with the nomination of T. Coleman Andrews for president.

Welch addressed the Memphis conference and made a very favorable impression, Barr remembered. Later, however, Barr was disappointed by a "little circular on integration" which Welch published not long after he had formed his Birch Society.

"He seemed to move in the direction that 'a little integration wouldn't hurt'—so I didn't even put it out [through the Federation for Constitutional Government]," said Barr. "But I think he's changed his opinion on it since then. He touches on the subject by pointing out the usurpation of power by the federal courts."

Through his Birch Society bulletins Welch—in acknowledged imitation of communist technique—advocates the use of "fronts" to combat America's Reds and Comsymps ("Comsymp" is the Birch Society term for "communist sympathizer").

He has suggested, for example, an organization called the Women Against Labor Union Hoodlumism and a Committee to Investigate Communist Influence at Vassar.

But by far the most popular of the John Birch Society "front" campaigns in the white South has been the Movement to Impeach Earl Warren.

Recently Welch announced that the Birch Society would give $2,300 in prizes for the eight best essays by college students giving reasons why the chief justice should be impeached. "We hope to stir up a great deal of interest among conservatives on the campuses on the dangers that face this country," said Welch.

Although his literature urging the impeachment of Warren has judiciously been kept free of anti-Negro statements—indeed Welch urges both "black and white" citizens to join in the impeachment effort—it is obviously a crusade that plays effectively on the Dixieland emotions aroused by the Warren court's 1954 school decision.

"We are aware," Welch writes companionably to Birch Society members, "that the whole Supreme Court is a nest of socialists and worse. . . . We believe that the impeachment of Earl Warren would dramatize and crystallize the whole basic question of whether the United States remains the United States, or becomes gradually transformed into a province of the worldwide Soviet system. . . ."

Welch has not exactly declared that Warren is, in fact, a Communist.

"But the man who has done the most specific direct damage to our Constitution, and to our whole system of safeguards which a constitutional republic offers against the power of demagogues to manipulate majorities, is Chief Justice Earl Warren," he says.

"The most important *specific* result of Warrenism in our federal judiciary, of course, has been the storm over integration. . . . The whole trouble has been brought on by Communists for their own purposes. Among their objectives are riots and civil disorders, promotion of interracial distrust and bitterness, a reopening of old animosities between North and South, the creation of 'civil-rights' programs and organizations which can attract gullible do-gooders and then serve many other communist purposes. . . ."

This sort of unrestrained polemic broadcast by the Massachusetts

candy man is, of course, music to the ears of Southern segregationists. It harmonizes beautifully with their own song that the
1954 decision and the whole civil-rights movement are nothing
more than parts of a communist plot to create chaos below the
Mason-Dixon line, "mongrelize" Southern white children, and turn
the whole kit and caboodle over to the Kremlin.

Battling the Dupes and the Diabolical-X

In keeping with the campaigns of the Federation for Constitutional Government and the State Sovereignty Commission to develop a coalition of segregationists with Northern groups, the
Association of Citizens' Councils of Louisiana distributes a
quantity of non-Southern "patriotic" literature from its main
office in Baton Rouge.

Among the material furnished a recent visitor to the Baton
Rouge CC office was a copy of Merwin K. Hart's *Economic Council Letters* denouncing the United Nations and calling for a constitutional amendment giving the several states sole control of
their public schools. Also available was a mimeographed reprint
of an *American Mercury* article by retired Marine Lieutenant General Pedro Del Valle, sometime unsuccessful candidate for governor of Maryland and a vice president of Hart's National Economic
Council. The Del Valle article hints that the untidy U-2 incident
and the failure of our "front man" (presumably Eisenhower) at
the 1960 Summit Conference debacle both were rigged by a "mys-
tery organization" which Del Valle chooses to identify as "Diabolical-X." This organization, he suggests, "exercises control over
both the USSR and the USA (and perhaps over other participants)." Although his presentation is a bit foggy, he does make
it clear that he suspects the said "Diabolical-X" is operated in
both America and the Soviet Union by "modern money-changers."

"[There] is a power which controls the mismanagement of both
countries," Del Valle writes. "Our objective, then, is not how to
end the top-heavy bureaucracies seeking self-preservation. Our
objective is enlightenment as to the long-range plan of the invisible power we are certain exists."

A stack of back issues of *American Mercury* is kept on file by the Louisiana CC. The *Mercury,* David Lawrence's *U.S. News and World Report,* and (among segregationists of higher brow) William Buckley's *National Review* are just about the only Northern publications that white supremacy leaders feel have not been unduly influenced by integrationists and Communists.

Not unexpectedly a popular item on the CC's shelf of reading material at Baton Rouge is the John Birch Society bulletin that calls for the impeachment of Chief Justice Warren.

There also is a brisk distribution of literature from another organization that shares the Birch Society's fear that the Reds have almost taken over the country—the Christian Anti-Communist Crusade, a rapidly spreading "movement" with offices in Long Beach and San Francisco, California, and Houston, Texas. It is an organization which, in the long run, may prove even more effective than the John Birch Society in spreading tidings of the "Red Plague" in America.

The Christian Anti-Communist Crusade, founded a few years ago by a middle-aged former Australian physician named Fred Schwarz, campaigns for a "revival of pure [Christian] religion" as a means of combatting world communism and the American "pseudo-liberals," "pseudo-intellectuals," and "liberal theologians" who are often "dupes" of the Reds.

The messages of the Crusade contain approximately the same points that have been made millions of times before by American politicians and patriots: Stalin *was* a bad guy, Khrushchev *is* a bad guy, the Communists are out to conquer the world, and if the Reds take over this country it will be a gloomy day for Christians and capitalists.

The messages are simple and familiar, but the energy with which they are delivered is extraordinary. The Crusade's program includes films and tape recordings, and the organization of anti-communist schools, seminars, "clinics," and neighborhood study groups. Crusaders are available to give lectures in churches, schools, clubs, and military and civic groups. And there is a dissemination of a seemingly endless amount of literature praising freedom and the House Un-American Activities Committee and denouncing foreign and domestic Communists and Comsymps.

The Crusade's firmest foothold in the South is in Texas, where it is directed by a vigorous young insurance-company executive named W. P. Strube, Jr.

Born in Missouri, Strube was educated at the Hannibal La-Grange Junior College, the University of Washington, and the University of California. Since 1954 he has been president of the Mid-America Life Insurance Company in Houston.

The Crusade does not concern itself with the "race problem." Although its literature is distributed by such a frankly racist organization as the Association of Citizens' Councils of Louisiana, it never addresses itself to the subject of integration v. segregation —one way or another.

Not long ago Strube was asked whether he felt that advocates of school integration in such cities of the South as New Orleans and Little Rock were "unconsciously dupes of communism."

"I don't believe the Communists fomented the troubles in Little Rock and New Orleans," he said. But, he added, it is true that Red tactics are designed to place "group against group."

A prime argument of integrationist groups is that racial segregation in America gives aid and comfort to the Communists internationally, particularly in the "uncommitted" nations of color in Asia and Africa. But an examination of the Christian Anti-Communist Crusade's literature fails to reveal that its leaders believe that eradication of racial discrimination in America would help to defeat world communism. This convenient exclusion of the race problem from its platform for the preservation of American freedom undoubtedly contributes to the Crusade's popularity in areas of the South where integration is considered the outstanding "communist threat" in America.

Nativism and Be-bop

But it would be a grave error, of course, to look upon the divers "anti-communist" and "patriotic" campaigns in the South as merely hypocritical manifestations of the desire of white Southerners to maintain racial supremacy over Negroes.

In much of the South the popularity of Comsymp-baiting organizations such as the John Birch Society and the Christian Anti-

Communist Crusade should be considered an expression of old-fashioned "nativism" as much as or more than an expression of segregationist sentiment.

There is in the South as well as in other parts of the country a growing desire to recapture the old patterns of life—the old faiths, the prides and glories of the past.

Certainly much of the Red-hunting and campaigning for "the American Way of Life" (interpreted below the Mason-Dixon line as "the Southern Way of Life") must be considered an agonized response to the United States' loss of prestige in the world—to our series of defeats and retreats and awkward semi-successes in the world since World War II: the communist victories in China, Southeast Asia, Cuba; the frustrating war in Korea; the apparent decay of our military might; the fact that a Russian was permitted to shout at our President and Latin Americans were permitted to spit on our Vice President.

Even less specifically, these blossomings of fear and suspicion and vague unrest must be considered a response, too, to the filth and flaccidity which somehow have become important characteristics of the American Way of Life: the warped, unclean quality of television programs from Manhattan and Hollywood; the flood of pornography in our books and magazines and movies; the growth of uncertainty among our religious leaders (the cracks in the rock of ages, the termites in the old rugged cross); the jungle libidinousness of the songs listened to by our children. It is not *merely* insanity that one of the South's leading white-supremacy crusaders for a time used as his main slogan: "Be-bop Promotes Communism."

VIII.   THE INVESTIGATORS

Politics and Panel Shows

1. THE LAWMAKERS

WHENEVER militant segregationists are pressed hard for evidence to prove their argument that race mixing in the schools "just won't work," many of them display a sort of grim pleasure in discussing the District of Columbia's experience with instant integration.

They observe that, in contrast with days gone by, the Washington educational experiment is nowadays not often eulogized by the Northern press as a "miracle in social adjustment." Nor is the city any longer pointed to with pride by Liberals as the "nation's showcase" for successful school desegregation.

On the contrary, the celebrated Washington experiment in education apparently has reached the stage where it is producing rapid resegregation. Rather than becoming more and more integrated, the District of Columbia school system promises soon to be attended almost entirely by Negro pupils—pupils segregated *in fact* while still integrated *in theory*.

At this writing (spring semester, 1962) 82 per cent of Washington's public-school pupils are Negroes—and only about 15 per cent of these Negro pupils are attending what (with any degree of realism) can be called "integrated" schools.[1]

[1] The figure, 15 per cent, is based on the National Association for the Advancement of Colored People's sensible rule of thumb that *de-facto* segregation exists in any school whose enrollment is more than 90 per cent Negro or less than 10 per cent Negro. As random examples in Washington, Mott Elementary School was attended by one white pupil and 1,059 Negro pupils during the 1961–62 academic year; Wilson High School had 1,345 whites and one Negro: the NAACP, while acknowledging that such schools as these are desegregated in theory, recognizes that they are segregated in fact.

Serious segregationists are often remarkably heavily equipped with facts and figures on education in Washington, and yet, too, it is often found that their statistics are just a few years out of date. The reason for both these things is that one of the most widely circulated large documents issued on the side of segregation has been the 1957 "Report of the Subcommittee [of the House Committee on the District of Columbia] to Investigate Public School Standards and Conditions, and Juvenile Delinquency in the District of Columbia." Among tomes above leaflet size probably only Tom Brady's *Black Monday* book has been more attentively perused by the South's leading segregationists.

The report was based on a two-week hearing held by the District of Columbia Subcommittee in September and October 1956, two years following the introduction of mass racial integration into Washington's public schools.

The hearing was plainly an uncomfortable experience for the dedicated integrationists who headed the District of Columbia education system, for the Subcommittee was led by and loaded with several of the most unyielding segregationists in the whole House of Representatives.

James C. Davis of Georgia was its chairman, and three other Southerners were members of it: John Bell Williams of Mississippi, Woodrow W. Jones of North Carolina, and Joel T. Broyhill of Virginia. Its only other two members were A. L. Miller of Nebraska and DeWitt S. Hyde of Maryland, neither of whom expressed any strong integrationist sentiment or, in fact, manifested any very active interest in the hearing.

The Subcommittee's most tenacious and most dedicatedly segregationist questioner by far was John Bell Williams of Raymond, Mississippi. Williams, a genial-looking, one-armed (he lost his left arm in a plane crash in South America when he was an Air Corps pilot during World War II), rugged-featured fellow who was then in his late thirties, is the person commonly given credit for employing the phrase "Black Monday" as a description of May 17, 1954, the day the Supreme Court handed down its portentous school-desegregation decision.[2] Plainly, Williams, an able

[2] " 'Black Monday' is the name coined by Representative John Bell Williams of Mississippi to designate Monday, May 17, 1954, a date long to be remembered throughout this nation," Tom Brady wrote in the fore-

lawyer and a politically ambitious Mississippian, came to the hearing loaded for bear—integrationist bear.

After two weeks of asking unsettling questions to Washington's desegregationist school supervisors and asking encouraging questions to teachers and principals who had become more or less disillusioned with instant integration, a majority of the Subcommittee —Georgia's Davis and Mississippi's Williams, along with Virginia's Broyhill and North Carolina's Jones—issued a scorching indictment of the District of Columbia school system and its national "showcase" of racial brotherhood.

Along the Road to Resegregation

The Subcommittee report, written, of course, by white men, expressed concern that so many white people were leaving the District of Columbia for suburban climes—particularly those Caucasians with school-age children.

"The records show, conclusively, that the elementary-school population was increasing after World War II until the first steps into integration were taken in public housing and other fields." But, the Subcommittee added: "At the first threat of integration, the white residents began to leave. . . . This exodus is continuing at this moment [and] there is a prediction that in the not-too-distant future the District of Columbia will be a predominantly Negro community.

"Where there were a few years ago 59,582 white students and 33,498 Negro students . . . the school census of October 1956 . . . shows that the school population is now 34,750 white students (32 per cent) and 73,723 Negro students (68 per cent)."

(The Subcommittee was correct in its prediction that the District of Columbia would soon become a "predominantly Negro community": in 1950, only 35 per cent of the District of Columbia populace was Negro; by 1960, 54 per cent was Negro.)

---

word to his book, *Black Monday*. "Should Representative Williams accomplish nothing more during his membership in Congress he has more than justified his years in office by the creating of this epithet, the originating of this watchword, the shouting of this battle cry. . . ."

The Subcommittee concluded that the mass of Negro pupils—many of them fresh from the deeper South—were inferior to white pupils in mental maturity and academic achievement.

For example, the results of a city-wide "California test of mental maturity" indicated that third-grade pupils at all-white schools scored five points *above* the national average; the average score of pupils at racially integrated school was four points below the norm; and pupils at all-Negro schools had scores that averaged thirteen points *below* the national norm.

A battery of achievement tests given to ninth-grade pupils indicated that the academic level at all-white schools was one grade *above* the national average, at integrated schools was one full grade below the norm, and at all-Negro schools was almost three grades *below* the national average.

To cope with the pedagogical problems posed by such challenging statistics as these, the Subcommittee noted, District of Columbia school officials had established a "four-track plan" in the schools. Under this plan, pupils in certain grades were separated into different classes according to their mental ability and scholastic achievement.

"These developments under the integrated program," the Subcommittee commented, "[have resulted] in a new form of segregation: instead of having a segregated-school system, they now have segregation in different classrooms under the same roof."

The most controversial part of the report—and the most spine-tingling to segregationists who have read it—was that which dealt with sex and violence in the newly "integrated" school system.

Stimulated by Representative Williams' questions, many school principals and teachers spoke of the problems that they felt integration had produced at their schools. Fairly typical was this testimony from John Paul Collins, retired principal of Eastern High School, a formerly all-white school which had become predominantly Negro by 1956 (459 Negroes and 94 whites):

After integration of the schools in 1954 . . . the problem of discipline was tremendous.

I found it necessary to require that all teachers leave their desks when the bell rang and keep order in the corridors.

At times I heard colored girls at the school use language that was far worse than I have ever heard, even in the Marine Corps. . . .

Fighting, including several knifings, went on continuously. While such incidents had occurred occasionally in previous years, they became more or less commonplace following integration. . . .

There have been more thefts at Eastern in the last two years than I had known in all my thirty-odd years in the school system. . . .

There were many sex problems during the year following integration. The first evidence of this came about when some colored boys began writing notes to the white girls, telling them their phone numbers and asking the girls for their numbers in return.

The white girls complained of being touched by colored boys in a suggestive manner when passing them in the halls.

One white girl left school one afternoon and was surrounded by a group of colored boys and girls. One of the colored boys put a knife at her back, marched her down an alley, and backed her up against a wall. While the group debated as to whether they would make her take her clothes off, she broke away and ran home. . . .

It [integration] has created grave social problems that cannot be solved under existing circumstances. This leads me to the obvious conclusion that our system of integration cannot be held out as any model to any community that has not, as yet, integrated its school system.

Actually, those problems of an *interracial* character have been solved at Eastern High since the time of Principal Collins' testimony. The solution has evolved through gradual *re*segregation. In the 1961–62 school year Eastern was being attended by 1,701 Negroes and 3 whites.

Collins' testimony was not exceptional. The Subcommittee reported that the "overwhelming majority" of the teachers and school administrators interviewed during the investigation testified that integration had been followed by a marked increase in disciplinary problems involving stealing, lying, cheating, fighting, vandalism, and obscene language.

Indeed the Subcommittee staff gathered a considerable amount of evidence from police and health authorities that seemed to indicate that many Negro parents of Washington had failed to instill in their children a wholesome respect for sexual proprieties and the law. For instance, while 39 white girls of school age (seventeen years and under) gave birth to illegitimate children in 1955, there were 670 illegitimate births among Negro girls in the same age group. During the same year 834 cases of gonorrhea were reported among Negro boys and girls of school age, while only 20 were reported among whites. And of the 1,814 juveniles (seventeen years and under) arrested on felony charges in the District of Columbia that year, 79 per cent were Negroes.[3]

The Subcommittee did not choose to give the statistics a thorough sociological interpretation—i.e., did not choose to "explain the figures away" in the Myrdalian manner commonly accepted by integrationist "experts on the race problem." Instead, the majority of the committeemen chose to view the whole matter with alarm.

The four Dixieland members of the Subcommittee—Davis of Georgia, Williams of Mississippi, Jones of North Carolina, and Broyhill of Virginia—concluded that integration had "seriously damaged" the public-school system in the District of Columbia.

"The evidence, taken as a whole, points to a definite impairment of educational opportunities for members of both white and Negro races as a result of integration, with little prospect of remedy in the future," the Southerners declared at the conclusion of the report. "Therefore, we recommend that racially separate public schools be re-established for the education of white and Negro pupils in the District of Columbia, and that such schools be maintained on a completely separate and equal basis."

Congressman Miller of Nebraska and Hyde of Maryland refused to sign the majority report or endorse the views of their Southern colleagues. They said they felt that many of the witnesses were asked leading questions, and they suggested that integration should not be blamed entirely for "the educational deficiencies in our school system." The 1954 Supreme Court decision, they said, "must be taken as final."

[3] Almost all of the white juvenile arrests resulted from either housebreaking or auto theft. Among the most serious of the alleged crimes, murder was charged to 3 of the Negro juveniles, none to the whites; rape was charged to 33 of the Negroes, none to the whites; robbery to 261 of the Negroes, 9 to the whites; aggravated assault to 84 of the Negroes, 12 to the whites.

Even so, the Miller-Hyde dissent was by no means simply an expression of the usual anti-segregationist sentiments. For one thing, they chose not to blame Negroes' social problems entirely on white people.

"The facts brought to light by this investigation," wrote Miller and Hyde, "seem to indicate that Negro leaders, and those actively interested in the advancement of the Negro people, have much work to do among the Negro people, and that all of the difficulties attended with integration are not caused by the seemingly uncompromising attitude of the white people."

Since the report was so alien to the integrationist temper of the times, no legislation resulted from it, of course. And because the Subcommittee was so obviously loaded with segregationist Southerners, it was inevitably attacked with vigor by large numbers of "racial-brotherhood" enthusiasts—by those who had read the Subcommittee report and by those who had not.

"The Miracle of Social Adjustment"

The most notable "reply" to the Subcommittee's findings and recommendations was a long treatise written later in 1957 by Carl F. Hansen, who was then assistant superintendent in charge of senior high schools in the District of Columbia, and later became superintendent in charge of all the District's schools. The title of his treatise was *Miracle of Social Adjustment: Desegregation in the Washington, D. C., Schools.*

His title was based on a comment he made while being questioned by Mississippi's John Bell Williams:

WILLIAMS: Do you think, Mr. Hansen, that integration in the District of Columbia schools has been carried on smoothly and without incident?
HANSEN: It would be fantastic to say "without incident." I think that the integration program in this city has been a miracle of social adjustment.

Hansen chose to counterattack the Subcommittee findings obliquely.

True, he said, whites have been swiftly moving to the suburbs as Negroes have been pouring into the District of Columbia. But:

"To what extent integration was a causative factor will never be precisely known. Out-migration to suburban areas is a widespread phenomenon throughout the United States. For example, in the period between 1940–50 the increase in suburban growth in the New York City area was almost 19 per cent, in Chicago, 31 per cent, in Los Angeles, 69 per cent, and in Cleveland almost 41 per cent. . . . A fair and reasonable assumption is that a significant amount of change of residence resulted from the reorganization of schools. Some of this withdrawal by out-migration, however, was caused by changes in neighborhoods. This was accompanied by lower social and cultural levels of the people moving in, by the dissimilarities in backgrounds, as well as by the differences in race. . . ."

True enough, said Hansen, "desegregation has added a new dimension to disciplinary problems." But the city's eleven high schools, for example, reported only 410 cases of "serious disciplinary offense" (defined by Hansen as an offense "which seriously interfered with the rights of other students with respect to their persons or property, morals, or educational opportunity)." Such offenses were committed by "only [sic] 3.1 per cent of the high-school population."

Rather than dwelling on the depressing aspects of the "social-adjustment miracle," Hansen preferred to look on the bright side —and to predict even better days to come:

"Anyone who views the Washington story in its entirety . . . will feel a glow of pride that in the nation's capital the ideal of individual dignity and worth, no longer simply an idle phrase in a textbook on American democracy, is now to a much larger extent a living reality in the lives of its citizens."

And, said Hansen in conclusion:

"The big fear, that integration will impair the education of some children in this community, is rapidly yielding to the concentrated drive to effectuate the big solution. The prevailing spirit in the District of Columbia is positive and dynamic. It looks forward to a growing and improving school system, to a betterment of educational opportunities for all children, and is resolved to let no transient troubles prevent the realization of the ultimate goal, a better community through brotherhood."

In the five years since Hansen made this declaration on the side of a "better community through brotherhood," the number of white pupils in his school system has decreased from 34,750 to 23,462, and the number of Negro pupils has increased from 73,723 to 103,806.

Yet Hansen—presumably still encouraged by the "positive and dynamic" spirit which he feels prevails in the District of Columbia —is still striving to make racial integration work in the schools of the nation's capital.

During the 1961–62 school year Superintendent Hansen announced that his school system will soon curtail its practice of permitting "hardship" transfers of students out of schools where they are part of a small racial minority. Ever since the integration attempt began in 1954, school officials had made it a practice to grant transfers to students of either race who were assigned to schools where they were in an extreme racial minority, "if there were indications that the situation might impair their emotional health."

But Hansen has now decided:

"There is too much fluidity in the school system. Children should stay in the schools where they belong. . . . It is apparent that children can attend school together successfully and that people are living together harmoniously in neighborhoods that are biracial to varying degrees."

He indicated that he feels this new policy will tend to reduce the number of all-white and all-Negro schools in Washington. And he added—in one of the more fascinating statements of the pedagogical season—that he believes the racial composition of the schools "is important only to the degree that it indicates an increase in the number of children needing the best kind of educational services."

It requires some gift of prophecy—but not much, really—to predict the result if this latest integrate-them-even-faster policy is actually enforced. Facts and figures from the past and inductive reasoning (as opposed to forthright statements about "brotherhood" and dreamy deductive reasoning) inevitably lead to the conclusion that this would simply accelerate the exodus of white pupils from the District of Columbia.

This transformation of the Washington school system into an even more predominantly Negro educational community—perhaps eventually entirely Negro—may or may not be socially desirable in the long run, but it is extremely difficult to see how it is compatible with the spirit of the 1954 Supreme Court decision.

The Law of Diminishing Integration

Of course the resegregation that has occurred in the Washington schools is not a singular phenomenon. The resegregation process has evolved in several other cities where attempts have been made to integrate white pupils with *large* numbers of Negro pupils.

There seems to be a sort of "law of diminishing integration" which goes into effect whenever the number of Negro pupils in any given school reaches a certain level. As long as Negro pupils make up no more than 10 or 20 per cent of a school's population, "integration" moves genially along. But when the number of Negroes begins to approach the halfway mark, white parents (Liberals and mossbacks alike) tend to take their children out of school and move with all deliberate speed to a more segregated suburb.

While the guiding spirits of the Washington, D. C., school system apparently have either missed this point or—for reasons altruistic, perhaps—have decided to ignore it, educators in several other "border area" states are expressing great concern over the effect of this new pattern of resegregation on their school systems.

The other two largest "border" cities—Baltimore and St. Louis, both of which have attempted mass school integration since the Supreme Court decision—report they are experiencing creeping resegregation of approximately the sort that Washington has undergone.

St. Louis—with a city population that is 29 per cent Negro—probably has more "actual segregation" in its school system than shortly after it was officially desegregated in September 1955, Deputy Superintendent William A. Kottmeyer said recently. This "stems from the tendency of white residents to move out of areas as Negroes move in."

Southern School News estimated that Negro pupils made up slightly more than half of St. Louis's school population in 1961–62 —but nobody is certain that this estimate is really accurate. In one of those ill-fated efforts to solve the race problem by discarding words, St. Louis school officials a few years ago decided to eliminate any mention of race on all the pupils' records. But even with the aid of that remarkable little exercise in semantics, the citizenry of St. Louis have not yet embraced the newfangled anthropological theory that there is no such thing as "race" and that the "Negroes" they see before their eyes do not, in truth, exist.

Baltimore, with a city population that is 35 per cent Negro, reports a resegregation trend perhaps even more pronounced than that of St. Louis. Until 1954 Baltimore's schools—like Washington's and St. Louis's—were racially segregated; then fast upon The Decision the city inaugurated a fairly comprehensive policy of school integration. But since then a great many formerly white schools have become predominantly Negro, and at least eleven schools have been built to serve Negro residential areas.

"That leaves more Negro children today in essentially segregated situations than we had when segregation was compulsory," Assistant Superintendent Houston R. Jackson, the highest-ranking Negro in the Baltimore school administration, said recently. "[Only] 27,000 out of 87,000 Negro children are in the formerly white schools. . . . Fewer than 53 white pupils attend Negro schools, and most of them are children of storekeepers who are interested not so much in integration as in the nearness of the Negro schools to their family shops."

An added problem for school administrators in Baltimore, as in other "integrated" cities, is the fact that large numbers of able and experienced white teachers and principals join white pupils and their parents in the great Caucasian exodus to the segregated suburbs.

"White staff members have run away, just as white pupils and, more important, the parents of white pupils have run away," said Jackson. "When the Negroes in a school reach 50 per cent, that's when the white teachers begin to ask for transfers. The white pupils have already begun to move out, and teachers follow."

The white flight to the suburbs is not, of course, merely a result of an increase in the number of Negro children in the Baltimore school system. It is also, among other things, a response to the changing cultural make-up of the city.

Between 1950 and 1960 Baltimore's white population declined by 113,000 while its Negro population increased by 102,000.

And yet "During the past ten years, despite a slight drop in [our city's] total population," Baltimore Mayor J. Harold Grady reported in late 1961, "welfare cases have increased in number by 27 per cent. The incidence of fires has increased 22 per cent; false alarms have tripled in number. Arrests for burglary have doubled. Arrests for robbery have tripled. Other crimes of violence are on the rise and commitments to jail by our courts have increased 28 per cent. In six years the cost of repairs for vandalism in the public schools has increased by 135 per cent."

Mayor Grady did not attribute changes in these statistics to his city's loss of whites and gain of Negroes. Nicely—in this genial age of now-you-see-it-now-you-don't sociology—the mayor chose not to dwell on any cause-and-effect relationship between the influx of Negroes and the unseemly increase in these municipal disasters.

Despite all the politically prudent unspeak, however, the truth remains that white people in such cities as Baltimore, St. Louis, and Washington, D. C., have *fled* from Negroes. And the fact that high public officials—whether motivated by Caucasic politeness or *Realpolitik*—do not deign to discuss this openly might well be recorded as one of the more striking sociological oddities of the twentieth century.

But it would be misleading to leave the impression that the resegregation process is peculiar to cities of the "border states." In several Northern cities, which theoretically operated desegregated school systems long before the Supreme Court decision of 1954, resegregation has progressed with fairly deliberate speed in recent years. *Time* magazine not so many weeks ago remarked on this long-apparent fact of life in the "integrated" North:

In large Northern cities a kind of resegregation results from ghetto housing. New York, Chicago, Detroit, and Philadelphia all have Negro populations that are at least twice as big as the South's largest Negro communities, those in New Orleans and Houston.[4]

[4] New York City has 1,087,931 Negroes (14 per cent of the city's total population); Chicago, 812,637 (23 per cent); Detroit, 482,223 (29 per cent); and Philadelphia, 529,240 (26 per cent). Houston has 215,037 Negroes (23 per cent), and New Orleans has 233,514 (37 per cent). Other non-Southern cities that have larger Negro populations than any

Hundreds of Northern city schools are predominantly Negro, and becoming more so. This ironic turn of events puts the Northern schools in a category somewhat like the "separate but equal" Southern schools that the Supreme Court outlawed. Believing that such *de-facto* segregated schools are inferior, Northern Negroes are starting legal attacks, calling for such solutions as taking students by bus to distant mixed schools.

And *Time,* traditionally a staunch crusader for school integration in Arkansas, Georgia, Louisiana, and elsewhere, reached this arresting conclusion:

But if the majority of a city's school children are Negro, "integration" may be a fairly elusive goal. The phenomenon of resegregation also suggests that the law can go only so far in correcting racial inequalities—and that stressing the fine points of integration is less important than insisting on excellent schooling for all United States children.

A Chorus of "Dixie" in D. C.

Time magazine does not often agree with Representative John Bell Williams of Mississippi, nor does Williams with *Time.*

Just this once, though, their conclusions about the elusiveness of integration and the limitations of the law are fairly similar—even though the routes of logic that Williams and *Time* took to reach the conclusions probably differed considerably.

"I'm inclined to feel," Congressman Williams said in his Washington office the other day, "that the more people are brought into personal contact with the race problem the less inclined they are to insist on forced intermingling of the races.

"The fewer Negroes there are in a community's population, the more intense pro-integration feeling becomes. But then when there is an increase in the number of Negroes, there is a corresponding decline in enthusiasm for integration."

---

city in the eleven states of the old Confederacy are Washington, D. C., 411,737 (54 per cent); Los Angeles, 334,916 (14 per cent); Baltimore, 326,589 (35 per cent); and Cleveland, 250,818 (29 per cent).

This, Williams suggested, is not merely a product of white supremacist sentiment.

"As Negroes move into a white area, property values go down and welfare costs go up—and that means less tax revenue and more expenditures for a city. As this makes itself felt on the pocketbooks of the whites, I believe there is—and will be more so in the future—a greater tendency for them to band together to protect their economic interests."

The husky Mississippian—who is now in his forties but still is boyish looking in a rough-cast, open-faced sort of way—sat contentedly relaxed with his feet propped easily on his desk. His office virtually sings "Dixie" aloud: draped behind him is a vast Confederate flag; the walls are clustered with pictures of Jefferson Davis and Robert E. Lee and several paste-ups of Confederate money in frames—along with a photograph of the World War II Air Corps airplane in which he crashed and lost an arm.

Williams' uncompromising segregationist philosophy is not an impersonal thing.

He and his wife have three young children—in the second, fourth, and sixth grades.

"They go to a segregated school over in Arlington County [Virginia]," said Williams. "We, too, are refugees from the District. We made a mad dash to Virginia, where we figured we'd be protected from integration. And we have been protected, despite some token integration over there."[5]

Predictably, the Mississippian spoke of the evils of racial intermarriage, but in a slightly unusual way.

"It's not fair to simply say that 'Southerners fear intermarriage.' Southern people have great pride in the integrity of their race—they regard race as a badge of honor; they fear for the future of the race, not for themselves as individuals.

"My children will have to live with the future, and my children's children. A person who doesn't care what happens to this world after he's gone—what happens to future generations—is indeed helpless. Certainly no person who believes in a Supreme Being could be unconcerned about the future of civilization."

[5] Of Arlington County's 25,730 public-school pupils, 2,298 are Negroes. Of the Negroes, 143 attended classes with whites in the 1961–62 school year.

Aside from his concern with the fate of Western civilization, it is only logical to conclude that Williams' fiery and frequent pronouncements on The Problem are also motivated in part by the fact that he has higher political ambitions, the fulfillment of which depends on the rigidly segregationist white electorate of Mississippi.

It is unlikely that Williams in the foreseeable future will run for the United States Senate against the veterans Jim Eastland or John Stennis, either of whom very possibly could make political hominy grits of him. But sooner or later—probably sooner, he indicated— he plans to run for governor of Mississippi.

One political advantage that he enjoys is the fact that he is the number-one political darling of the vastly influential Mississippi Citizens' Council apparatus. Williams never misses a chance to breathe a bit of eulogy in the direction of the CCs back home.

"The Citizens' Councils have served a very useful and worthwhile purpose in Mississippi, and will continue to do so as long as their leadership continues at such a high level of quality. As to the charge that the Council has used coercion and other questionable means to carry out its ends, a case of that kind has never been called to my attention.

"The Council's board of directors are not thugs: it [the Jackson CC board, for example] reads like a 'Who's Who in Jackson.' It's been a very effective channel for holding down lawlessness.

"Mississippi, when you think about it, has had less race trouble than any state in the Union since 1954—less violence and less litigation. That's excluding a few states like Montana and Colorado, of course; no trouble out there: no Negroes."

Williams takes pride in the fact that since he was first elected to the House in 1946 he has amassed "about as conservative a record as anyone in Congress."

"Actually, I'm a liberal by the historic definition of a 'liberal'— one who believes in a maximum amount of individual freedom with a minimum amount of Government control. Today it seems that a man is classified as a 'Liberal' in proportion to how much he advocates Big Government."

As a self-classified conservative, he said, he is encouraged by the reported increase in political conservatism on college campuses.

"Our students are beginning to see the evils associated with overcentralization of Government and will eventually demand a return to Constitutional principles."

Williams suggests that the Liberals' pressures to reduce local governmental authority and increase federal power might one of these days result in a backlash that will foul up their own eager humanitarianism.

"I'm afraid a demagogue could arise, one who could seize our centralized government by using the various hatreds that have been engendered and capitalizing on the grievances of the country's conservatives," he said. "I feel that the liberals are unwillingly providing the machinery by which another Hitler could come into being."

As for the struggle over The Problem:

The outcome, feels the congressman from Mississippi, depends primarily on how firm the segregationist spirit remains in the South.

"Nobody could say what would happen if the Southern leadership were to abandon its resistance [to integration and 'Big Government']. But, collectively speaking, the Southern white people are the last stronghold—the last frontier—of our historic American philosophy of freedom under the Constitution.

"If the South falls, our system of government will fall with it."

Rebel Yells on Capitol Hill

In their *legislative* function, Southerners in neither House of Congress have been effective in advancing the cause of segregation —except in a negative sort of way (e.g., the threat of obstructionist parliamentary tactics by Southerners prompted President Kennedy to keep civil-rights legislation out of his "new-frontier" program for 1961, at least).

On the floors of the Senate and House the South's legislators have, in the main, been forced to content themselves with orotund pronouncements and a few "rebel yells" for the pleasure of the folks back home.

The most notable of these was the richly worded "Southern Manifesto" of 1956, a document (officially entitled "Declaration of Constitutional Principles") signed by 19 senators and 77 representatives. With the exception of Senator W. Kerr Scott of Oklahoma, all of the signers were from the states of the old Confederacy.

The "Southern Manifesto" declares, in part:

We regard the decision of the Supreme Court in the [1954] school cases as a clear abuse of judicial power. It climaxes a trend in the Federal Judiciary undertaking to legislate, in derogation of the authority of Congress, and to encroach upon the reserved rights of the States and the people.

The original Constitution does not mention education. Neither does the Fourteenth Amendment nor any other Amendment. The debates preceding the submission of the Fourteenth Amendment clearly show there was no intent that it should affect the systems of education maintained by the States.

The very Congress which proposed the Amendment subsequently provided for segregated schools in the District of Columbia. . . .

It [the "separate but equal" principle] is founded on elemental humanity and common sense, for parents should not be deprived by government of the right to direct the lives and education of their own children. . . .

This unwarranted exercise of power by the Court [on May 17, 1954], contrary to the Constitution, is creating chaos and confusion in the States principally affected. It is destroying the amicable relations between the white and Negro races that have been created through ninety years of patient effort by the good people of both races. It has planted hatred and suspicion where there has been heretofore friendship and understanding. . . .

We commend the motives of those States which have declared the intention to resist forced integration by any lawful means. . . .

Even though we constitute a minority in the present Congress, we have full faith that a majority of the American people believe in the dual system of government which has enabled us to achieve our greatness and will in time demand that the reserved rights of the States and of the people be made secure against judicial usurpation.

Now and then a Southern congressman will propose a court-curbing segregationist bill just, if you please, for the hell of it. In 1961, for instance, Senator Herman Talmadge of Georgia introduced a group of bills that would (1) require Supreme Court justices to have at least five years of judicial experience; (2) require the Supreme Court to "accord full hearings to all parties before acting upon lower court decisions"; (3) require jury trials in all cases of contempt arising from the disobedience of any federal court order; and (4) "withdraw the jurisdiction of all federal courts over matters relating to the administration of public schools by the states and their subdivisions." In 1959 Talmadge and a handful of colleagues had proposed a constitutional amendment that would return the complete and exclusive control of the public-school system to Georgia and the other several states.

Aside from the question of the merits and demerits of Talmadge's proposals, it was obvious all along that they were nothing more than fine old cornpone Confederate gestures. They did not pass, and it is inconceivable that Talmadge did not know they would not pass. Indeed, his old segregationist political buddy, editor Roy Harris, made it plain in his Augusta *Courier* that he did not feel the Talmadge bills would have much more chance than would snowballs in Albany, Georgia—that the senator was merely indulging in an "exercise of futility."

The fact that the bills did not pass came, of course, as no ego-shattering surprise to Senator Talmadge. The senator was asked recently if he really thought there was any likelihood that legislation of that sort would pass in the Congress.

"At the present time, unfortunately not," he admitted.

The senator, rocking restively in a big swivel chair behind his desk in the Senate Office Building, puffed fiercely at a large morning cigar. He is a lanky man with an aggressive jaw and a back-woods-fashion dangle of hair that juts down across one region of his forehead; as the years have passed he has become more and more the spitting image (literally; he most always has a cuspidor within range) of his late father, the colorful Governor Eugene Talmadge of Georgia.

"If the present course of events is continued, before long we'll have a federal school system rather than local school systems," he said. "This would be catastrophic."

The only hope that the "catastrophes" of integration and the increase in federal power can be averted is that the American people will eventually "wake up to the threat." And what will rouse them? Talmadge admitted that he does not know for sure.

"It's difficult to foresee what'll wake the people up. I wouldn't speculate on what'll happen in the electorate's mind. No one can anticipate the trends of one hundred and eighty million people."

About a year after the Supreme Court's *Brown* v. *Topeka* decision, Talmadge wrote a little book which—along with Tom Brady's *Black Monday*—has been a standard volume in Southern segregationists' libraries, *You and Segregation* (Vulcan Press, Birmingham, 1955). In the book Talmadge presented, among other things, an abundance of Dixieland ethnological determinations:

In Cuba, in Mexico, and in the South American countries, segregation has never been practiced. As a result, the races have intermarried and become a mongrel race in which the strongest and best features of both races have been destroyed.

God Advocates Segregation

Ethnology teaches that there are five different races: white, black, yellow, brown, and red. God created them all different. He set them in families and appointed bounds of habitation. He did not intend them to be mixed or He would not have separated or segregated them.

Certainly history shows that nations composed of a mongrel race lose their strength and become weak, lazy, and indifferent. They become easy preys to outside nations. And isn't that just exactly what the Communists want to happen to the United States?

This position has nothing to do with Hitler's theory of the "super race." It is based on history and natural science.

Certainly a man with pure Negro blood will have a better opportunity to develop the finer characteristics and culture of his race than one of mixed blood. The same is true of the white man, of course. . . .

It is said by some that Herman Talmadge, who was not behind the door when the political acumen was passed out, has tended to become slightly more flexible—more accommodating—on the "race issue" in recent years. In truth, it did seem that his segregationist fires were banked, as it were, when the first "token" Negroes were admitted to the University of Georgia, Georgia Tech, and the grade schools of Atlanta. At least there were no notable alarums sounded from his Washington office.

Talmadge himself noted that the number of Negro voters in

Georgia has grown fairly large in recent years, and interestingly enough (considering the fact that the very name "Talmadge" has for half a century connoted uncompromising "white supremacy"), he has harvested quite a few votes from his "mongrel" and "pure Negro" constituents.

"When I ran for the Senate I received about 10 per cent of the Negro vote," he said. "We have about a hundred and eighty-five thousand Negroes voting in Georgia. They have the balance of power in many areas [of Georgia] and, in fact, have elected Negroes to public office."

In truth, the political genius of a Talmadge is not really necessary to recognize that for a Georgian the time is riper this season for public pronouncements on the poetry of the United States Constitution than for Mississippi-style denunciations of Negroes and human "mongrels."

Of the possible eventual effect of increased Negro voting in Georgia Talmadge conceded:

"I don't know what the result will be in that area [of practical politics.]"

But, vigorously swiveling and neatly sheltering himself in cigar smoke, the firm-faced senator from Georgia declared he feels that history is on the side of the (white) South.

"We've been through this [same sort of thing] before—in Reconstruction days. The pressure [of the North on the South] ultimately relented. Ultimately they got tired and pulled out their troops."

Being well aware of the problems of desegregation which had recently racked his home state, Talmadge emphasized that he did not wish his comments to be interpreted as official pronouncements in behalf of Georgia—or anent the hereafter of that sovereign state.

"I speak only for Herman Talmadge," he said, and added, perhaps unduly modestly, at least as far as politics are concerned, "I have no power to see the future."

2. THE RED HUNTERS

But ALTHOUGH congressmen from below the Mason-Dixon line plainly have had no success in passing segregationist legislation on Capitol Hill, they nevertheless have delivered some fairly telling blows in behalf of the Southern Way of Life through the gaudy old "quiz-show technique" which was so nicely perfected a few years ago by that remarkable man from Wisconsin, Joe McCarthy.

When the late senator from Wisconsin was riding high in the early fifties the spectacular investigatorial ceremony which was a featured part of "McCarthyism"—while it spread hysteria throughout the liberal establishment and much of the rest of Yankeedom—never became a fad down in the land of cotton.

Since McCarthy's political eclipse and ensuing demise, however, not a few Southern legislators have found his techniques nicely adaptable to the task of equating the integration movement with the evils of communism and other foul forms of radicalism.

The organization that has served as the favorite "punching bag" for the various Dixie-oriented investigating committees has been the Southern Conference Educational Fund, Inc., a New Orleans-headquartered outfit that describes its goal as "the elimination of all forms of racial segregation in the Southern and border states."

The president of the SCEF is Aubrey W. Williams of Montgomery, owner of the long-successful rural publication, *Southern Farm and Home,* and head of the old National Youth Administration back in the New Deal days. Its executive director is James A. Dombrowski, who has been engaged in one way or another in the fight against the "Southern Way of Life" for thirty years or so.

SCEF's chief field secretary and organizer has been Carl Braden, a former Louisville *Courier-Journal* copy editor who a few years ago was sentenced to fifteen years in prison under a Kentucky state sedition law after having helped a Negro purchase a house in an all-white Louisville neighborhood—a purchase which, quite predictably, enraged the white residents and resulted in an explosive bit of violence. However, the United States Supreme Court eventually reversed Braden's conviction on the sedition charge—after he had dwelled for eight months or so in Kentucky lockups. More recently Braden gave the federal appellate courts another juridical workout after he was sentenced to a year in prison for declining to tell a congressional committee whether he is or was a Communist (he based his refusal to answer primarily on the ground of the First Amendment of the Constitution rather than on the "safer" and judicially more acceptable ground of the Fifth Amendment).[1] At this writing Braden is in jail, his appeal of the contempt-of-Congress conviction having failed—at least for the time being.

Braden's unique and at times doubtless uncomfortable experience in the field of race relations has been described in *The Wall Between,* a book by his wife, Anne, who has worked with her husband as a field secretary for SCEF.

The Southern Conference Educational Fund (which should not be confused with either the Southern Regional Council of Atlanta or the Southern Education Reporting Service of Nashville) asserts that its primary aim is to "work toward that day . . . when racial segregation will no longer place its life-long blight on the bodies of Negroes and the spirit of white people [and] when Negro and white Southerners will build together . . . toward greater opportunity for all." However, following a series of New Orleans hearings con-

[1] The First Amendment rules (in part) that Congress shall make no law "abridging the freedom of speech or of the press; or the right of the people peaceably to assemble and to petition the Government for a redress of grievances." The Fifth Amendment says (again in part): "No person shall be held to answer for a capital or infamous crime unless on a presentment or indictment of a Grand Jury, except in cases arising in the land or naval forces, or in the militia, when in actual service in time of war or public danger . . . nor shall be compelled in any criminal case to be a witness against himself, nor be deprived of life, liberty, or property, without due process of law. . . ."

ducted in March 1954 by Senator James O. Eastland of Mississippi (who is, as a mattter of fact, of segregationist persuasion), the internal-security subcommittee of the Senate Judiciary Committee concluded that "subversive influence" existed in the Southern Conference Educational Fund, Inc.

SCEF, declared the Senate Subcommittee, was plainly a descendant and near-duplicate of the old Southern Conference for Human Welfare. According to the Subcommittee report:

The Southern Conference for Human Welfare was conceived, financed, and set up by the Communist Party in 1938 as a mass organization to promote communism throughout the Southern States. Earl Browder, former general secretary of the Communist Party in the United States, in a public hearing, identified the Southern Conference for Human Welfare as one of the Communist Party's "transmission belts." Under date of March 29, 1944, the Southern Conference for Human Welfare was cited by the Special Committee on Un-American Activities as a Communist front and, on June 12, 1947, by the Congressional Committee on Un-American Activities as a Communist-front organization "Which seeks to attract southern liberals on the basis of its seeming interest in the problems of the South," although its "professed interest in southern welfare is simply an expedient for larger aims serving the Soviet Union and its subservient Communist Party in the United States."

The Southern Conference Educational Fund, Inc., was initially an adjunct of the Southern Conference for Human Welfare. After the exposure of the Southern Conference for Human Welfare as a Communist front, it began to wither and was finally dissolved, but the Southern Conference Educational Fund, Inc., continued. The official paper, the *Southern Patriot,* which was published by the Southern Conference for Human Welfare, was taken over by the Southern Conference Educational Fund, Inc., which professed the same ostensible purpose. . . .

An objective study of the entire record compels the conclusion that the Southern Conference Educational Fund, Inc., is operating with the same leadership and purposes as its predecessor organization, the Southern Conference for Human Welfare.

The subcommittee accordingly recommends that the Attorney General take the necessary steps to present this matter before the Subversive Activities Control Board in order that a determination can be made as to the status of the Southern Conference Educational Fund, Inc.[2]

The Senate Subcommittee placed considerable emphasis on the fact that a striking number of the key executives of the old allegedly Red-dominated Southern Conference for Human Welfare had later become key executives of SCEF.

Aubrey Williams, SCEF's president, had been a board member of the predecessor organization, for example. Dombrowski, administrator of the Southern Conference for Human Welfare, had become SCEF's executive director. Mrs. Modjeska M. Simkins of Columbia, South Carolina, had been a board member of the Southern Conference for Human Welfare and was now a vice president of SCEF. Mrs. Virginia Durr, sister-in-law of Supreme Court Justice Hugo Black, had been a vice president of the earlier organization and later served for a time as a member of the board of directors of SCEF.[3]

It was in July of 1958 that the House Un-American Activities Committee, at hearings in Atlanta, focused particularly on Carl Braden and his role as a SCEF organizer. As at the 1954 Senate Internal Security Subcommittee hearing in New Orleans the remarkably energetic quizmaster, Richard Arens, served as chief questioner; and again, a Deep Southerner, Representative Edwin E. Willis of Louisiana, functioned as chairman of the hearing at which Braden appeared.

Braden spiritedly accused the Committee of holding its hearing for the purpose of "investigating" integrationists rather than "un-Americanism." And he chose to invoke the First Amendment as a ground for refusing to answer whether he was a Communist.

"Sir, it is our understanding," said Arens, "that you are now a

[2] The report was signed (without dissent) by the following senators: James O. Eastland of Mississippi, chairman; Olin D. Johnston of South Carolina; John L. McClellan of Arkansas; Price Daniel of Texas; William E. Jenner of Indiana; Arthur V. Watkins of Utah; Herman Welker of Idaho; and John Marshall Butler of Maryland.

[3] "Mrs. Durr," the Senate Subcommittee reported, "was identified by a witness [the late Paul Crouch, an articulate ex-Communist who for several years was one of the Washington Red hunters' favorite and most productive sources of information on matters of 'subversion'] as one who had not only accepted Community Party 'discipline' but as one who had 'plotted with the

Communist . . . part of the Communist Party which is a tentacle of the international Communist conspiracy. It is our information further, sir, that you as a Communist have been propagating the Communist activity and the Communist line principally in the South; that you have been masquerading behind a façade of humanitarianism; that you have been masquerading behind a façade of emotional appeal to certain segments of our society; that your purpose, objective, your activites, are designed to further the cause of the international Communist conspiracy in the United States. . . ."

"Mr. Arens has been grossly misinformed," Braden replied, "and it still remains a fact that my beliefs and my associations are none of the business of this committee."

"In other words," said Representative Willis of Louisiana, "you are maintaining your attitude of refusing to answer?"

"On the grounds of the first amendment to the United States Constitution, which protects the right of all citizens to practice beliefs and associations, freedom of the press, freedom of religion and freedom of assembly," Braden replied. "On that ground I stand, sir. . . ."

Meanwhile, the legislatures of many Southern states had created special committees for the apparent purpose of illustrating in a dramatic manner that the "civil-rights movement" in behalf of Negroes has really been a communist enterprise.

Probably the most undilutedly splendiferous investigation instituted by any one of these groups was that of the Louisiana Joint Legislative Committee headed by State Senator Willie Rainach of Homer, Louisiana, in March 1957. There was no question of awkward contempt citations here, for all of the witnesses—without exception—were "friendly" ones.

Communist leaders to exploit her relationship as sister-in-law of a Justice of the Supreme Court in the interest of the world Communist conspiracy and interest of overthrowing the Government.' Mrs. Durr denied that she had ever been a member of the Communist Party or that she is under Communist discipline. She stood mute when asked a number of questions, including questions pertaining to affiliation by her with numerous Communist-front organizations. She did not, however, invoke the fifth amendment to the Constitution in response to the questions."

The outstanding witness was Manning Johnson, a New York
Negro who identified himself as a former Communist. Although on
most days New York Negroes are rarely seen around the capitol
at Baton Rouge, Johnson received notably cordial treatment from
the Rainach Committee. An explanation for this hospitality perhaps is that he not only asserted that communist influence had existed in the Southern Conference for Human Welfare (predecessor
of SCEF) and the considerably less "activist" Southern Regional
Council, but Johnson also delivered a tirade against the Reverend
Martin Luther King which obviously satisfied the white Louisiana
committee:

Now, I'm not saying that Reverend King is a Communist, but I
am saying that Reverend King is doing the Negroes considerable
harm. Reverend King has none of the qualifications, nor the wisdom, nor the experience required to give leadership to the Negro
in the South in this period. He has at the present time organized
masses of Negroes, and he has got them worked up to a frenzy, to
the extent that they are willing to follow him though he is misleading them. Somebody has told him that he is the modern Moses.
Maybe he thinks that he has a magic wand or something that he
can wave and part the Red Sea and lead his people safely across
to the promised land. . . . Reverend King is absolutely wrong
when he is advocating to the Negroes a program of civil disobedience. Such a program can only lead to violence and bloodshed
in which many Negroes would be killed. Any policy that will set
white against black and result in Negroes losing their homes, losing
their jobs—it must be said that there is something radically
wrong with the policy. . . .
I will tell you why it is the wrong policy. . . . He [King] said,
"If they fire one Negro, make them fire 5,000. If they bomb one
Negro's home, make them bomb 10,000." Now, I would like to
ask Reverend King, the great Moses, the great Gandhi, if 10,000
Negroes lose their homes, is Reverend King going to build them
new homes? . . . I don't think so, but the Negro women who make
suds and chase dust and slave in white folks' kitchens—they will
get up the money to build him a new home if *his* is blown up. . . .
[If] 5,000 Negroes lose their jobs, will Reverend King be the one
to come up with the money to take care of their needs? Of
course he won't. . . .
[C]onsider the stark realities of this movement. That man is

playing around with the lives and hopes and the aspirations of his people. He is nothing but a dastardly misleader, and he is leading the Negroes in the South down the road to bloodshed and violence. . . .

Relative to the National Association for the Advancement of Colored People, a somewhat unpopular organization among the segregationist white populace of Louisiana, the Negro witness from New York was asked by Representative L. D. Napper, Committee member from Ruston:

NAPPER: The Negro race and/or the NAACP have been and are presently being exploited as allies for the Communist party toward world domination?
JOHNSON: That is correct.
NAPPER: . . . [F]rom facts within your own knowledge, is it your opinion that the so-called communist Trojan horse is stabled today within the NAACP?
JOHNSON: That's right.
NAPPER: Now, then, the point which is to me most crucial to this hearing is: if that is a necessity, then they must successfully overthrow the respective governments of the forty-eight states, one of which is the state of Louisiana?
JOHNSON: That is correct, sir.

Hearings similar to the Rainach Committee's "investigation" of "Subversion in Racial Unrest" have been staged by state legislative groups throughout the Deep South during the last five years. Invariably the committees have solemnly announced their conclusion that the various integrationist organizations such as the NAACP, SCEF, and sometimes even the respected Southern Regional Council are "fronts" for the Communist party's campaign to mongrelize the South and overthrow its sovereign states.

The most popular performer on the new Red-hunting "quiz-show" circuit down in the chitling country has been J. B. Matthews, who served as the late Senator McCarthy's staff director for a brief time back in the early 1950's (until he too much aroused the ire of American men of the cloth by declaring that "the largest single group supporting the communist apparatus in the United States today is composed of Protestant clergymen").

For the Florida Legislative Investigation in 1958 Matthews prepared a ninety-nine-page list of alleged Red "fronts" to which various NAACP leaders and luminaries had belonged or participated in during the past quarter of a century. Among the eye-opening intelligence reported in this document was the assertion that the name of poet Archibald MacLeish, sometime member of the "NAACP Committee of 100," appeared in 1937 on a letterhead of the American Pushkin Committee and in 1938 appeared on a letterhead of the Foster Parents Plan for Children in Spain.

Matthews declared that "Communists or communist influence were directly involved in every major race incident of the past four years since the Supreme Court 'legislated' on the subject of integration." Rather than dwelling in detail on data which would support this observation, however, Matthews devoted most of his testimony to discussion of communist activity in the field of race relations in decades past—drawing much of his material from the 1954 Eastland Subcommittee hearing and other long-ago investigations of "subversive activities."

The conservative Tampa *Tribune* remarked that the Florida committee sessions which starred Matthews had been "largely devoted to old charges and an intense study of the obvious."

Even so, Matthews' information was republished in two pamphlet volumes entitled *Communism and the NAACP* and since 1958 has been widely distributed in the South. Among the publishers was the Georgia Commission on Education.

Based in part on Matthews' research and in part on reports from its own undercover agents, the Florida Legislative Investigation Committee in early 1961 again probed the activities of the Southern Conference Educational Fund (SCEF) in the state. It came as no surprise that the Committee concluded that SCEF "is a communist-controlled-front organization." It also reported that "sworn testimony shows [Carl] Braden to be a member of the Communist party" and that Braden had been actively promoting SCEF's integrationist policies in the Sunshine State; moreover, the Committee declared, "the NAACP in Florida and many of its top officials have been closely associated with and have closely cooperated with Communist Carl Braden and his subversive SCEF."

Meanwhile, Matthews had continued riding the anti-communist trail—into Mississippi, creating a bit of a stir there in late 1959 when he testified to a legislative committee that Hodding Carter, the noted author and editor of the Greenville *Delta Democrat Times,* was one of the "50 interlocking officials . . . of the Southern Regional Council and also held official rank in the Southern Conference for Human Welfare and/or the Southern Conference Educational Fund." All three of these organizations—SRC, SCHW, and SCEF—are, Matthews declared, "more than slightly tainted" by communism.

Editor Carter, one of the bolder souls in Mississippi these days, promptly replied that it was true he belonged to the Southern Regional Council, an organization which is headed by a distinguished list of Dixieland "moderates" and "liberals."

"I belong to it openly," said Carter, "and believe it a worthwhile interracial organization in these unhappy times. In implying that I am in any way linked with the Southern Conference Educational Fund and in stating that the Southern Regional Council is communist-tainted, Matthews is a damned liar!"

Despite an occasional protest from the likes of Hodding Carter, the accusations that integrationist organizations are "Red fronts" or "Red-tainted" continue to move back and forth from federal investigating committees to Southern state investigating committees —and back again to federal committees.

At the 1959 hearing of the Subcommittee on Constitutional Rights of the Senate Judiciary Committee in Washington, for example, Attorney Leander Perez, Sr., of New Orleans introduced into the record no less than one hundred eighty-three pages of testimony and documents designed to prove that integrationist groups such as the NAACP are "fronts" for the Red campaign to destroy the South. Much of his material was the same stuff that had been introduced into the 1957 Rainach committee hearing—and much of that had been garnered from the investigatory files of Mississippi Senator James Eastland.

And, of course, the chairman of the Senate Judiciary Committee that received and reprinted this old Eastland-harvested material was none other than Senator James Eastland himself.

So it is that the Dixie-delighting anti-Communist, anti-NAACP, anti-integrationist committee music goes round and round—and it comes out most everywhere from the Potomac River to the Gulf of Mexico.

And the old maestro himself, Senator James Oliver Eastland of Sunflower County, Mississippi, takes an obvious pleasure in this lively roundelay.

The senator, a big, bespectacled, jowly fellow with a heavy delta drawl, sat in his Washington office one afternoon a while back and spoke of what he felt was the absurdity of the notion that Negroes can be successfully integrated with white folks in Mississippi or anywhere else in these United States.

"You can't legislate the social lives of citizens. No court decree is worth anything unless it's accepted by the people. The only enforceable law is one that follows the customs of the people. I think this whole thing [the current desegregation effort] is a plot of a few agitators; the great mass of Negroes want their own schools and teachers and churches and to live their own lives.

"And we [whites] are not going to permit our children to be indoctrinated with the idea that there are no racial differences and that there's nothing wrong with intermarriage," he said. "Over a long period of time people might be so indoctrinated. But we're not going to let that happen."

As Eastland talked, he puffed plumply on a large cigar and held his feet crossed restfully on his big desk—as had his Lower House colleague, John Bell Williams. (Both when questioning Senator Eastland and when questioning Representative Williams it was occasionally necessary for the interviewer to tilt in his chair and peer past the legislators' footgear in order to view their faces; the interviewer was never able to determine whether this was merely coincidence or whether it was some sort of significant exercise in Mississsippi shoe-sole two-upmanship.)

It is a commonly held belief that white supremacy—in Mississippi—and, consequently, the "protection" of white children from being indoctrinated with notions of racial equality—is maintained largely by the fact that the state's voting laws, in effect if not in theory, prohibit all but a few Negroes from voting.

"According to Mississippi's law, anyone can vote who's qualified," Eastland said. "There's no intimidation of Negroes in Mississippi—not as far as I know."

But as a senator away up in Washington, he explained, such state-level matters are not in his province.

"I have nothing to do with the enforcement of laws in Missis-

sippi," he said blandly, and smoked his cigar. "It's not my problem."

Eastland recognizes that racial developments in the North inevitably will have influence on racial developments in the South.
Does he predict that Northern whites will come around to the
white South's way of viewing the race question?

"They've already come around," he snapped. "What you have in
the North is *de-facto* segregation. Here in Washington we've seen
thousands and thousands of white people move out of the city as
Negroes have moved in; in other words, the pattern here is 'segregation through flight.' "

Through the years since the 1954 decision Eastland has continually pushed for the formation of a nationwide organization capable not only of defending segregation but of battling the "extreme
liberals," "socialists," and "Communists" on all the various political and economic fronts in America. However, such a single, unified
national organization has not yet come into being.

"I still think we need a national organization," said Eastland,
"but I think, too, that we've made tremendous strides. The national
campaign ["against federal usurpation of power, for a return to
states' rights and constitutional principles, etc."] is being handled
by several organizations; I expect I know of a dozen.

"Take the John Birch Society; it's an example." And the senator,
knowingly narrowing his eyes, added with a little smile: "The position they take is just not a happen-so. You don't think these things
[like the rise of the Birch Society] just *happen,* do you?"

True, the Liberals have made advances in some sectors. And,
true, the Supreme Court decision of 1954 has resulted in a smatter-
ing of integration here and there in Dixieland.

"But you'll remember that the Confederate Army made a 'token
capture' at Gettysburg. *Some* of Pickett's men reached the top of
the ridge. But who won the battle?" Senator Eastland clamped
down hard on his cigar. "Since the Decision in 1954 we've had
token integration in a few places, but *the South has not been
breached.*"

IX. THE DARK SEGREGATIONISTS

Jim Crow Among the So-called Negroes

1. THE BOOKER T'S

SOONER OR LATER almost every Dixie segregationist volunteers the opinion that the great majority of Negroes in the South like segregation. They have been happy in the past, and would be content today were it not for the agitation of integrationist-minded "outsiders": so goes the theme.

Some segregationists insist that 99 per cent of the South's Negroes oppose desegregation; some say 90 per cent; rarely does one settle for merely "most."

The remarkable thing about this is that an impressive number of them actually seem to be convinced that what they are saying is true. The conviction has sometimes even served as the basis for political action.

Back in 1954, a couple of months after The Decision, Governor Hugh White of Mississippi called a meeting of 90 Negro leaders in his state to ask their support of a "voluntary" segregation plan in exchange for a state financial outlay to bring Negro school facilities in Mississippi up to the level of those enjoyed by white pupils. Of the Negro leaders present at the meeting, only one endorsed the plan; the others issued a joint statement declaring that they were "unalterably opposed to any effort of either white or Negro citizens to circumvent the decision of the Supreme Court of the United States of America outlawing segregation in public schools."

It is noteworthy that Governor White seemed surprised, sincerely surprised, that the Negro leaders opposed his program to maintain segregation.

"I am stunned," said the governor. "I had believed that the vast

307

majority of Negroes would go along. Now I am definitely of the opinion you can't put faith in any of them on this proposition."

While such segregationists as Governor White cling to the belief that "the vast majority" of Negroes wish to "go along" with the South's system of apartheid, the National Association for the Advancement of Colored People claims the very opposite is true. Roy Wilkins, the NAACP's executive secretary, has on occasion mentioned a poll taken by *Catholic Digest* magazine, which, said Wilkins, "found that 94 per cent of Northern Negroes and 93 per cent of Southern Negroes support the views of the NAACP." And the NAACP's views, of course, include approval of The Decision and advocacy of complete freedom for Negroes to integrate with the white citizenry.

The truth of the matter probably dwells somewhere between the 90-odd per cent suggested by the segregationists and the 90-odd per cent suggested by Wilkins and the *Catholic Digest*. About a year before the *Catholic Digest* made its survey, the Gallup Poll reported that 53 per cent of the South's Negroes (in thirteen states) approved of the 1954 Supreme Court decision while 36 per cent opposed it and 11 per cent were undecided.

It is simply not true that a majority of Negroes—or even a significant minority of them—favor the kinds of segregation practiced either in the South *or* North at present. But it is true that a very significant portion of America's Negroes do not feel that their problems will be solved by being integrated with the whites; indeed, a substantial number of Negroes consider the integration effort a foolish pursuit—one that history has shown plainly will not succeed in the United States.

The Search for Uncle Tom

The movements to improve the lot of American Negroes since the Civil War have been of three main kinds: *integrationist* (as urged by the NAACP); *accommodationist* (to uplift the Negroes within the framework of the existing segregation system); and *separationist* (to transport the Negroes en masse out of the country or set up a "black republic" exclusively for them in one or more of these United States).

While white segregationists of the South occasionally flirt with the idea of separating (i.e., exporting) the Negroes from the United States, they more often relish the memory of Booker T. Washington's philosophy of accommodation. They frequently repeat Washington's statements, which were so comfortably different from those heard today from the NAACP and the Congress of Racial Equality. One of the most widely circulated Citizen's Council pamphlets quotes the late Reverend G. T. Gillespie[1] in praise of the Tuskegee educator:

All would-be leaders and promoters of better race relations in America today would do well to study [Booker T. Washington's] realistic approach to the problem and follow his wise leadership. In a notable and epoch-making address delivered at the Atlanta Exposition in 1895, pleading for cooperation between two races, he sounded the keynote of his philosophy, and provided for all men of understanding and good will a key to the solution of the problem. . . . He said: "The wisest among my race understand that agitation of questions of social equality is the extremest folly, and that progress in the enjoyment of all the privileges that will come to us must be the result of severe and constant struggle rather than of artificial forcing. . . . In all things that are purely social we can be separate as the fingers, yet one as the hand in all things essential to mutual progress."

Whenever editorials criticizing the NAACP's integrationist policies turn up in the Negro press, or a Negro—however uninfluential —speaks words of praise for Booker T-ism, white segregationist groups such as the CCs jump to reprint them for distribution—to shore up the sagging notion that most Negroes in the South really do not want to end segregation. Every batch of "educational literature" from the Citizens' Councils includes at least one reprint of an article written by some Negro warning of the evils of the NAACP.

Some of the favorite material for such reprinting has come from the pen of Davis Lee, a Negro editor of South Carolina.

"Someone has definitely sold the Negro leaders a bill of goods on integration to the extent that they are willing to sacrifice economic advantages for the mere privilege of associating with others on an equal basis." So says Lee in an editorial which has been reprinted

[1] For a discussion of Dr. Gillespie's *Christian View on Segregation,* see Chapter VI (1).

by several segregationist newspapers and organizations. "The unfortunate thing about this whole issue is that the masses of Negroes have had no opportunity to be heard. This integration movement is carried on by the so-called upper-crust Negro, the fortunate few, and they do not have the welfare of the masses of Negroes at heart. . . . These big Negroes who are running roughshod over everyone in their fight for integration [are] creating so much bitterness, hatred, and prejudice that before long [the] little Negroes won't be able to get the help in the future from white people that they have gotten in the past. . . ."

Lee denounces the "yellow and mulatto" leaders of the integration movement for themselves practicing color discrimination against Negroes with dark skins. And he adds: "At the rate they are going, in a few years there will not be a Negro race. You can hardly conceive of sensible leaders advocating a movement that is going to do away with our race. But that is what they are doing."

One of the earliest such pieces of anti-NAACP writing was published in at least two white South Carolina newspapers, the Spartanburg *Herald-Journal* and the Charleston *Evening Post,* within a month after the May 17, 1954, decision. It was in the form of a letter to the editor signed "JANIE S. JONES, A Colored Patron."

"I believe I'm speaking for other colored patrons and teachers when I say many of us don't belong to this so-called race-stirrer NAACP, and we are not in accord with what the NAACP is asking for in South Carolina, but what we sincere people want is 'equal facilities for our children but separate buildings,' " the letter said. "Our so-called NAACP leaders would not have anything but sympathy to offer and God knows you can't pay bills or meet responsibilities with the word 'sympathy.' "

The fiery Negro newspaper, the Pittsburgh *Courier,* reprinted the Janie S. Jones letter under the headline, "PLEASE SAY IT AIN'T SO!"

Similar letters from "colored patrons" have continually cropped up in the columns of white segregationist newspapers through the years since The Decision. The author's own home-town weekly, the Fayette County, Alabama, *Times,* has in recent months run several such. For example, one Sudie Mae Lewis of Chicago, who identifies herself as a former schoolteacher "raised in the cotton fields" of Mississippi, advises her fellow Negroes that "you've never had it so good as you have in dear old Dixie," and promises that she plans soon to return to Mississippi "where black is black, white is white, and all a friend to man." In another issue of the Fayette County *Times* two Negro men of New Albany, Mississippi, insist that segregation is "a part of God's program that every race or nation is to have its own language and society" and that the integration movement is the work of "communist and filtrated-minded people."

Some of the anti-integration letters to the editor are considerably more literate. One which has been reprinted and distributed energetically by the Mississippi State Sovereignty Commission and other segregationist groups is a letter written to the Orlando *Sentinel* by Zora Neale Hurston, Negro novelist-playwright of Florida, who is identified as a graduate of Barnard College.

Miss Hurston says in her letter that she considers the 1954 Supreme Court decision an insult to her race. The ruling, she says, is an expression of "the doctrine of the white mare."

"Since the days of the never-to-be-sufficiently-deplored Reconstruction there has been current the belief that there is no greater delight to Negroes than physical association with Whites. . . . Those familiar with the habits of mules are aware that any mule, if not restrained, will automatically follow a white mare. Dishonest mule traders made money out of this knowledge in the old days. Lead a white mare along a country road and slyly open the gate and the mules in the lot would run out and follow this white mare. . . .

"It is to be recalled that Moscow, being made aware of this folk belief, made it the main plank in their campaign to win the American Negro from the 1920's on.

"It was the come-on stuff. Join the party and get yourself a white wife or husband. To supply the expected demand, the party had this-and-that off of park benches and skid rows and held them in stock for us. The highest types of Negroes were held to be just panting to get hold of one of these objects. Seeing how flat that program fell, it is astonishing that it would be so soon revived. Politics indeed make strange bedfellows."

Sometimes the Negro gestures of accommodationist good will to white segregationists are expressed in behalf of some "organization." Last year the Louisiana State Sovereignty Commission was handing out mimeographed copies of what was identified as a letter to Governor Jimmie Davis from one Bertha Means Spears of the American Negro Division of the NAAAP of Luling, Texas.

"NAAAP," not to be confused with "NAACP," are the initials of the National Association for the Advancement of the American People.

Written during the first great New Orleans school crisis, the letter said: "I believe that if I could talk to the parents of those of my race who are taking part in the integration of your schools there, and show them what we are doing and receiving for our efforts, that they would be unselfish enough as to withdraw their children from the schools for the present. I feel that the white people have shown us their friendship and unselfishness often enough that it is time that some of my race return this kindness, as a favor to our race and our country.

"The founder of the NAAAP, Mrs. Virginia L. McCleary, assures me that such a kindness would be repaid many times, for all Americans in your area would be given aid with their employment, educational, and 'American-rights' problems—who would place the American cause, our children's future, and helping their neighbors—FIRST, by establishing a branch of the NAAAP, and opening special schools for teaching Americans of all races how we are being used and confused in the Communist's efforts to destroy us. . . ."

A group of Alabama Negroes called the Southern Negro Improvement Association sent a telegram to the White House awhile back urging that a poll be taken to determine whether Southern Negroes prefer integration or segregation. The Association, headed by one Samuel H. Moore of Birmingham and claiming 5,000 members, declared it was certain that the pollsters would find them "unalterably opposed" to integration.

The telegram also expressed some concern about the effect the integration campaign was having on the white people of Birmingham and other Dixie climes: "Racial hate and racial prejudice that were dead are now reconstructed. Threat of forceful integration has created fear and hate in many of our white friends."

A report of the telegram was dispatched from Birmingham on the wires of United Press International and was printed widely in Southern publications, including *The Georgia Klansman*.

Of the various white segregationist organizations and agencies in the South which make a practice of assembling such material, the Mississippi Sovereignty Commission has been especially diligent. This is in harmony with the belief expressed by Commission Director Albert Jones that "the percentage of Negroes in Mississippi who are interested in integration is very small."

In one editorial circulated by the Mississippi commission, J. W. Jones, Negro editor of the New Albany, Mississippi, *Community Citizen,* urges his readers to ask themselves: "What other state in the Union [has] as much peace as the state of Mississippi?" Moreover:

"What more should we want?" asks Editor Jones. "Negro teachers who have their degrees from colored colleges are receiving equal salaries to white teachers who have their degress from white colleges. The state is providing buildings with equal facilities for colored children to those of the white children, and equal transportation to that of the white children. . . . The NAACP is the worst enemy we have. Its objective is to create a disturbance among us and the white people of the South."

In the field of higher education, one of the Mississippi Sovereignty Commission's favorites has been Dr. J. H. White, president of the Mississippi Vocational College for Negroes at Itta Bena (the little delta home town of Robert T. Patterson, executive secretary of the Association of Citizens' Councils of America). The Commission has given a large distribution to a transcript of an address made by Dr. White at Mound Bayou, a Mississippi delta town notable for the fact that all of its citizens are Negroes.

Dr. White's message is right in the Booker T. Washington tradition. After roundly denouncing New York Congressman Adam Clayton Powell in much the fashion that Washington used to denounce the integrationism of W. E. B. DuBois half a century ago, White declared that the Negroes of the South "should have intestinal fortitude enough to rise up against those who are not sincere in their leadership during this troubled age."

"Citizens of Mound Bayou and friends," said White, "I don't believe you are going to throw away your churches, schools, hospitals, businesses, insurances, newspapers, refuse to sing—'Nobody knows de trouble I've seen, Nobody knows but Jesus.' No,

I don't believe you are going to throw all of this away just to sit, eat, and ride with a white person."

White quoted Booker T. Washington's advice to Negroes to "Cast down your bucket where you are." He also quoted a comment made to a friend of his by George Washington Carver, the famous Tuskegee Negro scientist, at the time a particularly brutal lynching of a Negro had occurred in a nearby town. "I know that a thing like this is almost enough to break your heart," Carver had said. "But never mind, my young friend, these things won't be always. There are plenty of good people in the South, and someday they are going to make themselves heard. Someday our Southland will be a wonderful place for all of us to live. I firmly believe that [the] good white people of the South will see that the Negro gets justice in the courts, the good white people will see that the Highway Patrols will protect him as a citizen rather than as a Negro, the good white people will see to it that after paying the same price for gasoline as anyone else will receive rest-room accommodations for their families, the good white people will see to it that the Negro is recognized on his merits."

Dr. White recommended that his fellow Negroes in Mississippi "cultivate friendly relations with the Southern white man who is our next-door neighbor," and to have faith. He defined "faith" as "the substance of things hoped for, the evidence of things not seen."

Another Negro writer whose statements occasionally are given bonus circulation by the Mississippi Sovereignty Commission— and he is a writer who has a degree of influence among the Negroes of his state—is Percy Greene, editor of the Jackson *Advocate,* the largest Negro newspaper published in Mississippi.

In one of the Sovereignty Commission's favorite editorials Greene suggests that Negroes in the South would be better off if the May 17, 1954, decision were repealed.

"Any view or study of American history, and of the American ideal of democracy, is bound to reveal that what brought peoples of all races, nations, colors, and creeds to these shores to join in helping make the United States the great nation it is today, was that each group could have their own churches, schools, and other institutions and organizations under the guarantee of equal protection."

In contrast with that happy ideal, writes Greene, "The idea of integration in this country was born in the minds, first of those who saw in it a means of creating the division, and stirring up strife and tension in the United States, as an aid to the cause and advancement of world Communism, and later by those who think the best way to combat Russia and Communism is to make the United States as nearly like Russia as possible. We see no reason why the aims of the Negro for equal protection under the law would suffer as a result of the repeal of the U. S. Supreme Court Decisions in the public-school integration cases. Indeed, the Negroes, particularly those in the South, might be far better off than they now are, by thus relieving the existing tension, and again making race pride a motivating incentive in Negro progress, and again making possible Southern interracial cooperation and good will. . . ."

Greene has served the "accommodationist" cause not only through the columns of his newspaper; it is noteworthy that he appeared before the Senate Subcommittee on Constitutional Rights in 1959 to testify *against* federal civil-rights legislation—a rare act indeed for a Negro to perform on Capitol Hill in recent years.

It was Greene's feeling, he told the senators, that the period from 1940 until May 17, 1954, was for Negroes "the brightest and most hopeful period in the history of Mississippi and in the rest of the South."

He recalled the progress he felt was being made back when he was president of the Mississippi Negro Democrats Association. In 1940, he testified, fewer than 250 Negroes were registered to vote in Mississippi, and "it was almost like committing suicide for a Negro to talk about voting." But by 1954 there were "some thirty-odd thousand" registered Negro voters in Mississippi—a great many more than there have been since the Year of Decision, 1954.

Greene has not been especially popular with the NAACP in recent years; things were different back in 1950. That year he was invited by the late Walter White, crusading executive secretary of the NAACP, to be a principal speaker at a civil-rights "mobilization" being held in Washington. But Greene said he disappointed White and the other militants at the meeting by proposing that the NAACP concern itself only with the right of Negroes to vote and not with such other matters as school desegregation and federal civil-rights legislation.

Greene told the senators that the inspiration for his proposal came from none other than Supreme Court Justice Hugo Black, generally considered to be the bench's foremost champion of racial integration at all levels. He had met Justice Black a few months before the NAACP "mobilization," while in Washington to accept a plaque from the Washington Committee on Race Relations in recognition of his work in behalf of Mississippi Negro voters.

As Greene recalled it, Justice Black said he was aware that the NAACP was planning to bring before the Supreme Court several suits attacking segregation in Southern grade schools. But the justice advised him to concentrate on Negro voting rights instead, he said.

"All the Southern states have now conceded that you have the right to vote. They have conceded that you have the right to enter the colleges and universities for graduate and professional training," Greene quoted Justice Black as saying. "But if the NAACP attacks the separation in the schools below the college level they are going to succeed only in arousing and rallying the most reactionary sentiments in this country against the Negro and defer rather than hasten full emancipation. But if you make it the vote, you can get by gradual learning the art of political participation. At the same time you will be making friendship with the responsible white people at the state and the local level. It is the best approach."

In his testimony to the senators, Greene compared the hazards of the present situation to those of the years following the Civil War.

"My father was born in slavery [and] he repeatedly told me about the things that happened between white people and Negroes during the Reconstruction and post-Reconstruction periods, how the efforts, the sending of the federal troops to the South, and certain other efforts had given the [Negro] people, who had not had a sufficient amount of experience with that kind of thing, a sort of arrogance, a forwardness, a something that made them lose sight of the value of relationships between white people and Negroes at the local level. . . ."

The chief counsel of the Subcommittee, Charles H. Slayman, Jr., closed the interrogation of Greene with a question that suggested the possibility that his receipt of money from a white segregationist agency might have encouraged him to oppose civil-rights legislation.

MR. SLAYMAN: In the Jackson, Mississippi, *Clarion-Ledger,* Sunday, July 7, 1957, in an Associated Press story about work of the Mississippi State Sovereignty Commission, there is a paragraph that reads: "Percy Greene, editor of the Jackson *Advocate,* the State's leading Negro newspaper, drew money in several categories. He was paid $35.00 last September for travel and $300 last February under the heading of 'Advertising,' and a $200 warrant was made out last October to National Association of Colored People of the South, care of Percy Greene." Is that an accurate report?

MR. GREENE: No, sir, that is not. I made a speech entitled—I would like to make this clear. I have certain views. I have expressed them for twenty years, and if it is anybody—sovereignty commission, [or] the man from down under, who wants to buy my paper and pay me for the service, I am going to sell it to them.

But in that case that was nothing but the propaganda of certain people who were trying to reflect or cast reflections on everybody who is not expressing agreement with them.

The Sovereignty Commission paid the Mutual Association of Colored People of the South and me for the privilege of circulating a speech that I made on parallel progress, which was subsequently produced as an editorial in my paper, and not as an employee of the Sovereignty Commission.

The speech Greene was referring to was made in Jackson at a 1956 "Statewide Goodwill Meeting" of the said Mutual Association of Colored People of the South. In it he pledged his paper's support of the Association in working with white people toward "parallel progress" for both races and the reduction of tensions created by the 1954 decision.

Greene's accommodationist statements have prompted some of the more uncompromising integrationists to consider him guilty of "Booker T-ism" and "Uncle Tom-ism." But in an *Advocate* editorial that was published in pamphlet form along with his "parallel-progress" speech, Greene argued that the South's outstanding Negroes in the past—leading educators and businessmen—had "made it a point to get along with white people."

"In the minds of this new Negro leadership ('the new crop of Negro leaders who have come forward since the 1954 decision') any Negro is an 'Uncle Tom' who, whatever the issues involved, seeks to maintain a friendly and respectful attitude toward the responsible white people of the community. . . . What this new and brash Negro leadership has succeeded in doing more than anything else is losing whatever welcome they might have had in the councils of authority, by vituperative, vindictive, calumnious speeches and newspaper statements, directed toward the responsible white citizens who form the councils of authority in the community. . . .

"Though somewhat slowly, the masses of Negroes of the South are beginning to see that they are being led over a precipice by the siren calls of the new Negro leadership to be repeatedly submerged in an ever-maddening whirlpool of hatred, fear, frustration, and bewilderment. . . . Looking backward at Negro history, in the light of present conditions as they affect the masses of Negroes, the greatest need of the Negro in Jackson, in Mississippi, and in the rest of the South, is more and more 'Uncle Toms.' "

Theology on Beale Street

Search as they might, the officials of the Mississippi Sovereignty Commission—and it is true of the other Southern states' apartheid agencies—have not yet managed to scrape up any Negro organization of consequence to support their thesis that most of their citizens of color prefer Dixie's traditional system of segregation.

Their best substitute for one is the group mentioned by Editor Greene, the Mutual Association of Colored People of the South, which has its headquarters in Memphis, just a few miles north of the Mississippi state line.

The Mississippi commission's largest Negroes-for-segregation publishing project to date has been the distribution of a forty-page "picture paper" prepared by the Mutual Association. Printed on slick paper stock in tabloid size, it bears the masthead, *Mississippi*

NEGRO PROGRESS EDITION, and features as its banner headline: "STORY OF NEGRO PROGRESS IN STATE HAS
NEVER BEEN SUFFICIENTLY TOLD."

The publication consists of numerous photographs of scenes at
several of the new public schools for Negroes in Mississippi, most
of them products of the building spree that started in the state—
as throughout the South—when the NAACP began focusing its
legal efforts in the late 1940's and early 1950's on the inequality
of educational facilities for Negroes. The stated purpose of the
PROGRESS EDITION "is to acquaint the people of Mississippi,
as well as those outside of Mississippi, with the progress that has
been made within the past ten years."

The lead article of the paper describes the Association's president, the Reverend Dr. M. L. Young of Beale Street, Memphis, as
a man "born in the halls of radical greed and nurtured by God and
Christian parents" and "one among the first of his race to combat communism." As an opponent of integration since he founded
the Mutual Association back in the 1940's, "he has been called a
Negro hater and accused of trying to hold the Negro back, but his
stand is that the Bible is right regardless of the stand anyone else
may take."

The publication concludes with an editorial that could well
have come right from the columns of *The Citizens' Council:* "If
the 'attitude of the North' is assumed to be indicated by the sporadic
muggings and window smashings and race riots in these areas, one
can as readily leap to the conclusion that there is no hope, anywhere, for integration. . . . The people of the North can help most,
we believe, by cleaning up their own mess, and this process might
well begin with a general soul searching to discover what residues of
prejudice remain there. When Harlem has been desegregated,
when Negroes have been welcomed as neighbors in the pleasant
suburbs of New York and Chicago, when Chinese and Filipinos
have been made to feel at home in San Francisco's Sea Cliff and
Pacific Heights, there will be time enough to point a finger at the
South. . . . WE ARE ASKING YOU TO 'THINK' AND, IN
YOUR THINKING, DON'T LET YOUR THOUGHTS BE
RADICAL, BUT SOBER."[2]

----

[2] In a recent issue of the Fayette County, Alabama, *Times,* there was a
"letter to the editor" signed by Horace Vailes and Howard Conner, who

The Mount Zion African Methodist Episcopal Church, of which
Dr. Young is pastor, is an unimposing structure—"It's one uh
them *lil'* ol' choiches," a Negro service-station attendant explained
with a measure of hauteur as he directed a visitor to it one recent
afternoon—a little square building of concrete blocks nestled
amid the flimsy, sagging houses of a south Memphis Negro slum.

An all-day "district conference" was in melodious progress at
the church, but Dr. Young said he would not at all mind taking an
afternoon break to explain the work of his Mutual Association of
Colored People of the South.

The middle-aged minister is a man full of bustle and laughter.
After suggesting a drive downtown to his office on Beale Street,
he expressed immense amusement at the difficulty he had squeez-
ing into his visitor's Volkswagen; Dr. Young is, in truth, endowed
generously with embonpoint—and not much height.

He is a pronouncedly dark man and he dresses in ministerial
black, yet there is about him an air of dash; he sports a small
mustache and favors hats that have a nifty snap. Although he has
on occasion attended Fisk University, Turner School of Theology,
and the University of Chicago, he has never chosen to acquire that
colorless Columbia Broadcasting System manner of speech which
is picked up by so many Negroes of the Deep South who have a
brush with college; Dr. Young speaks with an accent that is
frankly "cotton patch." Anyone who has been away from Dixie a
few years must listen closely to catch what he has to say—which
is a great deal, for he is a man who loves to talk.

Driving past an intersection crowded with Negroes, the minister
said: "The Chamber of Commerce here—they estimate only 35

---

identified themselves as Negroes of New Albany, Mississippi. The last two
paragraphs of their letter read:

"The people of the North can help most, we believe, by clearing up
their own mess—and this process might well begin with a general soul
searching to discover what residues of prejudice remain there. When
Harlem has disintegrated [*sic*.], when Negroes have been welcomed as
neighbors in the pleasant suburbs of New York and Chicago, when Chinese
and Filipinos have been made to feel at home in San Francisco's Sea
Cliff and Pacific Heights, there will be time enough to point a finger at
the SOUTH.

"We are asking you to THINK and, in your THINKING, don't let your
thoughts be radical, BUT sober."

or 40 per cent of the population in Memphis is Negro."[3] This gave him a laugh. "My guess is there's 275,000 of 'em in Memphis. Census takers—they can't find these Negroes; so many of 'em up in these little alleys and ain't to be found. Anyway, you know well as I do, Negroes ain't about to tell a white man nothing."

Speaking of his Mutual Association of Colored People of the South, Young recalled that it was incorporated in 1945 "with one member and a shoebox."

The Memphis *Commercial Appeal* reported in 1950 that the Association, "an anti-communist Negro group organized to promote better race relations," had chapters in 17 states and more than twelve thousand members.

"We did have close to eight or nine thousand members before 1954, but after that . . ." Young spread his plump hands philosophically. "We still got some very active people, but we've had no mass program in a long time."

Young's suite of offices is right in the heart of the Negro populace's separate-but-not-especially-equal section of downtown Memphis. It is on the second floor of a run-down building facing a little grassless patch of land that is named W. C. Handy Park in memory of the Negro composer who was probably Memphis' most famous citizen.

A plump, brown, cordial woman of about forty—introduced as the Mutual Association's secretary—was minding the office. This was not taxing much of her energy, since—in contrast with busier times before the 1954 decision—nothing much seemed to be doing.

The office rooms would be gloomy were it not for an abundance of framed pictures on the walls: divers photographs of Dr. Young, several maps, charters of Mutual Association chapters which are now no more, *Life* magazine cutouts of Africans in native costume —even a printed portrait of Confederate General Stonewall Jackson.

In his own small office Young displayed his layouts for a new "Negro Progress Edition" he was preparing in the name of the

[3] The 1960 census reported 184,320 of Memphis' 497,524 population were Negroes—37 per cent.

Mutual Association. Much attention was being devoted in it to Negroes famed for achieving success within the framework of Southern segregation—men such as Booker T. Washington and George Washington Carver.

"I've tried to show the good side of the Negro," said the minister. "When the Supreme Court came out with its decision and the word was handed down that everybody's gonna be integrated now, a lot of these folks like to had a baby. But I want to know: will desegregation be the answer to the progress of the Negro universally? I say we've got to work out some plan to meet the needs of the masses of our people. I say they must be technically trained —as workers in industry, schoolteachers, nurses' aides, and such. My approach is like that of Booker T. Washington."

There are certain forms of segregation that are humiliating, the minister conceded, but school segregation is not one of them. Moreover, he indicated that he believes that some of the Negro's best friends are white Southerners.

"In no section of the country does the Negro enjoy the educational, employment, and economic oportunities which the Negroes in the South enjoy," he declared in a recent speech. "The liberal [who sheds] crocodile tears over the plight of the poor Negro in the South will gladly give him integration but won't give him a job or provide his family with clothing or bread. . . . Negroes can't eat integration. They need jobs."

Dr. Young did not say whether the Mississippi State Sovereignty Commission planned to aid him in distributing his second "Progress Edition." Indeed, he said he had no comment at all to make about the white folks' segregation apparatus in the Magnolia State.

"I have to go *down in there,*" he said, laughing gustily. "When I'm asked about *that,* I just *hesh.*"

Just as pro-slavery and pro-segregation white ministers have asserted for well over a century, Young believes that the dark pigmentation of Negroes' skins is a product of long-ago sin. The dark races, he said, are descended from Ham as the result of the curse placed on him by his father Noah soon after the Great Flood.

To prove his point, he began leafing through a large booklet he had obtained from a Northern publishing house, *The Bible Story.* The booklet presents the history of earth, hell, and heaven in a series of simple drawings: of a Nordic-looking couple, Adam and Eve, lounging in a pleasant thicket; then a chasm representing the Fall; followed by a boat with animal passengers, the Ark; then a crumbling skyscraper, the Tower of Babel; an so on to Armaggedon.

He commented as he turned the pages:

"Here's Ham and the dark races. . . . There's Japheth. His crowd is ruling the world now: the gentiles. . . . Here the black folks are, ruling Egypt, then here they run over past Moses and zigzag down to Babylon. . . . Then comes the New Dispensation. . . . And here comes Christ: look at Him here."

Asked what had become of the dark descendants of Ham at this point the minister waved his hand casually and said: "Oh, they're out of it here."

The final picture of heaven, all of whose occupants are pictured as uniformly white, is preceded by a drawing of a spectacular explosion representing the end of the world.

"The NAACP or nobody else," he said, tossing aside *The Bible Story*, "is going to change the plan of God."

Everyone had just as well accept the fact that the "social order" of whites and Negroes is separate now and will remain so, he said.

"We're here in this office together," he said, "but when we part, I'll go back into my church and you'll go to the Peabody Hotel. We'll be going different ways."

It is a shame, he said, that he lacks the financial resources to get that message across to people North and South, black and white.

"This organization ain't near what it could be. If I just had a few thousand dollars, I could get 'em told."

Outside, the scene on Beale Street was approximately the same as it had been on most any midweek afternoon since the long-gone days when Handy was there to blow his golden trumpet and there was a song that ran:

> *Oh, the river's up and cotton's down,*
> *Mister Ed Crump, he runs this town.*

Fat women in basement-rack dresses and lean men in work-grimed overalls walked slowly past the cluttered show windows of dinky bargain stores; a slender butterscotch girl in a white satin frock clicked across the street on very high heels; and a few duded-up men with mustaches and wide-brimmed pastel hats stood at a corner across the way, dawdling, waiting for action.

In view of Dr. Young's opinion that desegregation will not take place on this side of the pearly gates, does he share with some white segregationists and some Negro groups the thought that it might be best for America's Negroes to resettle in Africa?

"You could never get twenty million Negroes to accept the idea of going to Africa," he said. "Anyway, there's no prophecy in the Bible for Negroes to move back to Africa. It wouldn't be like the Jews going back to Israel; there was a prophecy for that."

Arriving back at his church, where the district conference was still in progress, Young said the truth is that 50 per cent of the Negroes in the South are not concerned about the integration-segregation issue "either way." He would not fathom a guess as to how many Negroes share the accommodationist philosophy of the Mutual Association of Colored People of the South.

"Colored people won't talk much," he said. "It's hard to tell what they think. The reflexibility of their mind changes."

He shook his head thoughtfully.

"If I just had a little more money," he mused. "With just a few thousand dollars I could get 'em told. If I had a few thousand dollars I could move the earth."

And, chuckling at that pleasant thought, Dr. Young—as he had prophesied several minutes earlier—walked into his church as his visitor turned his car and drove off in the direction of the Peabody.

2. THE COLONIZERS

CHISELED INTO a panel in the majestic Jefferson Memorial at Washington are the most famous anti-slavery words ever uttered by the author of the Declaration of Independence:

"Nothing is more certainly written in the book of fate than that these people are to be free."

In truth—and present-day Jeffersonian Democrats of the South delight in pointing it out—the inscription is an out-of-context fragment of a sentence. When read as a whole, the sentence bears a message that has been bitterly meaningful to millions of Americans born long after the abolition of Negro slavery.

In full, the sentence written by Thomas Jefferson in 1821 reads:

"Nothing is more certainly written in the book of fate than that these people are to be free; nor is it less certain that the two races, equally free, cannot live in the same government."

Jefferson's next two sentences in the same essay asserted that "nature, habit, opinion, have drawn indelible lines of distinction" between the two races, and suggested that the best course would be to free the slaves and "peaceably" deport them from the United States.

Even as early as 1781 Jefferson had advocated that America's Negro slaves be emancipated and assisted to settle in Africa. In his *Notes on Virginia* he expressed a prophecy which still haunts the American mind:

"Deep-rooted prejudices entertained by the whites; ten thousand recollections, by the blacks, of the injuries they have sustained; new provocations; the real distinctions which nature has made;

325

and many other circumstances, will divide us into parties, and produce convulsions which will probably never end but in the extermination of the one or the other race."

The Great Emancipator, Abraham Lincoln, flirted for years with the idea of dispatching America's Negroes to Africa—or somewhere else afar.

"If all the earthly power were given me, I should not know what to do as to the existing institution [the 'peculiar institution' of slavery]," Lincoln conceded in one of his debates with Stephen A. Douglas, but he added: "My first impulse would be to free all the slaves and send them to Liberia—to their own native land. [But] if they were all landed there in a day, they would all perish in the next ten days. What then? Free them all and keep them among us as underlings? Is it quite certain that this betters their condition? What next? Free them and make them politically and socially our equals? Our own feelings will not admit of it, and if mine would, we well know that those of the great mass of whites will not."

Hodding Carter, in his excellent account of the first Reconstruction, *The Angry Scar,* emphasizes that the idea of Negro resettlement was not for Lincoln merely an idle speculation:

The problem plagued Lincoln even as the Union fought for its very life. Time after time during the war the President and his Cabinet discussed deportation of the Negroes as a way out. Mr. Lincoln espoused a non-compulsory colonization program to resettle Negroes in Panama and the West Indies; a promoter did ship 400 Negroes, the vanguard of 5,000 he intended to transport, to an island leased for the purpose from Haiti. The unprepared, sickened survivors among these volunteer migrants had to be brought home. Lincoln also thought of using the Navy, once the war had been won, to bear at least 150,000 Negro men to distant climes. . . .

Legislation was introduced in the early years of the Civil War to finance a large-scale colonization scheme, but it gained not much more than ridicule. General Ben Butler, later to become a leader of the integrationist Radical Republican program of Reconstruction, remarked sarcastically to Lincoln that it would be impossible for the Navy to ship the former slaves even to the nearest Caribbean island "half as fast as Negro children will be born here." By mid-1864 the last of the resettlement legislation had been abandoned.

Lincoln's "first impulse" to send all of America's Negroes to Liberia perhaps was inspired by the work of the American Colonization Society, the most active back-to-Africa movement of the nineteenth century. But while Lincoln thought of resettlement as an adjunct to emancipation, the dominant purpose—though not sole purpose—of the American Colonization Society was to protect the institution of slavery by ridding the country of its free Negroes, whose enjoyment of liberty obviously set a bad example for Negroes still in bondage.

From the time it was established in 1817 until the Civil War the Society arranged the transportation of several thousand Negroes to Liberia. But in the long run it had little effect on America's "race problem."

"In spite of great efforts," Ernest Sutherland Bates reflects in his *American Faith,* "the colonization scheme was a failure, owing to inadequate capital, the unwillingness of the free Negroes to emigrate, and the inability of those of them who did go to Liberia to develop any kind of prosperous community in that equatorial region—their failure, of course, being taken as conclusive evidence of the Negro's incapacity for self-government."

In a sort of revival of the spirit of the American Colonization Society, the late Senator Theodore Bilbo of Mississippi proposed in the 1930's that the federal government assist our Negroes to undertake a mass exodus to Africa; he claimed that more than two million Negroes had signed a petition endorsing his plan. In 1949 the late Senator William Langer of North Dakota introduced a bill to aid Negroes who wished to migrate to Liberia, and reintroduced it at several subsequent Senate sessions before his death. But the Senate never seriously entertained the thought of acting on either proposal.

Reflecting on the American Colonization Society and the more recent Bilbo colonization scheme, Gunnar Myrdal commented in

An American Dilemma: "The idea of sending American Negroes back to Africa or to some other place outside the United States has, in the main, been confined to the whites. As [Ralph J.] Bunche observes: 'The real significance of the colonization schemes is to be found in the conception of the Negro as an evil that had to be done away with.' "

Maybe so. It is a fact, though, that by far the largest back-to-Africa campaign in American history was strictly Negroid. Black was Marcus Garvey and black were his hordes of followers in the spectacular Universal Negro Improvement Association crusade of the late 1910's and early 1920's—"the largest mass movement in the history of the American Negro."

By 1919, three years after he "came screaming out of the British West Indies onto the American stage," Garvey was claiming 2,000,000 members in 30 branches of his UNIA.

In preparation for the imminent day when American blacks would return "home" to Africa, Garvey—described by one Negro scholar as "a Jamaican of unmixed stock, squat, stocky, fat, and sleek, with protruding jaws and heavy jowls, small, bright pig-like eyes and rather bulldog-like face"—soon organized a Universal African Legion, Universal African Motor Corps, the Universal Black Cross Nurses, and a Black Eagle Flying Corps, attiring them all in colorful costumes. And in the most elaborate gesture of all he raised a million dollars for a Black Star Steamship Line.

In practical economic moves he organized cooperative UNIA laundries, grocery stores, restaurants, hotels, and other businesses.

And in the spiritual realm he encouraged the establishment of a new African Orthodox Church. The clergyman chosen as its chief bishop, a minister of Episcopal cloth named George Alexander McGuire, was soon busy instructing the faithful to "tear down and burn any pictures of the white Madonna and the white Christ found in their homes." Within a few years the worship of a black Christ was being advocated, and pictures of the black Madonna and Child were common in the homes of Garveyite disciples of the new faith.

To a throng of 25,000 Negroes gathered in New York's Madison Square Garden for the Universal Negro Improvement's first international convention Garvey vowed:

"We shall now organize the 400,000,000 Negroes of the world into a vast organization to plant the banner of freedom on the great continent of Africa. . . . If Europe is for the Europeans, then Africa shall be for the black peoples of the world. We say it; we mean it."

Later, at a gathering of whites, he prophesied with striking accuracy:

"We say to the white man who now dominates Africa that it is to his interest to clear out of Africa now, because we are coming —400,000,000 strong. We shall not ask England or France or Italy or Belguim, 'Why are you here?' We shall only command them, 'Get out of here.' "

Apparently Garvey never really planned for his Black Star Steamship Line to boat off *all* of America's Negroes to Africa. "Some are no good here," he once said, "and naturally will be no good there." Dr. C. Eric Lincoln, the able student of black nationalism in America, comments:

His real intentions seem to have been not unlike those of modern Zionism. He wanted to build a state, somewhere in Africa, to which Negroes would come from all over the world, bringing with them a wealth of technical and professional skills. Within a few years, he hoped, the new state would gain such prestige and power that it would be recognized as a symbol of accomplishment and protection for Negroes all over the world. For Garvey was convinced . . . that the Negro can hope for neither peace nor dignity while he lives in a white society. [He] saw only one solution: the establishment of a separate nation "so strong as to strike fear" into the hearts of the oppressor white race.

Nevertheless, such white segregationist groups as the Ku Klux Klan, whose ascendancy in that period somewhat paralleled that of the UNIA, looked upon Garvey as a kind of Unpied Piper who would whistle all the Negroes out of Dixie, and they openly supported his movement.

Garvey's appeal caught fire in the urban North rather more than in the rural South, coming as it did simultaneously with the mass northward migration of Negroes following World War I. The flamboyant Jamaican's picture of Africa as the promised land of milk and honey understandably captured the imagination of dark-skinned Americans who had supported a war for democracy in Europe only to find Jim Crow waiting after the Armistice with his same old white subtleties and shackles.

The period immediately following World War I was, in fact, one of the most violent in the history of American race relations: 70 Negroes were lynched during the first year after the war; in the "Red Summer" of 1919 scores more died in an epidemic of twenty-five race riots that swept the country. For great numbers of Negroes it was a time for disillusion with their national leadership, of the NAACP integrationist variety as well as the Booker T. Washington accommodationist variety—both of which seemed to be taking them nowhere with all deliberate speed.

It was a thrill for the disillusioned to hear Garvey denounce well-known NAACP leaders as "weak-kneed and cringing" sycophants of the white man—as "Uncle Toms" who "must give way to the 'New Negro.'"

However, it was just such criticism of the established national Negro leadership that eventually led to the undoing of the president general of the UNIA and his dream of becoming "president of Africa."

Early in 1922 Garvey had been indicted for mail fraud in connection with his million-dollar promotion of stock in the Black Star Steamship Line. But the government let months pass without prosecuting the case, and seemed inclined to let the matter drop.

Then in January 1923 a former Garvey follower who was rumored to be a possible prosecution witness was murdered.

"There was no evidence linking Garvey or the UNIA to the crime, which remains unsolved," C. Eric Lincoln notes, "but the hostility of the responsible Negro leadership was whetted. Less than a week after the murder a 'Committee of Eight'—all prominent American Negroes, most of them active in the NAACP—sent an open letter to the United States attorney general. The letter condemned Garveyism as a philosophy seeking 'to arouse ill-feeling between the races' and urged that he 'use his full influence completely to disband and extirpate the vicious movement, and that he vigorously and speedily push the government's case against Marcus Garvey for using the mails to defraud.'"

Garvey was brought to trial the following May, convicted, and sentenced to the maximum prison term of five years.

In the summer of 1924, while Garvey's conviction was being appealed to a higher court, a mission of his UNIA members voyaged to Liberia to prepare for the first great back-to-Africa migration to begin the following October. But by then the Liberian government, strongly influenced by pressures from British and French colonial interests, had announced it was "irrevocably opposed" to the "incendiary policy" of the UNIA; and the lands that Liberia once promised Garvey were leased, instead, to the Firestone Rubber Corporation. When the Garveyite mission arrived, its members were promptly arrested for deportation.

Less than a year later, in February 1925, Garvey's last appeal effort had failed and he was resettled in the federal penitentiary at Atlanta.

He was freed in December 1927 by a commutation from President Coolidge, but because he had never become an American citizen and had been found guilty of a felony, he was quickly deported.

From the West Indies he tried to keep the movement alive, but interest in it soon faded. His colorful movement of the twenties could barely be remembered by readers of the few American newspapers that carrier an item in 1940 noting that Marcus Garvey had died in London at the age of fifty-three.

There still exist a few wisps of the old dream that American Negroes might solve their problems by "returning" to Africa. The decline and fall of the Garvey movement were followed by the formation of various black nationalist splinter groups with such names as the National Union of People of African Descent, the Peace Movement of Ethiopia, and the National Movement for the Establishment of a Forty-Ninth State. There is today a Garvey Club in Brooklyn, and a Universal Negro Improvement Association (the name of Garvey's organization) currently lists mailing addresses in Cleveland, Ohio, and Monrovia, Liberia. And three small Harlem-based organizations that still carry on a back-to-Africa campaign of sorts are the United African Nationalists; the Universal African Nationalist Movement; and the A.U.C. & C.L. (which encompasses an imposing array of organizational titles including the African Universal Church, the Commercial League Corporation, and the African Stock Exchange Association and Development Corporation).

They have little following in the North—and less in the South. However, a leader of one or another of them occasionally shows up below the Mason-Dixon line to denounce the NAACP integrationists and plea for a Negro exodus to the Dark Continent.

For example, Archbishop C. C. Addison of the African Universal Church, et cetera, who describes himself as "the Nation's Number-one African Nationalist and Segregationist," says he goes South every year to warn fellow members of his race that "the devil is the author of integration." In a pamphlet distributed by him while holding a week-long "national convention" recently in a Louisiana hamlet called Dutchtown (population: 7), the archbishop declared:

Integration on this planet begun in the Garden when evil integrated with good, which God forbid. . . . The devil knew that Eve was on the road to success knowing nothing but good, so he had to integrate good with evil in order to put his program over, so it is today the devil know that the Negro through segregated schools is on the road to success, so his only hope is to integrate all Negro schools in the South and give him so-called integration in the North. . . . Integration will move you on starvation street in the city of poverty.

Pointing out that the NAACP's president is a white man, Addison charges that the Association is actually a "white man's organization" fronted by Negro "Uncle Toms." Rather than following the NAACP's program of integration, says the archbishop, Negroes of Dutchtown and elsewhere should seek *separation*.

We have found a place: It is AFRICA, and as black men for three centuries have helped white men build America, surely generous and grateful white men will help black men build Africa. . . . I now appeal to the souls of white America. Let my people go. Tell them to build a government of their own in Africa. Do not encourage them to believe that they will become social equals and leaders in America without first on their own account proving to the world that they are capable of evolving a civilization of their own.

Just as the Ku Klux Klan and the Anglo-Saxon clubs of the 1920's were alert to the possibilities in the Marcus Garvey movement, white segregationist groups and individuals of both South and North have kept a sharp lookout since "Black Monday, 1954," for some organization that might entice the Negroes away to Africa or some other distant shore.

The Richmond, Virginia, *News Leader,* whose editor, James Kilpatrick, is perhaps Southern journalism's most articulate spokesman for segregation, has had occasion to print a letter from the Universal African Nationalist Movement urging federal support of a back-to-Liberia migration.

In the letter the organization's president, Dr. Benjamin Gibbons, claimed "from 10 to 15,000" members, and appealed for support of the old Langer proposal in the Senate.

"Our recent survey of prospective settlers to Liberia," Gibbons wrote, "shows a number of people running into the hundreds of thousands of families and millions of skilled and semi-skilled persons who want to live in Liberia; who do not have the necessary means to go there, but would gladly embrace such an opportunity with the assured backing of a substantial agency like the United States government to tide them over for a given time until said settlers could go on their own."

The racist white press of the "radical right" has, of course, found the idea of a back-to-Africa campaign congenial. For an example, the *Williams Intelligence Summary*—the segregationist, "anti-Zionist" paper long published in California by a Texas-born former military intelligence officer, Major Robert H. Williams—devoted the full front page of its May 1956 issue to a flattering description of Gibbons and his movement.

"Well," Williams declared, "If I ever saw a dream just ready to come true, this must be it."

The Negroes would have been transported back to Africa a century ago had it not been for the Jewish-Marxist "conspiracy" in America, commented Williams. "John Wilkes Booth was, of course, the grandson of a London Jewish tailor," Williams noted, "and he killed Lincoln just as the war was obviously won and as Lincoln was planning to resettle the freed slaves."

Young Dr. Edward Fields, leader of the anti-Jewish National States Rights party in Birmingham, said he planned to "prevail on"

South Carolina Senator J. Strom Thurmond to revive the old Langer back-to-Liberia bill. If the National States Rights party were ever to come to power in America, Fields mentioned, Negroes who volunteered to migrate to Africa would be subsidized; those who chose not to volunteer would be *sent*.

Back in 1940, noting Hitler's mass expulsion of Jews from Germany, W. E. B. Du Bois, the tireless old Negro campaigner for racial equality, wrote in *Dusk of Dawn* that he felt there was "no likelihood" that the Negroes would be chased out of the United States "just now." But he added:

So far as that is concerned, there was no likelihood ten years ago of the Jews being expelled from Germany. The cases are far from parallel. There is a good deal more profit in cheap Negro labor than in Jewish fellow citizens, which brings together strange bedfellows for the protection of the Negro. On the other hand one must remember that this is a day of astonishing change, injustice, and cruelty; and that many Americans of stature have favored the transportation of Negroes and they were not all of the mental caliber of [Bilbo]. As the Negro develops from an easily exploitable, profit-furnishing laborer to an intelligent, independent, self-supporting citizen, the possibility of his being pushed out of his American fatherland may easily be increased rather than diminished. We may be expelled from the United States as the Jew is being expelled from Germany.

The Red Dream

Not all "black nationalist" movements in America have envisioned a mass Negro journey out of the country—to Africa or anywhere else.

It is a fact—and white segregationists harp on it mightily these days—that the Communist party has campaigned with great vigor, especially in the 1920's and 1930's, for the establishment of a separate Negro nation in the "Black Belt" of the South.

In 1928 the Comintern instructed the party in this country to continue its campaign for "equal rights" for all races, but decreed that in the South "the main communist slogan must be: 'The Right of Self-Determination of the Negroes in the Black Belt.' "

A member of the party's campaign committee, C. A. Hathaway, described the Dixieland program in 1930 when he nominated James W. Ford, a Negro, as the communist candidate for vice president of the United States in the next national election:

In the first place, our demand is that the land of the Southern white landlords . . . be confiscated and turned over to the Negroes. . . .

Secondly, we propose to break up the present artificial state boundaries [and] to establish the state unity of the territory known as the "Black Belt," where the Negroes constitute the overwhelming majority of the population.

Thirdly, in this territory we demand that the Negroes be given the complete right of self-determination; *the right to set up their own government* in this territory and the right to separate, if *they* wish, from the United States.

The communist leaders, in their traditional pattern of consistent inconsistency, have run hot and cold on their southern plan since 1928. And from time to time they have juggled the geography of their dream of the "new Negro Republic."

"In 1948," the energetic student of communism, J. Edgar Hoover, recalls in his *Masters of Deceit,* "they described the belt as extending through twelve Southern states: 'Heading down from its eastern point in Virginia's tidewater section, it cuts a strip through North Carolina, embraces nearly all of South Carolina, cuts into Florida, passes through lower and central Georgia and Alabama, engulfs Mississippi and the Louisiana delta, wedges into eastern Texas and southwest Tennessee, and has its western anchor in southern Arkansas.'

"By 1952 the communist concept of the Black Belt had been narrowed to 'at least five Southeastern states, with port outlets at Charleston on the Atlantic and Mobile on the Gulf, encompassing the bulk of Mississippi and a good section of South Carolina, Georgia, and Alabama.'"

Four years later the American Communists' general secretary, Eugene Dennis, reported that the party had "reappraised" its Black Belt policy. It had decided that more emphasis should be placed on the struggle for Negro rights as a "national democratic task" desirable in the North as well as South.

No significant number of American Negroes ever publicly supported the idea of joining in a communist revolution to establish a black nation down among the magnolias. As one Negro remarked, "It is bad enough being black without being black and red."

The Negro author, James Weldon Johnson, commented in 1934 on the impracticalities of a mass Negro union with the communist cause:

[T]here is no apparent possibility that a sufficient number of Negro Americans can be won over to give the party the desired strength; and if the entire mass were won over, the increased proscriptions against Negroes would outweigh any advantages that might be gained. Every Negro's dark face would be his party badge, and would leave him an open and often solitary prey to the pack whenever the hunt might be on. And the sign of the times is that the hunt is not yet to be abandoned.

The Black Supremacists

Dead though it might be in its communist form, the basic idea of establishing a separate black nation within the continental United States is actually much more alive today than ever before. It is one of the main ambitions of the growing American Negro cult called the "Black Muslims."

Because it is just as bizarre as the soul-saving shenanigans of Father Divine and Sweet Daddy Grace, the Black Muslim crusade might well be dismissed as merely another crackpot Negro religious outburst were it not for the sobering fact that it is now the largest Negro mass movement in the country.

The Muslims, led by a former Georgia plowboy and sometime penitentiary inmate who calls himself Elijah Muhammad, "Messenger of Allah," have at least 100,000 members—all Negroes—in twenty-seven states.

So far most of the Muslim followers (not to be confused with the several thousand orthodox Moslem believers in the United States) have been recruited in the urban ghettos of Northern and Far Western cities.

But Muhammad has intensified his efforts to get a foothold in the South. By 1961 he had established "temples"—some of them still quite small, to be sure—in Richmond, Norfolk, Winston-Salem, Durham, Miami, Jacksonville, Tampa, Birmingham, Atlanta, and Orangeburg, South Carolina.

One of the short-range goals of the Muslims is to have 5,000,000 black American disciples by 1964. A fantastic ambition perhaps; but, as C. Eric Lincoln remarks in his brilliant study of the movement, *The Black Muslims in America,* "It is well to remember that only Billy Graham has attracted and converted more people in recent years than has Elijah Muhammad, Messenger of Allah."

The Muslims are even more "segregationist" than the Citizens' Councils and the Ku Klux Klans, and are just as fervently racist as the National States Rights party.

In his regular newspaper column, "Mr. Muhammad Speaks," which is carried by several of the country's most widely read Negro newspapers, the Messenger from Allah recently observed:

"The human beast—the serpent, the dragon, the devil, and Satan—all mean one and the same: the people or race known as the white or Caucasian race, sometimes called the European race. . . . Since by nature they are created liars and murderers, they are the enemies of truth and righteousness, and the enemies of those who seek the truth. . . ."

And in a sermon to 1,200 of the faithful gathered at the Magnolia Theater in Atlanta he added:

"There is no good in the white man. . . . All the whites are the children of the devil. We must separate ourselves as far as possible, for God did not intend for the two races to mix."

Elijah Muhammad, a slight, brown, intense man who was born Elijah Poole on a farm near Sandersville, Georgia, sixty-four years ago, has been directing his vast organization from an eighteen-room mansion in the once-fashionable Hyde Park district of Chicago. With him, in addition to his large family, has lived the memory of an impressive event in his Georgia youth—an event that gave his life a direction.

"After watching in fear the lynching of two of my own," he recalled to a crowd in Chicago awhile back, "I told myself then that I would get even with the white man for all the wrongs he has caused the black man."

Moving to Detroit in the 1920's, Poole found the integrated North not much more congenial to Negroes than the sovereign state of Georgia had been. Having a religious inclination—his father had been a Baptist preacher—Poole became a follower of one Wallace D. Fard, a Detroit peddler who solved the race problem at least on the spiritual level simply be deciding that there are no such things as Negroes. The so-called Negroes are, rather, members of the "Lost-Found Nation of Islam," preached Fard, who on occasion identified himself as Fard Muhammad and as "the Supreme Ruler of the Universe."

Fard gained a few thousand other devotees such as Poole, but he eventually ran into nettlesome difficulties. There was, for example, one especially untidy incident among his disciples in Detroit in 1932: one of them was convicted of killing one of his "brothers" in an old-fashioned human sacrificial ceremony, which is illegal in Detroit.

After a period of harassment by police in Detroit and Chicago Fard mysteriously disappeared in 1934, and the leadership of the cult was taken over by his chief lieutenant, Elijah Poole, who by then had been renamed by Fard as Elijah Muhammad.

The new Muhammad—also known as "The Prophet," "Divine Leader," and "Messenger of Allah to the Lost-Found Nation of Islam in the Wilderness of North America"—set up shop in Chicago. Soon he himself was having brushes with the law as a result of his singular beliefs.

In the year of Fard's disappearance, 1934, Muhammad (né Poole) was placed on six months' probation for insisting on sending one of his seven children to an "Islamic" school rather than the "integrated" public school in his neighborhood.

Then in 1942 he was convicted of sedition for allegedly encouraging Negroes to side with their "racial kin," the Japanese, in their war against the *Union* States. As a result of this he was confined in the federal prison at Milan, Michigan, until 1946.

But the movement continued to flourish even while the Messenger of Allah was behind bars. Indeed, some of his most highly prized converts are men who have spent a portion of their lives in the clink.

Muhammad's topmost aide in recent months is a former prison inmate, too—a trim, sharp-minded young man of upper Manhattan named Malcolm X (he was born Malcolm Little, but, as all good Muslims do, eschews his surname on the ground that it was inherited from the white "Slave masters").

Malcolm X now has for some time headed the affluent Muslim temple in Harlem, where not so many years ago he was pursuing a career of crime and was known as "Big Red."

One of eleven children of a Baptist minister, Malcolm Little grew up in Omaha, Nebraska, and Lansing, Michigan. The outspokenness of his father, an enthusiastic Garveyite, irritated some of the white citizens of Lansing; and when Malcolm was six, the Ku Klux Klan burned the Little family's home. It was a fire, Malcolm X recently commented, that "still burns my soul."

After his father's death (Malcolm feels sure he was murdered by white men) the Little family was forced to break up, and Malcolm was sent to an institution for boys. When he finished the eighth grade at a school near the institution Malcolm left for Harlem and began his apprenticeship in adult delinquency.

"By the age of eighteen Malcolm was versatile 'Big Red,' " Alex Haley has written. "He hired from four to six men variously plying dope, numbers, bootleg whisky, and diverse forms of hustling. Malcolm personally squired well-heeled white thrill seekers to Harlem sin dens and Negroes to white sin downtown. 'My best customers were preachers and social leaders, police and all kinds of big shots in the business of controlling other people's lives.' "

In boom times he stayed in business by "paying off the law from a $1,000 roll from the pockets of his $200 suits." But in the course of his criminal career it was necessary for him to go to prison several times.

It was in 1947, while in a Massachusetts maximum-security penitentiary, that Malcolm was converted to Muslimism.

"One reason [the Muslim faith] is strong in prisons," Malcolm X explained recently, "is that in prison a so-called Negro[3] has time to think."

Since his last release from prison in 1953 Malcolm X has come

---

[3] Muslims, who look upon the word "Negro" as a white slave-master term, prefer to speak of America's citizens of color as *"so-called* Negroes" or "Black Men."

to be the cult's main defender and salesman on college campuses and television shows. Still in his thirties, he is considered by many students of the Muslim movement as the heir apparent to the aging Elijah Muhammad.

Police authorities in cities where the movement is strong have expressed amazement at the overnight disappearance of crime among Muslim converts. It is, indeed, a faith that demands great self-discipline: Muslims are not permitted to drink, smoke, or eat pork; female Muslims wear (interestingly) *white* and are not allowed to use cosmetics. Also, temptation to sin might be reduced somewhat by the fact that the recommended "tithe" for Allah is one-third of the believer's wage earnings.

Some of the movement's financial resources are channeled into the establishment of small businesses run by and for so-called Negroes.

"We don't have any delinquency, either juvenile or adult," Malcolm X has said, "and if Mr. Muhammad is given a chance he will clean up the slums and ghettos—something all the leaders and the social workers and the policemen put together have not been able to do."

Delighted as the police are at the crime reduction resulting from the movement, they are obviously worried that the Muslim crusade has a great *potential* for physical violence.

The authorities are especially leery of the Muslim organization called the "Fruit of Islam," which has long been headed by Muhammad's son-in-law, Raymond Sharieff, and Muhammad's son, Elijah, Jr., both of whom must be considered along with Malcolm X as possible eventual successors to The Messenger.

The members of the Fruit of Islam, the best male physical specimens in the cult, are trained regularly in close-order drill and judo. Although the training is ostensibly dedicated to self-defense in the event of an attack by the "white devils," it is plain that the Fruit of Islam do not have in mind the sort of "passive resistance" advocated by Martin Luther King.

"We must return to the Mosaic law of an eye for an eye and a tooth for a tooth," Muhammad has said. "What does it matter if ten million of us die? There will be seven million of us left, and they will enjoy justice and freedom."

Attempts to rally American Negroes to a "cause" almost invariably have exploited the Protestant Christian faith, which is held by the great majority of them. But Muhammad commands that his followers renounce Christianity as a religion of slavery and death.

Behind the altar of the typical Muslim temple hangs a painting: on the right half of the canvas are the star and crescent of Islam, labeled "Freedom-Justice-Equality"; depicted on the left side are the United States flag and the Christian cross along with a black man hanging from a lynching tree.

The Christian Bible is discarded in favor of the Holy Quran, a book "which makes a distinction between the God of the righteous and the God of evil." Although some Muslims hold that the Christian Bible has some value when "rightly interpreted," Muhammad obviously has little use for the turn-the-other-cheek philosophy of Jesus.

" 'Love thy neighbor'; I have yet to meet one white man that loved his neighbor. . . . 'Thou shalt not kill'; I have yet to meet such a Christian," Muhammad has written to his followers. "[Y]ou fear and love [white Christians] though you are even disgraced, beaten, and killed by them. . . . You have made yourselves the most foolish people on earth by loving and following after the ways of Slavemasters, whom Allah has revealed to me to be none other than real devils, and that their so-called Christianity is not His religion, nor the religion of Jesus or any other prophet of Allah (God). . . ." And again: "There is no heaven or hell other than on earth for you and me, and Jesus was no exception. His body is still [in] Palestine and will remain there."

In addition to denouncing Christianity, various Muslim luminaries frequently deliver anti-Jewish pronouncements which could well warm the heart of a Conde McGinley or a Gerald L. K. Smith.

There is a certain divergence of opinion among Muslims on the subject of Jews. Some Muslims consider Jews "renegade Black Men" and despise them for that reason, while other Muslims merely classify them with other light-skinned Americans as "white devils."

"We make no distinction between Jews and non-Jews so long as they are all white," Malcolm X has said. "To do so would be to imply that we like some whites better than others. This would be discrimination, and we do not believe in discrimination." He added, however, "In America, the Jews sap the very lifeblood of the so-called Negroes to maintain the state of Israel, its armies and its continued aggression against our brothers [the Arabs] in the East. This every Black Man resents. . . . The European and American Christians helped to establish Israel in order to get rid of the Jews so that they could take over their businesses as they did the American Japanese [businesses] during the war. The scheme failed, and the joke is on the white man. The American Jews aren't going anywhere. Israel is just an international poorhouse which is maintained by money sucked from the poor suckers in America."

Like the white "radical rightists," many Muslim spokesmen look upon the National Association for the Advancement of Colored People as a Jewish "front" organization.

"In the early thirties," the Muslim-oriented Los Angeles *Herald-Dispatch* commented recently, "a large percentage of European Jews were engaged in trade, living in the rear of stores, markets, and generally making their living from the Negro in the Negro community. Thus they had an excellent opportunity to study the habits and weaknesses of the Negro. The depression of the thirties [and] the activities of the Communist party allowed the Jews to further intrench themselves into the community, to infect his thinking to the extent that by 1940 the Negro was almost entirely dependent upon the Jews and had accepted the thinking and ideology of the Jewish people. In the late thirties and by the early fifties the Jews had finally gained control of the NAACP."

Thurgood Marshall, the NAACP's chief legal counsel, has said he considers the Muslims a "vicious" group "run by a bunch of thugs organized from prisons and jails, and financed, I am sure, by Nasser or some Arab group."

In reply Malcolm X referred to Marshall as a "twentieth-century Uncle Tom."

The attitudes of white segregationists toward the Black Muslim movement are mixed—and seemingly somewhat hesitant.

It is rumored that a prominent Texas millionaire, apparently enthusiastic about the Muslims' desire to separate the so-called

Negroes from the white community, has contributed several thousand dollars to their cause.

Such groups as the Citizens' Council Association occasionally reprint and distribute some of Muhammad's more mildly-worded appeals for separation, presumably to support the old Dixieland dixit that "Negroes prefer segregation."

In his book about Muhammad and his followers Dr. Lincoln quotes a representative group of Muslims as saying "the crackers in the South disgrace the country and embarrass the nation. They can't keep out of the Black Man's bed, and they have to keep lynching Negroes to try to keep it covered up. . . . The Southern cracker [was] born a dog, and he'll be a dog."

Such views as these, of course, are not given any space in the "educational literature" published by the white-supremacy organizations down South.

At present most white segregationists who are familiar with the Muslim movement seem to enjoy it as an excellent joke on the integrationists—as a gratifying come-uppance directed at the NAACP.

And yet what would be the fate of all good white Citizens' Councilors if this zany crusade of the former Georgia plowboy just happened to click with a few million Negroes?

"The wicked must be punished for their wickedness poured out upon us," Elijah Muhammad has said. "This country is large enough to separate the two (black and white), and they both [might] live here, but that would not be successful. The best solution is for everyone to go to his own country. . . . The native home of the white race is Europe."

Muhammad promises his followers that white rule in the United States will be overthrown by 1970, and the black nation will "inherit the spoils."[4]

White advocates of racial *separation* are thus faced with the possibility that the "so-called Negroes," rather than the white folks, might be *doing the separating*. Recalling Judge Tom Brady's

[4] Muslim leaders have sometimes recommended that the "so-called Negroes" be given one state in the United States, at other times have proposed that they be given several states, and at still other times have suggested that the "white devils" all leave the country and leave it entirely to the black men.

idea of establishing a separate state outside the United States as a means of solving the race problem, is it possible that the United States will become a Black Muslim nation and the whites will all be dwelling in some other land—Lower California, say?

It is, in reality, unlikely.

But there is no doubt at all that old Elijah Poole, who has lived so long with his memories of a Georgia lynching and the gray terror of a prison cell, means business.

However peaceful the movement is described by its leaders, large numbers of Negroes—especially the younger ones—feel that they understand. As one young Harlem citizen commented to the scholarly Dr. C. Eric Lincoln:

"Man, I don't care what those cats [the Muslims] say *out loud* —that's just a hype they're putting down for The Man [i.e., the white man]. Let me tell you—they've got some stuff for The Man even the Mau Mau didn't have! If he tries to crowd them like he's been used to doing the rest of us all the time, they're going to lay it on him from here to Little Rock! I grew up with some of the cats in that temple—went to school with them; ran around with them. Man, those cats have changed. They ain't for no light playing. Those cats are for real, and you'd better believe it!"

At this writing the Muslims have still made no move to "lay it on" the so-called White Devils.

"[But] the expectation of an eventual racial clash is widespread among observers who know the Movement firsthand, whether as officers charged with the maintenance of public order or as Negro youths who visit the Muslim temples for a vicarious swing at 'white oppression,' " Lincoln remarks in *The Black Muslims in America.* "The belief that the Muslims plan some kind of overt attack against the Black Man's oppressors, or that they will retaliate in kind if attacked by the white man, is widely held by the youth of the 'Black Ghetto.' . . ."

X. POSTSCRIPT

A Few Stitches for the Bleeding Heart

As WE SAT with comfortable bourbons in the game room of a Memphis suburban home one evening in the warm months of 1961 the beautiful hostess expressed delight at the fact that I was preparing to write a book about the race problem. She—this tender-hearted, graceful woman of Memphis—thought it was shameful that the Underprivileged Colored People were segregated and she hoped something nice would be done to integrate them one of these days.

The fact was (I tried to tell her as gently as possible) that quite a bit of racial integration had already taken place right in Memphis. For one thing, the city's public transit system had recently been desegregated; a colored person, however underprivileged, now had the privilege of sitting right up front on a bus if he wished. Then, too, the traditional "Negro Day" at the Memphis city zoo had been eliminated; Negroes could go out to Overton Park and look at the animals any day the whites could. Also, the downtown Memphis Public Library had been desegregated. And, for another thing, a few dozen Negroes had for several months been attending classes with whites at the local public university, Memphis State.

She listened, eyes bright with fascination, and with a delicate cry of shock, declared:

"Jim Cook! You don't mean it!"

On reflection it is difficult to judge whether these tidings warmed her humanitarian spirit or simply were ungraceful expressions by me in exchange for really quite superior bourbon. In the South, perhaps even more so than elsewhere, many things are better left unsaid.

But the point for our purposes here is that "successful desegregation" had already taken place in her city and she was not aware of it.

And for very understandable reasons.

When she travels into the city of Memphis she does not go on any of the newly integrated busses; she drives in an automobile. She and her husband, a prosperous traveling salesman, take their children to the zoo now and then, but it simply had never occurred to the fair matron that it had ever been segregated in days gone by. The desegregation of the library had not been noticed by her because, although she is a college graduate, she is not really very "bookish" but rather keeps informed mostly through her subscriptions to various multicolored magazines. And the fact that Memphis State University was now integrated had not made an impression on her because her children are of grade-school age and not of college age (and, too, unless her husband loses his knack at salesmanship, they likely will not attend Memphis State when they do reach college age).

In truth, moreover, only a few months after the game-room chat aforementioned the public grade-school system of Memphis was officially "desegregated" when Negroes—thirteen first-graders —were admitted for the first time to previously all-white schools of the city.

Even so, the lovely matron's children have continued attending completely segregated schools because the suburb in which she and her family dwell contains—by reason of both elementary economics and traditional segregationist real-estate practices—no Negroes.

Unless I misinterpret it, this—the situation of the hostess and her husband and their handsome children—indicates the most serious weakness in the position now occupied by the major organizations and individuals warring for the maintenance of segregation.

The truth, in fine, is that large numbers of white people of affluence and influence in the South just do not give a damn about the integration-segregation controversy. Why? Because it simply

does not touch them. Prosperity and the safely segregated housing that almost invariably accompanies prosperity keep them
away from Negroes just as surely as if they lived in San Francisco's St. Francis Wood or in Long Island's Oyster Bay. And,
consequently, they are not inclined to join the CC or the KKK in
the crusade to "keep Negroes in their place."

Yet all the while Negroes are touched by the discomfort of
racial discrimination: they are touched by it in the morning, in
the evening, and in the night. In contrast to kindly white humanitarians who live in secure suburbs Negroes are forced by the
actualities of life to be aware of The Problem every day. And,
logically, they can be expected to act—to press on and on for
desegregation and for (as the slogan goes) "first-class citizenship."

In addition to the negative factor that so many of the "better-
class" white citizens show no really active interest in The Problem,
and the positive factor that almost all Negroes are vitally interested
in it (and a great many are willing to take personal action against
racial discrimination even at the risk of economic and physical
pain)—in addition to these, there are other colossal forces at
work against segregation.

There are, for example, the integrationist pressure of national
labor unions, the ready willingness of many business interests to
cooperate with civil-rights compaigners in order to avoid racial
difficulties which might adversely affect their balance sheets, the
steady pressure of the national church organizations and scores of
so-called "do-good" groups, and—second in importance only to
the force of the Negroes themselves—the integrationist thrusts
of the judicial and executive branches of the federal government.

All these things would appear to give mighty support to the
Liberals' insistence that "integration is inevitable," that the South's
whites—after a bit of squirming and complaining—will eventually
settle down and live compatibly with Negroes in desegregated accordance with "the American creed" that all men are equal.

Perhaps so. A reasonable conclusion is that integration is inevitable and the current Southern white crusade against it is
doomed to go down in history as another Lost Cause.

Reasonable, maybe. But it would be misleading, I think, to close
any discussion of the race struggle in the South without making

mention of a couple of *un*reasonable factors that tend to dim the prospect of that sweet day when whites and Negroes will dwell in integrated harmony. These are: the animosity that large numbers of white people feel toward Negroes in general, and the animosity that large numbers of Negroes feel toward white people in general.

One important fact—not to be dismissed as merely a psycho-neurotic oddity—is that significantly large portions of the white South's citizenry have a deep and quite sincere fear that Negroes, if freed from the reins of segregation, would commit acts of sexual mischief and violence against them.

A long-range fear is that desegregation would bring about more and more intermarriage and eventually a change in the racial composition of the United States as a whole and the South in particular.

Much of the segregationist literature that comes off Southern printing presses addresses itself to this fear. Still in circulation are reprints (reprints produced by the Citizens' Councils Association, among other organizations) of a statement on interracial marriage made back in 1955 by a South Carolina NAACP official and reported by the Associated Press.

"[O]nce the two races are integrated, intermarriage is the natural consequence," remarked Albert A. Kennedy, state counselor for the NAACP. "Psychologists say that a girl's chances of getting married are governed by the number of her male associates."

Integration will result in white girls being associated with Negro boys, he said, and "naturally intermarriage would result. . . . [I]ntermingling can't be regulated by the state and if the state tries to regulate it you will find the same thing in every particular—in the dark, behind closed doors and in automobiles."

Kennedy said he was "speaking as a private citizen," but many readers of his comments took them to be in behalf of the NAACP. Actually, the NAACP as an organization has taken care to treat the subject of interracial marriage gingerly. Although campaigning in several states against old "anti-miscegenation" statutes—the NAACP's national spokesmen have tended to stress that the purpose here has been to eliminate discrimination and not necessarily to promote intermarriage.

Even so, such comments as those of Albert Kennedy give many

white Southerners the shivers. And reports of actual marriages
of Negroes and whites in the North—especially weddings of
Negro males and white females—have been vigorously exploited
by the Southern segregationist press under such headlines as
"Mongrelization Actual Goal" and "Total Mongrelization." For
instance, a simple wedding in Cassopolis, Michigan, recently was
deemed news worthy of considerable space in Roy Harris' Augusta
Courier away down in Georgia. The *Courier* report read, in part:

STOP, READ AND
THEN PRAY
The Augusta *Chronicle* [has] carried the following story from
Cassopolis, Michigan:
"An interracial romance which began on the Indiana University
campus has resulted in the marriage of the first Negro president of
the IU student body and a white IU graduate.
"Thomas Atkins, Elkhart, Indiana, a senior honor student, and
the former Miss Sharon Soash were married Friday by Justice of
the Peace Frank McCormick in the Cassopolis courthouse. . . .
"The bride's father, Howard Soash, a South Bend postal clerk,
said he and Mrs. Soash had known of their plans for about a
month and had tried to talk Sharon out of the marriage."

Of course the "mixed marriage" which exercised the South's
segregationist press above and beyond all others was the late 1960
wedding of entertainer Sammy Davis, Jr., and actress May Britt.
Aside from their fame, the aspect of the union which so fascinated
the segregationists was the color contrast of the couple; Miss Britt,
so blond, so fair, fit so well the white Southern male's stereotyped
dream concept of what a "typical Anglo-Saxon girl of the South"
looks like.

At the annual meeting of the American Anthropological Association in December 1961 the delegates unanimously adopted the
following resolution—by a vote of 192 to 0.

The American Anthropological Association repudiates statements now appearing in the United States that Negroes are biologically and in innate mental ability inferior to whites, and re-
affirms the fact that there is no scientifically established evidence

to justify the exclusion of any race from the rights guaranteed by the Constitution of the United States. The basic principles of equality of opportunity and equality before the law are compatible with all that is known about human biology. All races possess the abilities needed to participate fully in the democratic way of life and in modern technological civilization.

The need for such a "reaffirmation" by the Association was felt, obviously, because of a large and apparently growing body of "scientific literature"—written by scientists both North and South, both foreign and domestic—which insists that whites are biologically superior to Negroes, and implies that intermarriage will weaken the mentality of the present majority race in the United States and other "Western" nations.

Among Deep Southerners probably the most popular pro-segregation book since the publication of Brady's *Black Monday* and Talmadge's *You and Segregation* in the mid-1950's has been Carleton Putnam's *Race and Reason: A Yankee View* (Public Affairs Press, Washington, 1961). Putnam—a New Englander, lawyer, biographer of Theodore Roosevelt, and former head of two large airlines that operated in the South—fills the pages of his book with a sort of recapitulation of the various doctrines of white supremacy, heavily emphasizing the data of anthropologists who presumably do not attend annual conventions of the American Anthropological Association. His conclusion, in brief, is that segregation is good and that the integration movement is a thing "of alien background and design"—and poses a grave threat to the genes of the white man.

The book so pleased the Citizens' Councils Association in Mississippi that Governor Ross Barnett was prompted to proclaim October 26, 1961, as "RACE AND REASON DAY." At a twenty-five-dollar-a-plate dinner in his honor in Jackson's Heidelberg Hotel that night Putnam spoke and posed for toothy photographs with Governor Barnett, former Governor Hugh White, Congressman John Bell Williams, *et al.*

So far, so Southern.[1]

[1] The Louisiana State Legislature in July 1961 had passed a resolution ordering high schools of the state to assign "selected mature students" to

But it is perhaps significant—and just possibly portentous—to observe that four fairly notable biological scientists saw fit to write a joint introduction to Putnam's book, praising its "scientific validity."

The four scientists—Dr. R. Ruggles Gates, former associate professor of zoology at the University of California and professor of botany at the University of London; Dr. Henry E. Garrett, professor emeritus who headed the psychology department at Columbia University for fifteen years; Dr. Robert Gayre, a Scot, editor of *Mankind Quarterly* and former head of the postgraduate department of anthropogeography at the University of Saugor in India; and Dr. Wesley C. George, professor and former head of the department of anatomy at the University of North Carolina—express in their introduction discontent that "nonscientific, ideological pressures have harassed scientists in the last thirty years, often resulting in the suppression or distortion of truth."

One gathers that Gates, Garrett, Gayre, and George would not have voted for the equalitarian American Anthropological Association resolution of 1961.

"We do not believe," they declare in the introduction to *Race and Reason,* "that there is anything to be drawn from the sciences in which we work which supports the view that all races of men, all types of men, or all ethnic groups are equal and alike, in anything approaching the foreseeable future. We believe, on the contrary, that there are vast areas of difference within mankind not only in physical appearance, but in such matters as adaptability to varying environments, and in deep psychological and emotional qualities, as well as in mental ability and capacity for development. We are of the opinion that in ignoring these depths of difference modern man and his political representatives are likely to find themselves in serious difficulties sooner or later. . . ."

Dr. George of North Carolina, probably the segregationist South's most admired biologist, ended a monograph some few years earlier with the conclusion that "we cannot consider the Negro to be genetically acceptable." While recommending that

---

study *Race and Reason,* in view of the "evidence that the sciences of biology and anthropology are being distorted and perverted to serve the purposes of certain pressure groups whose aims are inimical to the customs, mores, and traditions of this nation. . . ."

"we" allow the Negro "every reasonable opportunity to develop his race and culture," George insisted that "we cannot afford to take the chance of having him destroy our race and our civilization."

There is in the South (and elsewhere), in short, a very noteworthy fear by Caucasians that racial desegregation would change the color of their descendants. And this, of course, disturbs the vision of the future to which a great many men dedicate their lives.

But aside from long-range ethnology there exists strongly among many white men of the South the old, old, insecure feeling that Negro males, if given "social equality," might be sexually preferred by white women.

Here, plainly, is the fulminate for the explosive Southern cliché: "How would you like it if your daughter married a nigger?"

An intimate analysis of the ingredients of this attitude would be beyond the scope of this book. In one way or another the psycho-sexual relationship between whites and Negroes has been the subject of almost all of the readable literary works which have come out of the South this century.

As superficial evidence that such a fulminate does exist, however, it probably would be appropriate to mention briefly the case of Professor Roosevelt Williams.

Back in 1956 the Citizens' Councils showered the South with tape recordings and mimeographed texts of what was labeled a speech by "Professor Roosevelt Williams of Howard University" at a "secret NAACP meeting in Mississippi in December of 1954." According to the tape that was distributed, the Negro professor said, among other things:

As many of you are aware, some of the most outstanding Americans ever produced were the products of white men crossed with generate [sic] Negro women without benefit of clergy, and the whole world knows that the white man strongly prefers the Negro women with [their] strong, rich ancestors and warm, full-blooded passions than recline in the spiritless women of his own race. . . .

We, the Negro man, have long known that the white woman is violently dissatisfied with the white man and we know of the millions of clandestine meetings sought by the white women. They . . . demand the right to win and love the Negro man of their own

choice and shout to the world, "This is my man and he is a man
in every respect." They are likely to be doomed to disappointment
when the average Negro is of the attitude, "Why buy a cow when
I can get plenty of milk and butter for nothing?" But we demand
the right for any Negro man or woman to marry a member of the
white race if he [or she] can find one fit to marry. . . .

Circulation of this "secret speech," pinching as it did some of
the white Southerners' most sensitive nerve ends, gave a nice
stimulus to CC recruiting efforts for several months in 1956. An
extra boost was supplied by the office of Attorney General Eugene
Cook of Georgia, which began distributing copies of the speech in
official envelopes of the Georgia State Law Department.

However, the participation of Attorney General Cook's office
in disseminating Professor Roosevelt Williams' words ceased
abruptly in early September 1956. The cessation occurred quickly
after a small south Georgia daily, the Columbus *Ledger-Enquirer,*
reported there was no Professor Roosevelt Williams on the faculty
of Howard University and there never had been. At the same
time NAACP headquarters in New York insisted that it had never
had a "Roosevelt Williams" on its staff and suggested that he was
perhaps a "phantom professor" dreamed up by white folks down
South.

Attorney General Cook, blaming the distribution of the speech
on subordinates in his law department, said he telephoned Robert
Patterson, executive secretary of the Citizens' Councils Association, and asked him about Professor Williams. Cook said Patterson told him:

"We never claimed it [the speech] to be authentic."

According to Attorney General Cook, Patterson of the CC
Association said he got a tape recording of the speech "third or
fourth" hand.

But the fact that the speech of "Professor Roosevelt Williams"
apparently was not authentic should not be permitted to blunt the
point of the story. However inauthentic, the words of the "phantom
professor" can properly be taken to represent the Southern segregationists' interpretation of what "the Negro" has in mind.

Segregationists, then, are concerned about the color of their posterity, and many of them are hooked on the fear that the pedestaled white ladies of the South secretly lust for a "Negro man of their choice."

But an even more immediate fear in the white South is that Negro males, if freed from the restraints of segregation, would forthwith set about assaulting and insulting white women.

This is no new thought in the South, no strange flower grown particularly from the 1954 Supreme Court decision. It has been right there all along—since slavery days.

Always a significant number of Southern whites have felt with the mulatto Massachusetts author, William Hannibal Thomas, who asserted in *The American Negro* (1901) that:

All who know the Negro recognize [that] the chief and over-powering element in his make-up is an imperious sexual impulse which, aroused at the slightest incentive, sweeps aside all restraints in the pursuit of physical gratification.

And Thomas Nelson Page, who very accurately articulated the racial philosophy of the bulk of white Southerners, gave credit to Thomas for his conclusion (in *The Negro: The Southerner's Problem,* 1904) that:

He [the Negro] does not generally believe in the existence of actual assault. It is beyond his comprehension. In the next place, his passion, always his controlling force, is now . . . for the white women.

Page expressed fear of that "class" of Negroes who are "wholly ignorant" or whose "so-called education is unaccompanied by any of the fruits of character which education is supposed to produce." Of this "class" he wrote:

It is like a vast sluggish mass of uncooled lava over a large section of the country, burying some portions and affecting the whole. It is apparently harmless, but beneath its surface smoulder fires which may at any time burst forth unexpectedly and spread desolation all around. It is this mass . . . which constitutes the Negro question.

The abundance of atrocities committed by diverse Congolese citizens upon resident Caucasian women in 1960 was taken by many white Southerners as proof that William Hannibal Thomas and Thomas Nelson Page and their literary descendants have been correct in their insistence that Negroes have an "imperious sexual impulse" which differs from that of white men. One of the more popular pieces of segregationist literature in late 1960 and 1961 was the Belgian Government Information Center's *Preliminary Report on the Atrocities Committed by the Congolese Army against the White Population of the Republic of the Congo before the Intervention of the Belgian Forces.* A sample of the dozens of reported atrocities is this description of the experience of two white ladies in the province of Leopoldville:

Mrs. ———— was arrested by approximately ten soldiers of the Force Publique at her home in the Seke-Banza territory on the 9th of July. She was taken to Sanda. She was assaulted, kicked over her whole body, and dragged over the ground by her hair. [She and another lady] were severely injured.

Back home, the two ladies were separated. One of them was raped three times by [a] noncommissioned officer, according to what Mrs. ———— heard.

Mrs. ———— herself was raped three times by three different soldiers.

The following morning Congolese soldiers twisted her hand, which is still bandaged.

A third and fourth lady . . . could avoid being raped by offering 500 francs to soldiers during the same night. . . . Like the others, they were forced to pluck weeds under the menace of death.

Roy Harris' Augusta *Courier,* which might truly be counted as one of the more "moderate segregationist" journals of the South, expressed some further disapproval of certain unharmonious happenings in 1961 in the Portuguese African colony which is ironically called Angola. The *Courier* headlined:

Negroes on Rampage in Angola, Africa, Killed Women
By Thrusting Large Branches of Trees into Their Bodies

The *Courier* presented a sample incident reported by the Portuguese-American Committee on Foreign Affairs:

[T]he small village of Buela between Maquela do Zombo and Sao Salvador was attacked and the local administrator and his wife were tied to boards then sliced methodically into pieces. All the other members of the village, except the wife of the guard, also were slaughtered, including a businessman, Snr. Fernandes, who had first to watch his wife, a negress, being raped and then obscenely mutilated, despite her advanced state of pregnancy.

[That same morning] a group of some 400 terrorists attacked the experimental farm at M'Bridge. One of the few survivors of this attack, Manuel Lourenco Alves, relates what happened:

". . . My African boy, Joao, ran to the house next door to try and get some ammunition but he was caught halfway and beheaded and castrated before my eyes. The white, mulatto, and negro women were dragged out of their houses together with their children. In front of the mothers, the terrorists then proceeded to cut off the legs and arms of the children and then started to play a grotesque game of football with the twitching bodies. The women and girls were then led away, stripped, raped, and cut up. Many of them were killed by stuffing large branches of trees into their vaginas. They tied one young girl of eighteen to a tree, crucified her, and whilst she was still alive, they cut off her breasts and put one in each of her outstretched hands."

Harris of the *Courier* concluded that Portuguese attempts at peaceful token integration had not been totally successful.

"So," said Harris, "after five hundred years of race mixing in Africa these are the results."

Along with the general white Southern fear that integration would stimulate Negro males to atrocious sexual activity is the less complex fear that desegregated Negroes would also commit violent acts—breaches of the peace of the South—which are not necessarily related to "sex."

In a noteworthy speech to the House of Representatives in 1956—a speech reprinted by the Citizens' Councils Association in pamphlet form under the title *Where Is the Reign of Terror?*—John Bell Williams of Mississippi presented a mass of figures to show that Negroes were far more likely to commit crimes and go to prison in the "integrated" North than in the segregated South.

According to 1950 Department of Justice census figures, Williams reported, in 13 non-Southern states with 100,000 or more

Negroes each, the number of Negroes in state prisons on felony convictions was (on a per-capita basis) 681 per cent higher than the white prison population. In comparison, the Negro rate was just 248 per cent higher in 10 segregated Southern states.[2]

Williams made a point of comparing the great bastion of segregation, Mississippi, with the great seat of integration, New York.

"According to the 1950 census, Mississippi's Negro population exceeds New York's Negro population by 68,303. Yet official Justice Department figures show that New York sent twice as many Negroes to prison in 1950 [as] Mississippi. . . .

"Those figures must prove conclusively one or two premises: either that Negroes are more law-abiding in a segregated society, or Southern courts are far more lenient with Negro defendants," declared Williams. "This, in my opinion, puts the lie to the left-wing and NAACP propaganda to the effect that a 'reign of terror' against Negroes prevails in the South. . . . Where is the real reign of terror against Negro citizens, if such prevails? Is it in Mississippi and the South, as the bleeding-heart liberals contend, or is it in the integrated states?"[3]

Despite the great pains that the mass of America's social scientists have taken to prove that the exceptionally high crime rate among Negroes is a result of environmental forces, most white Southerners believe—and feel—that it is a matter of racial heredity. It is—as the Southern thought pattern goes—because Negroes are "not far removed from the African jungles" and therefore have a "more violent nature."

Then, too, there is the Southern feeling that Negroes might take violent revenge for all the decades of insults and outrages which

[2] The 13 non-Southern states in the report were California, District of Columbia, Illinois, Indiana, Kentucky, Maryland, Missouri, New Jersey, New York, Ohio, Oklahoma, Pennsylvania, and West Virginia. The 10 Southern states were Alabama, Arkansas, Florida, Louisiana, Mississippi, North Carolina, South Carolina, Tennessee, Texas, and Virginia. Two other states with large Negro populations, Georgia and Michigan, were omitted from the tabulations because they had not submitted prison reports to the Justice Department for the year 1950.

[3] Williams has indicated that he would enjoy updating those prison population figures from 1950 to 1960. But:

"We have been unable to secure prison population figures by race from

whites have committed against members of their race. This is not so often voiced aloud by segregationists (for how could it be reconciled with another part of their dogma which insists that Negro and white Southerners have great affection for each other?), but it is a feeling which is deeply ingrained.

The events of the last eight years leave no room for doubt that the Supreme Court decision of May 17, 1954, produced—inevitably—an atmosphere for interracial violence in the South. In this atmosphere police officials in various Southern communities have taken various extraordinary steps to be prepared.

The Jackson, Mississippi, Police Department's employment of a new "canine corps" to disperse Negro pickets from a public library in the capital in 1961 was an excellent example. In Birmingham, Alabama, police officials have readied a couple of heavily armored trucks—or "tanks," as they are called locally— for use in the event rioting breaks out.

Some Dixie communities have gone to lengths of preparation quaintly reminiscent of Civil War days. During the Little Rock crisis in 1957 the state legislative delegation from Union County, South Carolina, announced that it had arranged the purchase of nine new submachine guns for their county sheriff's office. State Senator John D. Long said they would be used to beat back "any invasion of federal troops" such as took place in Little Rock. Senator Long said he was confident that Union County Sheriff J. Harold Lamb and his eight deputies could handle any such situation that might arise.

Actually how much more racial violence can be expected in the South as integration proceeds "with all deliberate speed" in the years ahead? It is frustratingly difficult to guess.

---

the Justice Department," Congressman Williams' administrative assistant, Charles H. Griffin, reported in a 1961 letter to the author. "It would seem that 'Where Is the Reign of Terror?' caused the Department of Justice to refuse to release, or maybe compile, crime figures by race. . . . You are well aware of the fact, I am sure, that the NAACP has worked hard to eliminate the dissemination of any kind of information which lists the race of the people involved. This has been particularly true with reference to newspapers publishing the race of the person involved in a crime. . . ."

Having for some years been a workaday news reporter in the South and having written of many "race incidents" (lynchings and floggings and dynamitings and such), I felt in the mid-1950's that when school integration was seriously attempted in some Dixie communities there would be rioting the likes of which had not been seen below the Mason-Dixon line since Reconstruction days. I was, as it happened, wrong. Not totally wrong, of course: since 1954 there has been racial mob violence at Little Rock in Arkansas, New Orleans in Louisiana, Jacksonville in Florida, Birmingham and Montgomery and Tuscaloosa in Alabama, Clinton in Tennessee, Jackson and McComb in Mississippi, and at several other points South. Some of it, in truth, has been quite spirited, quite sanguinary; sticks and stones have broken bones, teeth have been scattered, skulls have been cracked. But by mid-1962 not a single death had occurred as a result of these clashes, if I recall correctly; not one race riot worthy of the term had taken place in the South since the Supreme Court decision of 1954.

My slight miscalculation—let me say in a bit of self-defense—should not be attributed simply to stupidity. It should be attributed, instead, to that remarkable man named Martin Luther King.

Who in 1954 or 1955 could have possibly guessed that such a man would crop up in—of all places—Montgomery, Alabama, and in no time at all channel the Southern Negroes' rage for equality into a Gandhian "nonviolent protest" movement?

The personal influence of King, as well as the approach he has advocated—and, more important, *has practiced*—has undoubtedly reduced the potential for race riots in the South in the last few years. (As much as the white Southerners fear him at present, in days to come they might well reflect on King in much the same wistful way that they now reflect on good old peace-provoking Booker T. Washington.)

But how long will King's turn-the-other-cheek Christo-Gandhianism continue to interest Negroes who were told eight years ago that the Day of Jubilee was at hand and yet have so far gained little more than an up-front seat on the bus to work and a breath of not-now-but-later-maybe school integration?

Perhaps on and on. Who can really say?

But without doubt old Elijah Poole from Georgia—the Messenger of Allah—has managed to tap the well of hatred that boils just beneath the surface of American society. Only the most feather-headed of the nation's "liberal humanitarians" can fail to realize that this well is a deep and deadly one.

The much-publicized hatred that white "bigots" feel for Negroes is a fact of life, but can it compare at all with the hatred that so many Negroes feel for them?

As James Baldwin, probably the most thoughtful Negro writer in the country today, observes in his *Notes of a Native Son:*

Negroes live violent lives, unavoidably . . . and, further, in every act of violence, particularly violence against white men, Negroes feel a certain thrill of identification, a wish to have done it themselves, a feeling that old scores are being settled at last. It is no accident that Joe Louis is the most idolized man in Harlem. . . .

And again:

[T]here is, I should think, no Negro living in America who has not felt, briefly or for long periods, with anguish sharp or dull, in varying degrees and to varying effect, simple, naked, and unanswerable hatred; who has not wanted to smash any white face he may encounter in a day, to violate, out of motives of the cruelest vengeance, their women, to break the bodies of all white people and bring them low, as low as that dust into which he himself has been and is being trampled; no Negro, finally, who has not had to make his own precarious adjustment to the "nigger" who surrounds him and to the "nigger" in himself.

Mrs. Ruby Hurley of Atlanta, the able and attractive Southern regional head of the National Association for the Advancement of Colored People, has observed this animosity among Negroes of the South. But, as is the custom of most NAACP leaders and professional Liberals, she also sees hopeful signs.

"Few people know—or at least talk about—the bitterness and hatred which many Southern Negroes feel toward whites," she remarked awhile back. "I suppose I notice it particularly because I didn't grow up in the Deep South, but it scared me when I first came down here."

She added, however:

"Now, since the Montgomery protest, Dr. King's philosophy has helped tremendously in stemming it."

Like Dr. Martin Luther King and Mrs. Ruby Hurley, James Baldwin believes that *"segregation is dead."* However, he suggests:

"The real question which faces the Republic is just how long, how violent, and how expensive the funeral is going to be. . . . It need scarcely be said that our racial situation is far more complex and dangerous than we are prepared to think of it as being— since our major desire is not to think of it at all. . . ."

At this time in American history the agonizing probability— the true and bitter inevitability—is that many so-called Negroes and so-called whites will have gone to their graves long before segregation is buried.

INDEX

DATE DUE

MAY 12 '65			
FEB 22 '66			
FEB 15 '68			
APR 22 '68			
MAY 8 '68			
MAR 26 '69			
APR 6 '71			
AP 21 '83			
AP 27 '83			
OCT 20 '86			
GAYLORD			PRINTED IN U.S.A